Lean Culture in Higher Education

Justyna Maciąg

Lean Culture in Higher Education

Towards Continuous Improvement

Justyna Maciąg
Institute of Public Affairs
Jagiellonian University
Kraków, Poland

ISBN 978-3-030-05685-8   ISBN 978-3-030-05686-5   (eBook)
https://doi.org/10.1007/978-3-030-05686-5

Library of Congress Control Number: 2019931938

This Palgrave Macmillan imprint is published by the registered company Springer Nature Switzerland AG
The registered company address is: Gewerbestrasse 11, 6330 Cham, Switzerland

To Ania, Kasia, Asia and my Parents.

Preface

Observations of the higher education sector indicate that despite numerous attempts at reforms, universities change more slowly than is expected by their stakeholders. A considerable emphasis is put on changes in the organisational and technical spheres, while too little attention is paid to their social dimension, including organisational culture. Changes are usually implemented on a top-down basis, hence they are met with misunderstanding and resistance on the part of university employees. Therefore, more and more higher education institutions make use of the change philosophy, methods, and tools offered by the concept of Lean Management. They believe that Lean Management has the potential for change in higher education organisational culture towards the continuous improvement of the processes which create value for stakeholders. A true change in a university management model is possible only if the new approach becomes a part of a given school's organisational culture, culture of everyday work manifesting itself in employees' proper behaviours and attitudes. Thus questions are posed as to whether the implementation of the Lean Management concept changes academic organisational culture, how such changes can be diagnosed and managed, and also how the meaning and understanding of the Lean

Management concept changes in the process of its implementation in higher education institutions.

These questions became an inspiration for me to carry out in-depth research on Lean Culture in higher education institutions. The objective of this book is to present the results of this research in the form of an original Lean Culture model and a tool based on this model and used to examine Lean Culture maturity in higher education institutions. It is difficult to assess changes taking place in organisational culture. Such an assessment requires going beyond the traditional functionalist research perspective and adopting a new research approach based on the interpretative-symbolic paradigm. This makes it possible to broaden research on Lean Culture with the humanistic perspective. Man becomes a point of interest, and Lean Culture is created in the networks of various relations and meanings, in people's interpretations.

The book is the effect of many years of research, and particularly a research project carried out in twenty-three higher education institutions in the United Kingdom, Norway, the Netherlands, Canada, and Poland. In the book, I discuss the external and internal conditions for implementing process-based management concepts in higher education institutions, present the Lean University concept, define a theoretical framework for research on Lean Culture, present a Lean Culture model, characterise in detail the dimensions of Lean Culture, propose a new research tool for assessing Lean Culture maturity, as well as a programme for building a mature Lean Culture in higher education institutions. The book allows a better understanding of what Lean Management contributes to university management models in their organisational, technical, and cultural dimensions; which areas are compatible and where contradictions may appear between the Lean Management principles and higher university management models (collegial, bureaucratic, enterprising); what Lean Culture is, how it can be diagnosed and shaped by means of organisational culture change programmes; how the Lean Management concept can be enriched by using experiences of higher education institutions.

The character of the book is both conceptual and applicative. It anticipates the expectations of the institutions which are already in the process of implementing Lean Management or are about to make binding decisions in this respect. The book makes it possible to systematise and supplement the knowledge of the subject; offers concepts, models, methods, and tools to implement changes in university management models on the basis of Lean Management and other process-based management concepts. The book is addressed to the theoreticians and practitioners of managing higher education institutions. The theoretical and applicative solutions proposed in the book can be also used in public organisations and service businesses.

Kraków, Poland   Justyna Maciąg

Acknowledgements

Many people have contributed to the writing of this book, inspiring me to undertake research and supporting me in its performance. First of all, I would like to thank Professor Grażyna Prawelska-Skrzypek and Professor Marek Bugdol from Jagiellonian University in Cracow, Poland. The execution of my research project would have been impossible without the support of the members of the international network LeanHE Hub, in particular Ms. Rachel McAssey from University of Sheffield, Mr. Stephen Yorkstone and Mr. Brent Hurley from Edinburgh Napier University, Mr. Mark Robinson from University of St Andrews, Ms. Marilyn Thompson and Ms. Kimberley Snage from University of Waterloo, Dr. Tammi Sinha from University of Winchester, Mr. Svein Are Tjeldnes from Arctic University of Norway, Ms. José Franken from University of Twente, and Mr. Vincent Wiegel from HAN University of Applied Sciences. Furthermore, I want to thank the Rectors of Polish higher education institutions for allowing me to conduct my research in their respective, particularly, Jagiellonian University in Cracow, Medical University of Łódź, Wrocław University of Science and Technology, Wrocław University of Environmental and Life Sciences, and University of Wrocław. My special thanks go to all those people who agreed to share with me their knowledge and experience during the conducted interviews. An important contribution to the development of the research tool presented in the book was expert opinions; for these, I would like to thank Dr. William K. Balzer from Bowling Green State University, Professor Bob Emiliani from Connecticut State University, Professor Grażyna Prawelska-Skrzypek, Professor Marek Bugdol, Professor Łukasz Sułkowski from Jagiellonian University in Cracow, as well as Dr. Iwona Burka and Ms. Rachel McAssey. The execution of the research project and the preparation of the book for publication would have been impossible without financial support from the National Science Centre provided under the Miniature I programme (Decision No. 2017/01/X/HS/00619) and from the Faculty of Management and Social Sciences, Jagiellonian University in Cracow.

December 2018   Justyna Maciąg

Contents

List of Figures

List of Tables

1

Research on Lean Culture in Higher Education—A Theoretical Framework

1.1 Reasons for Undertaking Research on Lean Culture in Higher Education

The contemporary university is an organisation full of tensions (Geppert and Hollinshead 2017), "suspended" between tradition and modernity (Leja 2013; Kwiek 2015; Antonowicz 2015; Sułkowski 2016). Some researchers are of the opinion that in the globalising economic, cultural, and social environment, the mission of the university as an institution dedicated to the education of the nation for the purpose of strengthening the state is being exhausted (Kwiek 2001). The severance of the strong connections between knowledge and power causes a change in the nature of knowledge and the process of its creation, accumulation, and transfer. Knowledge becomes the subject of commercialisation, a mainly private product/service provided based on competitive conditions and in the *quasi* market conditions. The market viewpoint manifests itself through the shared conviction of the adequacy of the concepts of New Public Management (NPM) and the enterprising university for the understanding of the nature of the contemporary university and the manner of its management. Universities implement

© The Author(s) 2019
J. Maciąg, *Lean Culture in Higher Education*,
https://doi.org/10.1007/978-3-030-05686-5_1

process management concepts coming from manufacturing enterprises (Maciąg 2016). It is assumed that these two concepts will be as effective in universities as they are in business organisations, despite the fundamentally different character of the former. However, it may be problematic to maintain the continuity and permanence of introduced changes. This may result from the fact that universities often implement pseudo-changes in order to appear more attractive to stakeholders (Alvesson 2013). Their lethargy, inertia, and focus on self-recreation are explained by compulsive isomorphism (Santana et al. 2010), conflicts of values (Lenartowicz 2016), strong organisational identities (Sułkowski 2016) or traditional organisational culture (Balzer 2010; Emiliani 2015).

An analysis of the literature on the subject indicates that universities turn away from process approaches popular at the end of the twentieth century such as Total Quality Management (TQM) or Business Process Reengineering (BPR), opting for the concept of Lean Management in the belief that its implementation would contribute also to changes in organisational culture. In order to stress the specificity of the Lean Management concept in higher education researchers use such terms as Lean Higher Education (Balzer 2010), Educational Lean for Higher Education (Waterbury 2011), Lean University (Emiliani 2015).

There are more and more publications on Lean Management in higher education. Conducted research indicates that Lean Management generates positive effects in the organisational and technical system, but there are doubts about the permanence of such results (Radnor and Bucci 2011; Balzer 2010; Emiliani 2015; Antony 2014; Hines and Lethbridge 2008; Yorkstone 2016; Francis et al. 2017; Balzer et al. 2016). Resistance and a lack of continuity of introduced changes are explained by too little attention being paid to the development of an organisational culture of Lean Management—a Lean Culture (LC) (Francis et al. 2017).

An analysis of the literature of the subject shows that the issue of cultural conditions for implementing Lean Management in higher education has not been discussed sufficiently enough. There is a lack of definitions, theoretical models, concepts, methodologies of building a Lean Culture and assessing its maturity as a higher education organisational culture. Furthermore, in the functionalist paradigm used currently to assess the effects of cultural changes, which is based on superficial "production-oriented" measures, it is impossible to understand fully the essence and maturity of the university for the implementation of Lean Management. The objectivist approach causes researchers to study organisational culture from the outside, similarly to how representatives of natural sciences do this (Jo Hatch and Schultz 1997). Therefore many authors propose broadening the research perspective based on the functionalist approach with a humanistic approach based on the interpretative-symbolic paradigm (Jo Hatch and Schultz 1997; Kostera 2003; Alvesson 2009; Czarniawska 2010; Sułkowski 2012; Zawadzki 2014; Weick 2016). In such an approach, Lean Culture is defined as an epistemological metaphor of an organisation (Kostera 2003). It is considered at the level of people's relationships and personal experiences (Sikorski 2009, p. 13). Sharing this opinion, the author decided that adopting this ontological approach would allow her to acquire a deeper understanding of the sense of implementing Lean Management in higher education.

The main reasons for writing this book were the author's need to discover in what way the concept of Lean Management changed higher education organisational culture and how its meaning, the way in which it is understood and developed in the process of its implementation in higher education institutions. For this purpose, it became necessary to create a theoretical framework and a model solution ensuring a holistic approach to searching and assessing the maturity of Lean Culture in higher education. So far no research has been undertaken in which Lean Culture is regarded as an epistemological metaphor of an organisation (Kostera 2003).

1.2   Methodological Premises

Before starting to work on the book, the author had conducted a study of the literature on the subject which had resulted in identifying a cognitive gap which can be summarised in the following question:

What is Lean Culture in higher education institutions, taking into consideration the interpretation of its notions, values, symbols, meanings, and senses and what are the critical descriptors used to assess its maturity?

The question framed in this way allowed the author to formulate the paradigmatic premises, the main objectives, the cognitive objective, and the methodological objective of the book.

The author adopted a number of paradigmatic premises. In the ontological perspective and referring to the functionalist paradigm (Schein 2004; Ott 1989), the author adopted the following assumptions:

- Lean Culture exists as a part of organisational culture of higher education;
- Lean Culture is a tool to manage organisational behaviour. It is an organisational mechanism of control, informally approving or restricting certain models of behaviour depending on their compliance with the philosophy, values, and principles of Lean Management.

Keeping in mind restrictions resulting from basing her research on Lean Culture on the functionalist paradigm only, the author supplemented it with the relational approach to defining Lean Culture. In the relational perspective, Lean Culture is analysed at the level of people's individual experiences in the organisation. As Sikorski observes, the relational approach is close to the interpretative-symbolic approach (Sikorski 2009). Adopting such an approach allows the author to broaden the ontological perspective of the research with the following premise:

- Lean Culture is a construct created by the behaviour and the attitudes of higher education employees.

The adoption of this ontological attitude causes the research on Lean Culture to be broadened with the humanistic perspective. Man becomes a point of interest, and Lean Culture is created in the networks of various relations and meanings, in people's interpretations. Such ontological premises are characteristic of the constructivist approach (Czarniawska 2010). It means that the structure of Lean Culture is created through people's behaviour and manifests itself in their attitudes.

The adopted ontological premises consistently translate into the epistemological premises adopted in the research on Lean Culture.

Formulating the epistemological premises, the author adopted the position of epistemological pluralism (Sułkowski 2012; Kawalec 2017). The following premises were adopted:

- Lean Culture is monolithic at the level of a theoretical framework (it is a harmonised, consistent, and coherent whole).
- Lean Culture allows university employees to understand and give sense to events and symbols related to the implementation of a Lean strategy.
- Lean Culture constitutes a basis for ensuring the permanence of continuous improvement.
- Lean Culture is the result of learning processes in the individual and organisational dimensions.
- Lean Culture in higher education is unique because its shape is influenced by the organisational culture of a particular university as well as the external and internal contexts of its functioning.

Taking into consideration the adopted paradigmatic premises, the author formulated the objectives of the book. The main objective of the research presented in this book is to define the notion and maturity of Lean Culture in higher education institutions as well as to determine its key dimensions and descriptors in the light of the adopted ontological and epistemological premises. The cognitive objective of the research was formulated as defining the notion of Lean Culture as well as the dimensions and descriptors of its maturity; the methodological objective was formulated as developing and testing the author's original model of assessing the maturity of Lean Culture in higher education (Lean Culture Maturity Model in Higher Education—LCMMHE) and tool for testing the maturity of Lean Culture (Lean Culture Maturity Questionnaire—LCMQ), as well as determining conditions for their implementation.

The conducted analysis of the literature on the subject and the identified research gaps allowed the author to formulate detailed objectives of the cognitive character (CO) and the methodological character (MO), to pose research questions, to propose research theses and hypotheses, as well as to adopt adequate research methods (Table 1.1). The theses

Table 1.1 Detailed objectives, research questions, theses and hypotheses, research methodology

Research gaps	Detailed objectives	Research questions	Detailed theses	Research methods	Book chapters
There is insufficient critical analysis of the external and internal contexts of the functioning of higher education institutions from the point of view of implementing process-based management concepts	CO1: To identify the factors of the internal and external contexts of the functioning of the modern university and to determine their influence on the university's ability to implement effectively process-based management concepts, including Lean Management	Is a process-based approach, e.g. Lean Management, an effective method of changing the model of management in the university, taking into consideration the external and internal contexts of its functioning?	Changes resulting from the application of process management, including Lean Management, allow a holistic and systemic change in the university's management model, taking into consideration its mission, goals, as well as external and internal contexts of functioning	1. Critical and systematic analysis of the literature on the subject 2. Interviews conducted in higher education institutions in Poland and abroad 3. Observation	Chapter 2
There is no standard concept of a Lean University determining the scope and direction of required changes in management models	CO2: To present the developed model concept of a Lean University	Does the specific character of the processes conducted in higher education institutions require a redefinition of the qualities of a model organisation implementing Lean Management or the Lean university model?	The processes carried out in higher education institutions have specific qualities and division criteria, which require the adoption of a new approach to a model presentation of the university in the Lean Management concept	1. Critical and systematic analysis of the literature on the subject 2. Interviews conducted in higher education institutions in Poland and abroad 3. Observation 4. The method of induction at the stage of generalising the research results 5. The method of deduction at the stage of verification and formulating conclusions	

Research gaps	Detailed objectives	Research questions	Detailed theses	Research methods	Book chapters
There is a lack of research on the external and internal context for the building of the maturity of Lean Culture in higher education institutions	CO3: To identify the external and internal contexts for the building of a Lean Culture in higher education institutions	What factors condition the effective building of a mature Lean Culture in higher education?	Lean Culture is strongly influenced by factors resulting from traditions, the models of organisational culture in higher education, and the national culture of a particular country	1. Analysis of the literature on the subject. 2. Interviews conducted in higher education institutions in Poland and abroad 3. Observation 4. The methods of analysing the results of qualitative research (the open coding method) 5. The method of incomplete enumerative induction at the stage of generalising the results of interviews and observations, and creating a model	Chapter 3
There is a lack of research and studies proposing a comprehensive and holistic approach to Lean Culture in universities as their organisational culture (there is a lack of definitions, research approaches, and systematics of elements). There is no model presentation of Lean Culture in higher education which would identify its dimensions and the most important descriptors constructing such dimensions	CO4: To define the notion of Lean Culture and to create a model of the maturity of a Lean Culture in higher education (Lean Culture Maturity Model in HE) as well as to determine its dimensions and descriptors	Will the application of the point of view of the relations definition of organisational culture based on the interpretative-symbolic paradigm in research on organisational culture in higher education institutions reveal anything new that could not be seen in the functionalist approaches to the definition and modelling of Lean Culture?	The application of the relational definition of organisational culture based on the interpretative-symbolic paradigm in research on Lean Culture allows the identification of new, previously undefined dimensions and descriptors of organisational culture as well as their prioritisation with respect to importance		

(continued)

Table 1.1 (continued)

Research gaps	Detailed objectives	Research questions	Detailed theses	Research methods	Book chapters
There is a lack of research on organisational culture with respect to Lean Management implementation conducted from research perspectives extended beyond the functionalist paradigm to include the interpretative-symbolic paradigm	CO5: To identify interdependences, contradictions, and gaps in higher education organisational culture and Lean Culture.	Will the broadening of the research perspective with the interpretative-symbolic paradigm make it possible to identify interdependences, contradictions, and gaps in higher education organisational culture and Lean Culture	The interpretative-symbolic perspective makes it possible to capture the fundamental premises of organisational culture in higher education and to identify interdependences, contradictions, and gaps in Lean Culture		
So far there has been no comprehensive research aimed at showing how manufacturing concepts such as Lean Management introduced in educational or public organisations change their definitions, meanings, ways of understanding and implementing	CO6: To determine the extent to which the Lean Management concept changes during the course of its implementation in higher education	Does the Lean Management concept change its definitions, meanings, ways of understanding and implementing in higher education institutions?	The external and internal contexts of higher education institutions, including their organisational culture, cause changes in the understanding of the essence of Lean Management as compared to business organisations		

Research gaps	Detailed objectives	Research questions	Detailed hypotheses	Research methods	
A lack of basic definitions of such notions as Lean Culture maturity, Lean Culture maturity model, Lean Culture maturity assessment level A lack of a concept of and tool for the assessment of Lean Culture maturity in higher education	MO1: To define a conceptual framework for the examination, assessment, and testing of Lean Culture maturity (Lean Culture Maturity Model in Higher Education) and to create a tool for assessing Lean Culture maturity (Lean Culture Maturity Questionnaire LCMQ) and to determine the conditions for its application	Does the Lean Culture Maturity Questionnaire allow a reliable assessment of Lean Culture maturity in higher education?	The Lean Culture Maturity Questionnaire allows a correct and reliable assessment of Lean Culture maturity in higher education	1. The method of incomplete enumerative induction at the stage of generalising the results of observations and formulating statements in a research questionnaire 2. The expert assessment method. 3. Questionnaire research based on the use of an Internet questionnaire 3. The statistical analysis methods	Chapter 4
Fragmentary research on Lean Culture maturity assessment in higher education as well as conditions for building such assessment. A lack of a typology of Lean Cultures in higher education institutions A lack of research on factors diversifying Lean Culture assessment	MO2: To test the Lean Culture Maturity Questionnaire and to determine the factors conditioning Lean Culture maturity assessment	Is Lean Culture maturity assessment diversified with respect to a university management model? Do the results of Lean Culture maturity assessment indicate the existence of a separate subculture created by a university's top management? Do the results of Lean Culture maturity assessment indicate the existence of separate subcultures created by administration employees or academic employees? Do participation in restructuring projects and possession of experience in Lean Management influence Lean Culture maturity assessment?	Lean Culture maturity assessment is higher in private universities and universities implementing quality management models and other process management concepts University management assesses Lean Culture maturity at a higher level (there is a separate subculture) With respect to maturity assessment levels, it is possible to distinguish two subcultures: the subculture of administration employees and the subculture of academics University employees who have experience in implementing process management concepts are more critical in assessing Lean Culture maturity (an assessment level will be lower)	1. Questionnaire research based on the use of an Internet questionnaire 2. The statistical analysis methods	
Limited and fragmentary research on the implementation of the Lean Management concept in higher education. A lack of a systematic approach to Lean Culture maturity improvement. Fragmentary descriptions of programmes aimed at building Lean Culture maturity in higher education	MO3: To develop a plan of a programme for building Lean Culture maturity in higher education institutions	Taking into consideration the diversified external and internal contexts of functioning, including organisational culture, is it possible to develop a model programme of change in higher education organisational culture?	It is possible to develop a model programme of change in organisational culture oriented towards the building of a Lean University which will be possible to apply in every higher education institution	1. The method of induction at the stage of generalising the research results 2. The method of deduction at the stage of verification and formulating conclusions	

Source The author's own work

Table 1.2 The relations among the research objectives

The detailed cognitive objectives of the research

CO1: To identify the factors of the internal and external contexts of the functioning of the modern university and to determine their influence on the university's ability to implement effectively process-based management concepts, including Lean Management	CO2: To present the developed model concept of a Lean University	CO3: To identify the external and internal contexts for the building of a Lean Culture in higher education institutions	CO4: To define the notion of Lean Culture and to create a model of the maturity of a Lean Culture in higher education (Lean Culture Maturity Model in HE) as well as to determine its dimensions and descriptors	CO5: To identify interdependences, contradictions, and gaps in higher education organisational culture and Lean Culture	CO6: To determine the extent to which the Lean Management concept changes during the course of its implementation in higher education

The main cognitive objective of the research

CO: To define the notion of Lean Culture as well as the dimensions and descriptors of Lean Culture maturity

The main objective of the research

To define the notion and maturity of Lean Culture in higher education institutions as well as to determine the key dimensions and descriptors of Lean Culture maturity in the light of the adopted ontological and epistemological premises

The main methodological objective of the research

To develop and test the author's original model of assessing the maturity of Lean Culture in higher education (Lean Culture Maturity Model in Higher Education—LCMMHE) and tool for testing the maturity of Lean Culture (Lean Culture Maturity Questionnaire—LCMQ), as well as to determine conditions for their implementation

The detailed methodological objectives of the research

MO1: To define a conceptual framework for the examination, assessment, and testing of Lean Culture maturity (Lean Culture Maturity Model in Higher Education—LCMMHE) and to create a tool for assessing Lean Culture maturity (Lean Culture Maturity Questionnaire—LCMQ) and to determine the conditions for its application	MO2: To test the Lean Culture Maturity Questionnaire and to determine the factors conditioning Lean Culture maturity assessment	MO3: Developing a plan of a programme for building Lean Culture maturity in higher education institutions

Source The author's own work

were formulated in the chapters in which the cognitive objectives were achieved (Chapters 2 and 3). The hypotheses were put forward in Chapter 4, in which the author reached the methodological objectives.

In order to attain the formulated research objectives, the author used a wide range of research methods and tools applied in social sciences and discussed in such works as, for example: Babbie (2013), Charmaz (2009), Creswell (2013), Kvale (2010), Easterby-Smith et al. (2015), Spencer (2013), Tabachnick and Fidel (2014), and Sobczak (2002).

Table 1.2 presents a diagram of connections among the particular objectives of the book.

In the next section, the author will present the methodology of her research.

1.3 The Methodology of the Research

1.3.1 The Subject Matter, Scope, and Stages of the Research

In preparation for the writing of the book, the author carried out an extensive research programme consisting of the following three stages: a study of the literature on the subject, qualitative research, and quantitative research conducted in higher education institutions. Writing the book, the author relied also on many years of experience gained in connection with her teaching career, training courses, academic, and application projects in the area of process-based concepts, including Lean Management. The picture below presents the chronology of the particular stages of the research (Fig. 1.1).

The subjective scope of the research included higher education institutions declaring that they were or were not implementing the Lean Management concept, and their employees. Interviews and questionnaire research were conducted in the schools which had declared the implementation of Lean Management. Only questionnaire research was conducted in the schools which had not declared their interest in the concept. The objective scope of the research comprised Lean

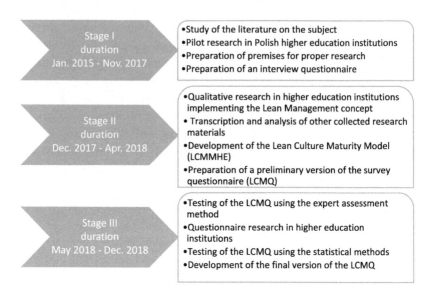

Fig. 1.1 The stages of the own research on Lean Culture in higher education institutions (*Source* The author's own work)

Culture in higher education. The research was carried out in the years 2015–2018.

The particular stages of the research and the respective adopted research strategies are described in detail below.

1.3.2 Stage I—Preparation for the Research

At the first stage of the research, on the basis of the conducted analysis of the literature on the subject, in 2016 the author carried out the pilot research in 5 higher education institutions in Poland (Maciąg 2016, 2018). The objective of the research was to identify the qualities of higher education organisational culture in the context of implementing the concept of Lean Management and to determine the scope of necessary changes. The research was based on the analysis of the literature on the subject, questionnaire research (the survey questionnaire had been designed using the Lean Culture dimensions described in the book "The Toyota Way" by Likert [2005]), interviews with employees, and the author's own experience. The results of the questionnaire research confirmed the hypothesis according to which the organisational cultures of the examined schools constituted a barrier to the implementation of Lean Management. In consequence of the conducted regression analysis, the author concluded that the variables which strongly influenced differences in the assessments of Lean Culture included a school type, a position held in a university (superior, subordinate), and a length of employment. The research results showed that technical and organisational changes were taking place in parallel to and were integrated with social changes only if restructuring projects were implemented using the bottom-up approach as well as that the application of the functionalist paradigm in research on higher education organisational culture was insufficient because it did not allow to notice all other components and areas of Lean Culture. Therefore the author proposed broadening the research perspective with the humanistic approach based on the interpretative-symbolic paradigm. The results of the performed pilot research became the reason for undertaking further research on Lean Culture in higher education institutions. On the basis of these results and a further study of the literature, the author drew up theoretical premises for a model of assessing the maturity of Lean Culture in higher education. They became a foundation for the preparation of a categorised interview questionnaire. An interview model is included in Enclosure 1. At the same time the author was successful in applying for a research grant. The project entitled *The Conditions for the Maturity of the Lean Management Culture in Higher Education Institutions* received financing from the MINIATURA 1 programme run by the National Science Centre (the project execution period: 25 September 2017–25 September 2018 No. DEC. 2017/01/X/HS/00619). Additionally, the author secured for her research the patronage of the Minister of Science and Higher Education. The project received also support from the international network LeanHE Hub.

The next stage of the project was qualitative research carried out in universities implementing the concept of Lean Management.

1.3.3 Stage 2—The Strategy of the Qualitative Research Conducted in Higher Education Institutions

At the second stage of the research, in accordance with the adopted strategy, the author conducted qualitative research, i.e. in-depth interviews, observations, and an analysis of documents in the schools implementing the Lean Management concept. The research comprised the following seven selected universities implementing the Lean concept: Napier Edinburgh University, St. Andrews University, University of Winchester in the United Kingdom, University of Twente, HAN University of Applied Sciences in the Netherlands, Arctic University of Norway in Tromso, Norway, and University of Waterloo in Canada. Thus the research participants were three universities from the United Kingdom, 1 university from Norway, 2 universities from the Netherlands, and 1 university from Canada. The criteria for selecting universities from outside Poland were membership in LeanHE Hub (the only worldwide network of higher education institutions implementing Lean), the adopted implementation approach, as well as the organisational and legal form. Each of the examined universities follows a different approach to the implementation of Lean Management and has a different period of experience connected with this concept. Within the framework of the project, the author undertook five days' visits to all universities during which she conducted interviews with people involved in Lean Management implementation processes, both administration employees and academics. Her interviewees were consultants, experts, coaches, lecturers, team members, team leaders, and management representatives. Each of the participating institutions appointed a coordinator, who selected such persons in accordance with the author's suggestions. Altogether thirty-six interviews were carried out. The structure of respondents is presented in Table 1.3.

An analysis of the structure of respondents shows that the decisive majority of them were administration employees as well as persons involved in various activities related to Lean Management and continuous improvement in a given university. More than 50% of the structure included management employees (senior managers, line managers). The average length of the respondents' experience in Lean Management

Table 1.3 The structure of respondents in the researched higher education institutions

No.	Employee in Lean Management (LM)/continuous improvement (CI) department	Department manager/independent position in CI/LM	Person involved in various activities related to Lean Management and continuous improvement (lean leader, lean facilitator, team member, etc.)	Administration employee	Academic	Senior management	Line manager	Subordinate	Length of the respondent's experience in Lean Management	First experience in Lean Management
1	1			1				1	4	HEI
2		1	1	1	1			1	4	HE
3			1	1					18	Production, business
4			1	1		1	1		15	Master's degree
5			1	1	1				16	Production, business
6			1	1			1	1	10	NGO
7			1	1			1		6	HEI
8			1	1		1	1		6	HEI
9			1	1				1	48	Health care
10			1	1					12	Production, business
11			1	1				1	6	HEI
12			1	1				1	2	HEI
13		1	1	1					15	Production, business
14			1	1			1		2	HEI
15			1	1			1		3	HEI
16				1		1	1			HEI
17				1				1	8	HEI
18			1	1					6	HEI
19			1	1				1	6	Tax administration
20			1	1					12	HEI

(continued)

Table 1.3 (continued)

No.	Employee in Lean Management (LM)/continuous improvement (CI) department	Department manager/independent position in CI/LM	Person involved in various activities related to Lean Management and continuous improvement (lean leader, lean facilitator, team member, etc.)	Administration employee	Academic	Senior management	Line manager	Subordinate	Length of the respondent's experience in Lean Management	First experience in Lean Management
21			1	1			1		12	HEI
22			1	1			1		10	HEI
23		1		1			1		10	HEI
24			1	1			1		12	HEI
25			1	1					10	HEI
26			1	1					10	HEI
27			1	1		1	1	1	12	Health Service
28			1	1					3	HEI
29			1	1					12	HEI
30			1	1				1	15	Financial industry
31			1	1				1	27	HEI
32			1	1	1			1	6	HEI
33			1	1	1			1	8	HEI
34			1	1	1				9	HEI
35			1	1			1		14	Production, business
36	1		1	1					18	Financial industry
	1	3	32	32	6	4	15	17	387	

Source The author's own work

was 10.75 years. The decisive majority of the respondents gained such experience in higher education institutions. As it has been noted earlier, the selection of the respondents was deliberate and consulted with the research coordinators in the particular universities. The information presented in the table confirms that it was appropriate for obtaining representatives opinions of the Lean community. Within the scope of the study visits the author conducted also observations during various project meetings, seminars, conferences, workshops and while walking around university premises or analysing documents. The whole collected material was used in the subsequent research.

At the next stage the interviews were transcribed (the interviews were recorded with the consent of the respondents, who received detailed information on how the recordings would be used). An analysis of the transcribed interviews and the notes taken during observations indicated the most important descriptors of Lean Culture. They were divided into 7 dimensions, thus creating the LCMMHE. The model comprises the following dimensions: a process approach, values, management (with a distinction between top management and immediate superiors), employees in an organisation, relations and work in teams, artefacts (tangible artefacts, behavioural artefacts, and language), as well as relations with the environment. The descriptors defined in the particular dimensions concerned the notions, values, symbols, meanings, senses, and interpretations through which Lean Culture is expressed. The details of the research results are discussed in Chapter 3. On the basis of the developed Lean Culture model, the author prepared a preliminary version of the LCMQ, which will be discussed in the next section.

1.3.4 Stage 3—Developing and Testing the Lean Culture Maturity Questionnaire

1.3.4.1 The Development and Qualitative Assessment of the LCMQ

The first version of the LCMQ consisted of 91 statements divided with respect to the 6 dimensions of Lean Culture. In view of the fact that the dimension of relations with the environment is difficult to research by means of questionnaires, the author recommended other methods of assessing its maturity. The survey questionnaire was drawn up in the Polish and English language versions.

For a preliminary qualitative assessment of the survey questionnaire, the author used the expert assessment method. The questionnaire was sent to seven experts specialising in the implementation of the Lean concept, as well as organisational culture, humanistic management, and process management. Selecting persons to perform the function of an expert, the author paid special attention to ensuring that they were people who had not had any influence on the shape of the questionnaire at the stage of the research conducted in higher education institutions. She also tried to ensure a balanced selection of experts with respect to their theoretical and practical knowledge of Lean Management as well as their nationalities. Five professors, three from Poland and two from the USA, participated in the research. Additionally, assistance was requested from the person managing the international LeanHE network, as well as an expert in Lean Management holding a doctoral degree and running their own consulting business in Poland. Thus the group of experts consisted of: 3 women and 4 men; 4 persons from Poland, 1 person from the United Kingdom, 2 persons from the USA; 5 active Lean Management practitioners, including 4 active practitioners and researchers associated with higher education institutions. The experts were asked to review and comment on the survey questionnaire. The experts' opinions and comments on the particular statements included in the questionnaire were put together in an Excel spreadsheet. There were slight differences in the assessments. The experts were generally consistent in their opinions, which allowed the broadening of the survey questionnaire with issues related to the humanistic approach, from the point of view of organisational culture, process management, management psychology, as well as the practice of implementing Lean Management in organisations.

Additionally, the experts analysed the questionnaire with respect to the Lean Culture descriptors. The grouping of the questionnaire statements in various configurations allowed the author to reduce their number to 80 (first of all, the repeating statements were eliminated). Eventually, the prototype of the questionnaire consisted of 80 statements divided according to the six dimensions of Lean Culture (the questionnaire omitted the dimension connected with relations with the environment because, taking into consideration their specific character, the more appropriate research methods are document analysis and interviews).

The assessment of the statements was based on a five-point Likert scale. The author's decision to use this scale was preceded by an in-depth analysis of its practical application in qualitative research (opinion and attitude surveys) and research on organisational culture (a detailed description is included in Chapter 4).

1.3.4.2 Statistical Testing of the LCMQ

At the next stage, the LCMQ was prepared in the form of a survey questionnaire, in two language versions (Polish and English), and was sent to the selected higher education institutions which had given their consent to participate in the research. The research was conducted using Google forms. The author complied with all ethical principles in order to ensure the anonymity of the research.

The Polish higher education institutions participating in the research were selected in a different way. In view of the fact that none of the universities in Poland declared having implemented the Lean Management concept at the stage of research project preparation, candidates for the research were selected based on the criteria established by the author (the so-called success criteria). They were as follows:

1. Universities which had implemented a quality management system based on the ISO 9001 standard[1]; the condition was the implementation of such a system in a whole university or in at least one faculty.
2. Universities which were placed on the Forbes Diamonds list[2] in the years 2016–2017.

---

[1]The list according to POLON; the status as at 28 March 2017 (www1).

[2]Analysts and experts of the business intelligence consultancy Dun&Bradstreet assessed the value of enterprises based on the Swiss method, taking into consideration the value of assets and financial results from the years 2008–2010 (www2).

3. The best universities in Poland according to the Centre for World University Rankings 2016 (www3).
4. The best three universities in the seven groups of criteria according to the university ranking organised by the magazine Perspektywy—rankings in the groups of criteria 2016 (www4).

A few institutions met all adopted criteria. Thirty-three universities were selected as candidates for the research and were sent requests for granting their consent to participate in the research project. Twenty-two institutions granted their written consent; four universities did not respond to the request, and seven institutions refused to participate in the project. The author accepted twenty-one Polish universities for participation in the research. They were as follows: the Feliks Nowowiejski Academy of Music in Bydgoszcz, The State University of Applied Sciences in Elbląg, the Medical University of Gdańsk, the Polish Naval Academy of the Heroes of Westerplatte in Gdynia, the Gdynia Maritime University, the Adam Mickiewicz University in Poznań, the Maritime University of Szczecin, the Pomeranian Medical University in Szczecin, the Kozminski University, the University of Warsaw, the Medical University of Warsaw, the University of Applied Informatics and Management in Warsaw, the Wrocław University of Science and Technology, the Wrocław University of Environmental and Life Sciences, the University of Wrocław, the WSB University in Wrocław, the Jagiellonian University in Kraków, the Medical University of Łódź, the Warsaw School of Economics, the Academy of Fine Arts in Katowice, and the Białystok University of Technology. Eventually, twenty-three universities took part in the research, including institutions from the United Kingdom, Norway, the Netherlands, Canada, and Poland (5 universities failed to complete and return the questionnaire).

The questionnaire research comprised 771 people (a detailed description of the structure of respondents is included in Chapter 4).

At the next stage the LCMQ underwent statistical tests aimed at checking its reliability as a research tool to measure the maturity of Lean Culture in higher education. For this purpose, the following methods were applied:

- A confirmative analysis based on the method of main constituents (Spencer 2013; Tabachnick and Fidel 2014).
- Standardised Cronbach's alphas.

The execution of the research programme described above allowed the author to obtain original research results and to indicate further areas for research on Lean Culture and conditions for the implementation of the Lean Management concept in higher education institutions. The results of the review of the literature on the subject and the author's own research are presented in the next two chapters of the book.

1.4   The Structure and Addressees of the Book

This book consists of 5 chapters.

In this chapter, the author presents the reasons for undertaking the research on Lean Culture in higher education institutions, the applied research paradigm, the cognitive and methodological objectives, the research questions, theses, hypotheses, as well as methods. She describes the research process comprising studies on the literature of the subject, as well as qualitative and quantitative research conducted in selected universities in the United Kingdom, Norway, the Netherlands, Canada, and Poland.

The objective of Chapter 2 is to identify the factors of the internal and external contexts of the functioning of the modern university, to determine their influence on the university's ability to implement effectively process-based management concepts, including Lean Management, and to present the developed model concept of a Lean University.

Chapter 3 has a conceptual character. Its objective is to present the author's proposal of a model of Lean Culture maturity in higher education as well as conditions necessary for the building of such maturity. The detailed objectives of this chapter are the following: to identify the external and internal contexts for the building of a Lean Culture in higher education, to define the notion of Lean Culture, to create a LCMMHE, to determine its dimensions and descriptors, and to determine interdependences, contradictions, and gaps in higher education organisational culture and Lean Culture. Also in this chapter, the author reflects on the extent to which the Lean Management concept changes during the course of its implementation in higher education institutions.

The general objective of the chapter is to present the author's original tool for the assessment of Lean Culture in higher education, i.e. the LCMQ, to determine the conditions for its application, and to present a concept of a programme for the building of Lean Culture maturity.

Chapter 5 summarises the results of the conducted research. The author presents the contribution to the theory and practice of research on Lean Culture and Lean Management in the cognitive, methodological, and applicative dimensions. The book ends with recommendations concerning the areas of further research on this subject.

The book is addressed to management theoreticians and practitioners, particularly those specialising in process management, Lean Management, and higher education management. It may be of special interest to researchers, lecturers, coaches, experts, managers, and employees dealing with Lean Management and other process-based management concepts (e.g. quality management, TQM, BPR, Business Process Management (BPM)), change management, continuous improvement, as well as the shaping of organisational culture in universities and other educational and training institutions. The theoretical and applicative solutions proposed in the book can be also used in public organisations and service businesses.

References

Alvesson, M. (2009). At home ethnography: Struggling with closeness and closure. In S. Ybema, D. Yanow, H. Wels, & F. H. Kamsteeg (Eds.), *Organizational ethnography: Studying the complexity of everyday life* (pp. 156–217). London: Sage.

Alvesson, M. (2013). *The triumph of emptiness: Consumption, higher education, and work organization.* Oxford: Oxford Unversity Press.

Antonowicz, D. (2015). *Między siłą globalnych procesów a lokalną tradycją. Polskie szkolnictwo wyższe w dobie przemian* [Between the power of global processes and the local tradition. Poland's higher education in the period of changes]. Toruń: Wydawnictwo Naukowe Uniwersytetu Mikołaja Kopernika.

Antony, J. (2014). Readiness factors for the Lean Six Sigma journey in the higher education sector. *International Journal of Productivity and Performance Management, 63*(2), 257–264.

Babbie, E. R. (2013). *Podstawy badań społecznych* [The basics of social research]. Warszawa: Wydawnictwo Naukowe PWN.

Balzer, K. (2010). *Lean higher education.* New York: CRP Press, Taylor & Francis Group.

Balzer, W. K., Francis, D. E., Krehbiel, T. C., & Shea, N. (2016). A review and perspective on lean in higher education. *Quality Assurance in Education, 24*(4), 442–462.

Charmaz, K. (2009). *Teoria ugruntowana. Praktyczny przewodnik po analizie jakościowej* [Constructing grounded theory: A practical guide through qualitative analysis]. Warszawa: Wydawnictwo Naukowe PWN.

Creswell, J. W. (2013). *Projektowanie badań naukowych: metody jakościowe, ilościowe i mieszane* [Research design: Qualitative, quantitative, and mixed methods approaches]. Kraków: Wydawnictwo Uniwersytetu Jagiellońskiego.

Czarniawska, B. (2010). *Trochę inna teoria organizacji. Organizowanie jako konstrukcja sieci działań* [A little bit different theory of organization. Organizing as constructing a network of activities]. Warszawa: Poltext.

Easterby-Smith, M., Thorpe, R., & Jackson, P. R. (2015). *Management and business research.* London: Sage.

Emiliani, B. (2015). *Lean university: A guide to renewal and prosperity.* Wethersfield: CLBM, LCC.

Francis D. E., Krehbiel T. C., & Balzer W. K. (2017). *Lean applications in higher education.* Downloaded from https://the-lmj.com/2017/03/.

Geppert, M., & Hollinshead, G. (2017). Signs of dystopia and demoralization in global academia: Reflections on the precarious and destructive effects of the colonization of the Lebenswelt. *Critical Perspectives on International Business, 13*(2), 136–150.

Hines, P., & Lethbridge, S. (2008). New development: Creating a Lean university. *Public Money and Management, 28*(1), 53–56.

Jo Hatch, M., & Schultz, M. (1997). Relations between organizational culture, identity and image. *European Journal of Marketing, 31*(5/6), 356–365.

Kawalec, P. (2017). Ewaluacja – teoria i metodologia [Evaluation—Theory and methodology]. In G. Prawelska-Skrzypek (Ed.), *Ewaluacja w procesie tworzenia polityki naukowej i innowacyjnej*. Warszawa: Dom Wydawniczy Elipsa.

Kostera, M. (2003). *Antropologia organizacji. Metodologia badań terenowych* [Anthropology of organizations. Field research methodology]. Warszawa: WN PWN.

Kvale, S. (2010). *Prowadzenie wywiadów* [Doing interviews]. Warszawa: Wydawnictwo Naukowe PWN.

Kwiek, M. (2001). Filozofia – demokracja – uniwersytet. Wyzwania epoki globalizacji [Philosophy – democracy – university. Challenges in the epoch of globalization]. In P. W. Juchacz, K. Kozłowski, & A. Cooper (Eds.), *Filozofia a demokracja, t. III*. Poznań: IF UAM.

Kwiek, M. (2015). *Uniwersytet w dobie przemian* [The university in the period of changes]. Warszawa: PWN.

Leja, K. (2013). *Zarządzanie uczelnią. Koncepcje i współczesne wyzwania* [University management. Concepts and contemporary challenges]. Warszawa: Oficyna a Wolters Kluwer Business.

Lenartowicz, M. (2016). *Natura oporu Uniwersytet jako samowytwarzający się system społeczny* [The nature of resistance. The university as a self-creating social system]. Poznań: CSPP UAM.

Liker, J. K. (2005). *The Toyota Way*. Warsaw: Esensi.

Maciąg, J. (2016). Uwarunkowania wdrożenia koncepcji Lean Service w polskich szkołach wyższych [The conditions of implementing the lean service concept in Polish higher education institutions]. *Zarządzanie Publiczne, 1*(33), 51–64.

Maciąg, J. (2018). Kultura Lean Management w polskich szkołach wyższych (wyniki badań pilotażowych) [The lean management culture in Polish higher education institutions (pilot studies results)]. *Nauka i Szkolnictwo Wyższe, 1*(51), 69–95.

Ott, J. S. (1989). *The organizational culture perspective*. Chicago, IL: The Dorsey Press.

Radnor, Z., & Bucci, G. (2011). *Analysis of lean implementation in UK business schools and universities*. London: Association of Business Schools.

Santana, S., Moreira, C., Roberto, T., & Azambuja, F. (2010). Fighting for excellence: The case of the Federal University of Pelotas. *Higher Education, 60*(3), 321–341.

Schein, E. H. (2004). *Organizational culture and leadership (Jossey-Bass business & management series)*. San Francisco: Jossey-Bass.

Sikorski, C. (2009). *Kształtowanie kultury organizacyjnej: filozofia, strategie, metody* [The shaping of organizational culture: Philosophy, strategies, methods]. Łódź: Wydawnictwo Uniwersytetu Łódzkiego.

Sobczyk, M. (2002). *Statystyka.(wyd. IV)* [Statistics (edition IV)]. Warszawa: PWN.

Spencer, N. H. (2013). *Essentials of multivariate data analysis*. Boca Raton: Chapman & Hall and CRC Press.

Sułkowski, Ł. (2012). *Kulturowe procesy zarządzania* [Cultural management processes]. Warszawa: Difin.

Sułkowski, Ł. (2016). *Kultura akademicka. Koniec utopii?* [The academic culture. The end of a utopia?] Warszawa: Wydawnictwo Naukowe PWN.

Tabachnick, B. G., & Fidel, L. S. (2014). *Using multivariate statistics* (6th ed.). Harlow: Pearson.

Waterbury, T. (2011). *Educational lean for higher education: Theory and practice*. Lulu.com.

Weick, K. (2016). *Tworzenie sensu w organizacjach* [Sensemaking in organizations]. Kraków: Wydawnictwo Uniwersytetu Jagiellońskiego.

Yorkstone, S. (2016). Lean universities. In T. Netland & D. J. Powell (Eds.). *The Routledge companion to lean management*. Abingdon: Taylor & Francis (Routledge).

Zawadzki, M. (2014). *Nurt krytyczny w zarządzaniu: kultura, edukacja, teoria* [The critical trend in management: Culture, education, theory]. Warsaw: Wydawnictwo Akademickie SEDNO Spółka z oo.

(www1) polon.nauka.gov.pl/opi/aa/instytucja/wsj/zestawienie?execution=e1s1.

(www2) https://www.forbes.pl/diamenty/2016.

(www3) https://www.timeshighereducation.com/world-university-rankings/2017/world-ranking#!/page/0/length/25/sort_by/rank/sort_order/asc/cols/stats.

(www4) http://www.perspektywy.pl/RSW2016/ranking-uczelni-akademickich.

2

Lean Management as a Concept of Management in Higher Education

2.1 Introduction

A public university is a special kind of an organisation in which the tensions of the modern world converge as if in a lens. It is "suspended" between the tradition of the liberal university and the modernity of the neoliberal enterprising university (Leja 2013; Kwiek 2015; Antonowicz 2015; Gibb et al. 2012; Etzkowitz et al. 2000), between collegiality and managerism (Sułkowski 2016). On the one hand, the operational framework of the university is determined by market forces (customers, consumers) and entities providing financing (the state, the business sector, sponsors), but on the other hand, the academic world defends its position consolidated by centuries-old traditions. Academics perceive ongoing changes as threats to the unhindered development of science and knowledge (Maciąg and Prawelska-Skrzypek 2017). What is particularly noticeable is a continuous dispute about the university's identity, values, principles of functioning, and roles. This exerts a strong influence on the selection and effectiveness of implemented management concepts and models. Universities' lethargy, inertia and focus on self-recreation are explained by compulsive isomorphism

© The Author(s) 2019
J. Maciąg, *Lean Culture in Higher Education*,
https://doi.org/10.1007/978-3-030-05686-5_2

(Santana et al. 2010), conflicts of values (Lenartowicz 2016), or strong organisational identities (Sułkowski 2016). Appreciating the role of universities in social and economic development, decision makers simultaneously demand that they be able to demonstrate their value for money (Kwiek 2015, p. 27). On the tide of the New Public Management (NPM), the university of the twenty-first century has to face the challenges coming from such categories as quality, effectiveness, efficiency, flexibility, transparency, and accountability. The indicators of the university's development are the achievement of scientific and didactic excellence with the support of efficient management systems. Higher education institutions make use of management concepts and methods coming from the business sector. Researchers indicate the usefulness of the practical application of Strategic Management (Leja 2013; Cyfert and Kochalski 2011; Koźmiński 1999; Rudolph and Steffens 2012), Marketing Management (Nowaczyk and Lisiecki 2006, p. 74; Nowaczyk and Kolasiński 2004), Knowledge Management (Leja 2013), the concept of Corporate Social Responsibility (Geryk 2010; Shek and Hollister 2017), process-based concepts such as Business Process Management (BPM) and Business Process Reengineering (BPR) (Tsichritzis 1999; Ahmad et al. 2007; Mircea 2010; Ciancio 2018), as well as the concept of Total Quality Management (TQM) (Tarí and Dick 2012; Manatos et al. 2017; Papanthymou and Darra 2017; Wawak 2011; Bayraktar et al. 2008, pp. 551–574; Maciąg 2011a; Piasecka 2011). However, questions are asked about how far universities may go in adopting the business approach without violating their fundamental principles and values or which management concept is optimal for a given university.

The first discussions on applying the concept of Lean Management in education were initiated in 1995 in connection with analyses of the issue of leadership in Total Quality Management (TQM) and possibilities of cost reduction by way of eliminating waste in educational institutions (Suárez-Barraza et al. 2012, p. 370). At present the concept of Lean Management is one of the important topics addressed in the process of reforming management in institutions of higher education. It is shown in the growing number of academic publications, practical implementations, or activities undertaken by communities of Lean Management practitioners established all over the world (e.g. the international

LeanHE network) (www1). With respect to the institutions of higher education, Lean Management is referred to as Lean Higher Education (LHE) (Balzer 2010; Francis et al. 2017), Lean University (Emiliani 2015; Yorkstone 2016), or Educational Lean (Waterbury 2011). The chapter includes a systematic review of the literature on BPM, BPR, TQM, and Lean Management in the institutions of higher education. The performed analysis of the literature allowed the author to indicate the following research gaps: there is insufficient critical analysis of the external context of the functioning of higher education institutions from the point of view of implementing process management concepts; there are deficiencies concerning the identification of the internal context of managing the university taking into consideration the requirements of the process approach; there is no standard concept of a Lean University determining the scope and direction of required changes in management models.

The objective of this chapter is to identify the factors of the internal and external contexts of the functioning of the modern university and to determine their influence on the university's ability to implement effectively process management concepts, including Lean Management, and also to present a developed model concept of a Lean University. In this chapter, the following research questions are formulated:

- Is a process-based approach, e.g. Lean Management, an effective method of changing the model of management in the university, taking into consideration the external and internal contexts of its functioning?
- Does the specific character of the processes conducted in higher education institutions require a redefinition of the qualities of a model organisation implementing Lean Management or the Lean university model?

In order to answer the above questions, the following theses were advanced:

- Changes resulting from the application of process management, including Lean Management, allow a holistic and systemic change in the university's management model, taking into consideration its mission, goals, as well as external and internal contexts of functioning.

- The processes carried out in higher education institutions have specific qualities and division criteria, which requires the adoption of a new approach to a model presentation of the university in the Lean Management concept.

In order to find arguments supporting the correctness of the premises, the following research methods were applied: an analysis of the literature on the subject as well as interviews conducted in higher education institutions in Poland and abroad as part of a research project carried out by the author.[1] The performed analysis draws on the achievements of higher education research (Kwiek 2015, p. 45) and falls within the scope of institutional research (Webber and Calderon 2015).

The author performed a critical review of studies on higher education systems, focusing on these factors which directly condition the implementation of process management concepts such as Lean Management. The factors were selected on the basis of earlier publications (Grudzewski et al. 2010, pp. 14–15; Yokoyama 2006, pp. 523–555; Balzer 2010, p. 7; Goranczewski 2013; Leja 2013, pp. 63–69; Kwiek 2015, pp. 12–47; Robins and Webster 2002, p. 10). In view of the above, the chapter will discuss the external context of implementing modern process management concepts, including Lean Management, the essence and the possibilities of using the process approach, the main values and principles of Lean Management in higher education institutions, the standard solutions and advantages of implementing this concept. Filling in the identified research gap, the author described the features of processes carried out in universities, focusing on their specific character and proposed new criteria for their classification. She also emphasised the basic differences between business organisations and higher education institutions which determine the course of implementing process management concepts in universities. The final part

[1]The project was financed from the MINIATURE 1 programme, The Conditions for the Maturity of the Lean Management Culture in Higher Education Institutions in the period from 25 September 2017 to 25 September 2018 (No. DEC. 2017/01/X/HS/00619).

of these deliberations is the author's original proposal for a model presentation of the university in the concept of Lean Management.

The chapter ends with conclusions and recommendations for further research on the concept of Lean Management and its implementation in higher education institutions.

2.2   The External and Internal Contexts for Developing Process Management Concepts in the University

In the contemporary globalised world, higher education institutions as knowledge organisations are regarded as a key element in the process of achieving competitive advantage by countries or regions. Hence they are the objects of interest of numerous organisations dealing with social and economic development such as The Organisation for Economic Co-operation and Development (OECD), EURYDICE, The United Nations Economic, Scientific and Cultural Organization (UNESCO), CER. At the same time the goal of many governments' marketing communication was to position their respective countries by attaching great importance to the quality of their educational systems (Alvesson 2013, p. 73). The new role of higher education stimulates a large number of various researches. They include comprehensive reviews in the area of higher education conducted by international organisations with a view to support the implementation of public policies (e.g. Santiago et al. 2008; Crosier et al. 2011; Altbach et al. 2009; Lambert and Butler 2006; Kwiek 2010, 2015). There are many intensive researches at the level of individual systems or institutions (e.g. Leja 2013). The author's intention is to arrange this knowledge and indicate the most important factors influencing the implementation of process management concepts in higher education institutions.

The university is a special organisation. Its roots can be traced to antiquity and the Platonic Academy. At present it is defined as a public utility institution, a public organisation (Rybkowski 2015), a part of the public sector (Antonowicz 2015, p. 87). The term university comes from the word *universus* (in Latin: whole, complete, extensive) consisting of the two segments *uni* and *versus* meaning making up a whole, complex (Szczepański and Śliz 2015, p. 23). The word university is used in many different contexts, e.g. as a proper name of an institution of higher education, a word indicating an institution which offers education and conducts academic research Oxford Dictionary (www2), a reference to those who learn and those who teach as subjects of universities (Szczepański and Śliz 2015, p. 23). Because of their growth and strong diversification, nowadays we use many different notions to define institutions fulfilling the functions of a university. The broadest of them is a higher education institution which includes universities, institutes of technology, colleges, academies, specialised or professional institutes, trade schools, and other organisations awarding academic degrees or professional certification (www3). This is the meaning which the author uses throughout this work.

Formulated in the Middle Ages, the academic principles constitute the traditional conditions for the organisation of a university and its activities (Woźnicki 2000, p. 59):

- the principle of creativity (in academic research and teaching),
- the principle of academic freedom (corporatism, the principles of co-optation, election, and autonomy).

These principles are derived from universal ethical values (truth, moral standards) and academic values (the academic community, the master-disciple relationship, supranational universality) (Woźnicki 2000, p. 59). Relying on the academic principles and values, a university builds its own traditions, creates its own culture, and determines its own mission in the national and international environments. Traditionally, universities are assigned various roles in the processes of teaching, education, research, creating, supporting and preserving national culture, and serving the public (Charta 1988, p. 2). It is noted that a university's identity is based on the integral combination of teaching and academic research (Lenartowicz 2016, p. 55).

In the contemporary world there is no single universal concept of a higher education model or university management. There is diversity, which is the heritage of a fairly autonomous development of higher education in various parts of the world in the past. However, the intensification of globalisation processes and the role played in them by higher education caused the strengthening of tendencies towards institutional isomorphism—the growing similarity among higher education systems, policies, and management methods (Geppert and Hollinshead 2017, p. 139). This isomorphism manifests itself in the spreading of various HEI management concepts. It consists in public-sector institutions' adapting management methods originating from and developed in business organisations; one of such methods is process management. In view of the above, the author conducted a review of the dominant and, from the perspective of the evolution of management concepts, the most important factors of the external contexts of the functioning of universities (the selection is consistent with the requirements of the standard ISO 9001:2015). These factors can be divided into the following groups:

- political and legal factors,
- economic and market factors,
- social and cultural factors, and
- technological factors.

The author would like to emphasise that this classification of the factors aims to organise the course of the argumentation only; in reality all of them interpenetrate strongly.

From the political and legal perspective, the main carrier of changes in the HEI management concepts is the evolution of views on the functions of the state in the process of addressing the society's needs in the area of education, academic research, and the development of new knowledge. From the very beginning of their history universities were established in different ways, as institutions created and controlled by students themselves (e.g. the University of Bologna), ecclesiastical, state, or borough authorities (Szczepański and Śliz 2015, p. 25). The traditional model of a liberal state based on the traditions of the Platonian Academy gave rise to a model of a collegial and liberal university independent of political influences in which freedom was the dominant value (Szczepański and Śliz 2015, p. 23; Sowa 2009, p. 40).

As it is emphasised by Allan Bloom, freedom of thinking and freedom of speech are both theoretical and practical demands, *a free university exists only in a liberal democracy, and liberal democracies exist where there are free universities* (Bloom 1997, p. 338). Knowledge was an autotelic value and pursuing the truth was the principle organising the functioning of the university (Zeller 2011, p. 51). It was in this period that the university formed its fundamental structural qualities based on the principles of self-government and autonomy (Sowa 2009, p. 12). There are two basic types of universities: a unitary type and a federated type (Sowa 2009, p. 40). Universities functioned, as it were, in the peripheries; they were building their exclusive character on the basis of the academic ethos (Sowa 2009, p. 28). However, with the passing of time their role in the creation of culture was appreciated. The seventeenth century witnessed the birth of two concepts which remain valid until today: Newman's cultural and liberal model of the university oriented towards the instrumental treatment of knowledge, education, and students (student-centred) and Humbolt's cultural and national model of the university focused on knowledge as an autotelic value, the needs of the faculty, and the creation of national culture (faculty-centred) (Zeller 2011, p. 51).

The nineteenth and twentieth centuries brought deep changes in views on the role of the state in addressing social needs, which was reflected also in changes in how universities were managed. On the tide of scientific management (e.g. Max Weber's concept of bureaucracy; Denhardt 2011, p. 28) and state interventionism, the dominant position was assumed by the concept based on the bureaucratic approach. The state guarantees universities stable financing and political autonomy in return for their support for national culture and the education of public-sector functionaries (Antonowicz 2015, p. 79). A new model of the university comes into being: the bureaucratic or etatistic university (Lacatus 2013, p. 424). The dominant value is the law and the central authorities are to fulfil regulatory and supervisory functions (Rybkowski 2015, p. 104). Universities start to be dominated by bureaucratic management systems based on hierarchisation, depersonalisation, legalism, formal qualification criteria for promotion and remuneration, specialisation and work division; assessments are based on audits and procedures (Sześciło 2015, p. 19). The bureaucratic university focuses first of all on its own management systems and the functions carried out within it (this is explained, among others, by the concept of bureaucracy as an autopoietic system) (Anders-Morawska and Rudolf 2015, p. 21; Lenartowicz 2016). The university is a service provider and the student is a customer. Leadership is based on the principle of *primus inter pares*, and the administration performs the ancillary function with respect to academics (Rybkowski 2015, p. 104). Legal regulations are complied with irrespective of changing circumstances; in consequence, the administration does not react appropriately to appearing problems (the promotion of trained ineptitude) (Anders-Morawska and Rudolf 2015, p. 16). The compliance of made decisions with the law is more important than the sense of justice and rightness (the justice paradox) (Anders-Morawska and Rudolf 2015, p. 19). Universities are becoming some kind of hybrids combining structural elements of the collegial university and the bureaucratic university, which does not result in any significant tensions thanks to the continually high level of financing. The 1960s witnessed the twilight of the institutional perception of the university. The university loses its unique status and becomes an instrument used to pursue the state's social and economic goals within the scope of the broadly understood public policy (Antonowicz 2015, p. 85).

In the 1980s, under the influence of the neoliberal concept of NPM (New Public Management), the state changes its function into that of the organiser and coordinator of public services (Sześciło 2015, p. 19). Marginson emphasises that NPM is a hybrid collection of organisational practices as it combines in itself business models and market patterns with bureaucratic control systems based on audit and accountability and the ideas of transparency and individualisation (Marginson 2015, p. 13). What appears is a new model of enterprise oriented towards the utilisation of existing resources in a new manner with a view to maximising the effectiveness and efficiency of public organisations (Denhardt 2011, p. 148). The university becomes accountable to not only academics but also first of all society at large and various groups of stakeholders (Antonowicz 2015, p. 86). It is also assigned important roles in social and economic development based on the execution of the following four missions: the formation of human capital by means of teaching, the building of knowledge by means of research, the dissimilation and application of knowledge by means of interactions with its users, as well as knowledge management, its storage and transfer among generations (Santiago et al. 2008, p. 23). The state continues to be the basic guarantor of the right to education and provides a general outline of a comprehensive educational policy. At the same time it reduces sources of financing, thus beginning to play a more passive role. The concept of an evaluative state is strengthened (Neave and Van Vught 1991, p. 13). The university's effectiveness is measured by means of the achievement of goals defined in public policies applicable to the various aspects of its activities such as governance, funding, quality assurance, equity, research and innovation, academic career, links to the labour market and internationalisation (www3, p. 17). These policies are formulated at regional and international levels by such organisations as The United Nations Economic, Scientific and Cultural Organization (UNESCO), The Organisation for Economic Co-operation and Development (OECD), The International Network for Quality Assurance Agencies in Higher Education (INQAAHE), The European University Association (EUA). These organisations' activities are a carrier for the process of globalisation. They also enhance the process of institutional isomorphism by enforcing the standardisation of activities, processes and services in higher education institutions as well as their transparency (e.g. the implementation of standards and guidelines concerning education quality assurance) (Kwiek 2010, p. 125; Vaira 2004).

Universities start to introduce business management concepts oriented towards professionalism in management, clearly defined standards and measures of activities, control of achieved results, deaggregation of activities, increasing competitiveness, and more effective utilisation of organisational resources. They implement modern management systems based on the TQM concept and quality models such as CAF (Common Assessment Framework) or EFQM Excellence Model (European Foundation for Quality Management). What comes into being is a model of a corporate university or an enterprising university similar to the market models of operations (Lacatus 2013, p. 424). In a corporate university, the dominant value is loyalty, and its authorities have a directive role to play (Lacatus 2013, p. 424). Researchers develop the concepts of academic capitalism in which borders among businesses, non-governmental organisations and public organisations are blurred. The market and market behaviours such as competing for financing, partnership with businesses, establishing spin-off companies or demanding tuition fees are becoming an integral part of universities' activities (Slaughter 2001). In an enterprising university, the dominant value is competences, and its authorities have a supportive role to play (Lacatus 2013, p. 424). A definition of an enterprising university comprises the following two dimensions of activities: adaptation to changes and a proactive approach consisting in future-oriented innovations and changes allowing the university to face future challenges on its own conditions (Yokoyama 2006, p. 523; Pluta-Olearnik 2009, p. 7; Hansson and Mønsted 2008, pp. 651–670). Marginson notes that the implementation of NPM certainly resulted in the more effective management of universities, but there is no evidence for improvement in research quality or the frequency of groundbreaking discoveries (Marginson 2015, p. 15).

Another wave of changes in university management is associated with the implementation of the Public Governance model in public organisations (the beginning of the twentieth century) (Sześciło 2015, p. 19). The state performs the function of a partner. A new management paradigm is used on an increasing scale. It is based on creating cooperation networks by combining public and private resources in the process of developing public services (Lambert and Butler 2006, p. 50). Universities enter various networks, federations, or alliances with other domestic and foreign education organisations in order to take advantage of external resources and acquire important personal and institutional contacts (www3, p. 11). New models of universities are being developed, e.g. a virtual university (based on technology and globalisation) (Robins and Webster 2002, p. 11), or a networked university. The dominant values are networks and cooperation (in both the internal and external aspects). Consequently, we can observe the growing importance of coordinating and managing networks of actors and various activities allowing the acquisition of the synergy of conducted operations.

Economic and market factors constitute another group of factors exerting strong influence on the development of approaches to HEI management concepts. Depending on which of the entities—the state, the market, or the academic community—dominates, it is possible to distinguish various organisational models of higher education (Thieme 2009, p. 46 and subs.; Santiago et al. 2008, pp. 68–69). One of them is the model proposed by Burton Clark and based on the so-called triangle of influence determining the space in which higher education systems of particular countries are located. A particular country's system can be dominated by the state, the academic oligarchy, or the market. We can distinguish a model with the dominant role of the state (France, the Soviet Union), a market-based model (the USA, the UK) and a model with a significant role of the academic oligarchy (Germany) (Clark 1986).

In the decisive majority of countries, it is the state that continues to be the main source of financing for research and education (the average for OECD countries is over 90%; the average for the EU is slightly less than 90%), but there is a noticeable trend of changes in the structure of financing (OECD Science 2016, p. 133). The expenditures of the private and non-governmental sectors are rising faster than public-sector spending. Another major trend concerns the state's gradual withdrawal from financing particular areas, e.g. education or applied research whose results can find economic applications. We can observe the process of the marketisation of the activities of higher education institutions which manifests itself in treating the student as a customer, adopting the idea of corporate responsibility and management systems, establishing individual contacts with academics and teachers or emphasising the importance of brand building (Robins and Webster 2002, p. 10). Education at the higher level becomes more accessible and some universities have transformed themselves from elite institutions into flexible service providers (mass "producers" of knowledge and practical skills). The massification of education changes student-related logistic processes, the course of such processes, and organisational structures. Education becomes a form of investment. Competition for students and funds for conducting research takes place among not only universities themselves but also universities, other education institutions and research institutes.

Changes in the political and legal as well economic and market spheres interact strongly with changes of a social and cultural character.

The knowledge-based economy is characterised by the society's increasing educational aspirations and the necessity of lifelong learning. The possession of higher education is still associated with a higher social and economic status (although there are considerable differences between countries in terms of the internal rate of return from investment in education) (Blöndal et al. 2002). This has been caused by the massification of education at the higher level. Demographic tendencies are another important factor determining changes in the environment of higher education. According to forecasts, the population of young people aged 15–24 is to increase in 2050 in Africa only (Council 2017). This represents new challenges of the dwindling numbers of students and the internationalisation of education. NPM causes also changes in the approach to the student in the university. The student is treated as a customer, user, buyer, investor, co-creator, assessor, graduate, potential donator (Slaughter and Rhoades 2004, p. 2; Budd 2017, p. 24). Depending on adopted strategies, universities undertake various marketing activities in order to attract a group of required (more or less talented) students (Mause 2009, p. 1109). An important selection factor is a university's brand and reputation based, among other things, on various national and international rankings (Council 2017). Competition for students is based on a university's status (such a status is of a symbolic character); it is confirmed by students and graduates, the manner of selecting students, the elitist character, and excellent research results (Marginson 2015, p. 27).

Based on the liberal and neoliberal concepts of the university, there is a dispute whether a student can be perceived in terms of a customer (Bay and Daniel 2001). The opponents claim that the relationship between a student and a teacher has the character of partnership and may not be regarded as a typical business relationship between a customer and a service provider. Furthermore, students are not customers because they are not always right, are not fully aware participants of the teaching process, and are not able to determine precisely their requirements and assess the quality of the teaching process (Scrabec 2000). It is emphasised simultaneously that an educational service is not a typical service because its qualitative result depends on not only the proper execution of the service provision process but also individual factors closely related to the student's personality and commitment (which cannot be fully controlled by the university). There are concerns that the introduction of tuition fees will lead to a situation where the student expects having a good time and a degree at the end, adopting a passive approach to the teaching process (Budd 2017, p. 26). Researchers indicate that the student's loyalty is strongly influenced by such factors as psychic attachment and a sense of belonging to a brand. A sense of satisfaction itself is not a sufficient guarantor of loyalty (Bowden 2011). Studies become a form of investment (Budd 2017). In view of the costs of studying, there occur changes in the model of making decisions about higher education studies; it becomes similar to a typical buying process (Chapman 1986). Authorities more and more often oblige universities to take actions aimed at improving the so-called student experience (Temple 2012). Student experience comprises the entirety of processes carried out and services provided for the benefit of the student (including social, cultural, accommodation, psychological assistance, and other services).

In the cultural context, the literature on the subject discusses paradigmatic changes in the models of higher education institutions. Questions are posed whether it is still possible to comply with the primary versions of the principles of the unity of research and teaching based on academic freedom and institutional autonomy (Sułkowski 2016, pp. 15–16; Antonowicz 2005, pp. 31–32; Leja 2013, p. 32). In adopted public policies, institutional autonomy is more and more often combined with accountability (Rybkowski 2015, p. 97; www3, p. 20). Numerous discussions focus on distinguishing between formal autonomy and "true" autonomy (Rybkowski 2015, p. 103). Autonomy is to defend academic freedom (Rybkowski 2015, p. 103), which, as Bloom emphasises, undergoes gradual erosion because the differences between this notion and the guarantee of employment granted by the government, businesspeople, or trade unions become blurred (Bloom 1997, p. 339). There appear questions about how to join teaching and research in view of the differences between stakeholder groups and their expectations. In which direction will the models of universities develop? Antonowicz indicates that universities have become very complex organisations on which the public imposes various, frequently mutually exclusive objectives (Antonowicz 2015, p. 93). Bloom is of the opinion that the university is under pressure exerted by student communities and mass movements, which may result in undermining its culture-creating role, sense of value, research on such movements and providing information on them, as well as in the university's surrender to the spirit of a nation, the spirit of time or mere fashion (Bloom 1997, p. 410). Cultural tensions are described the best by means of metaphors used by authors in discussions about the modern university. In these metaphors, the university is described in terms of a factory (Szadkowski 2015, p. 236), a quasi-enterprising business (Marginson 2015, p. 14), a public corporation (Rybkowski 2015, p. 102), or a living laboratory (Graczyk 2015).

The last group of factors exerting significant influence on the contemporary university comprises the development of the Internet and modern technologies. The quick development of the Internet and related technologies broadened the scope of the traditional teaching methods with possibilities of distance learning and e-learning. There appears a new wave referred to as M-learning where teaching processes make use of modems, mobile devices such as smartphones, laptops, personal digital assistants (PDAs), and tablets (Iqbal and Bhatti 2015, p. 86). At present universities are occupied by the so-called millennial generation which since its early years has been a recipient and user of modern information technologies in all spheres of life and has taken advantage of non-standard and personalised services. Researches show that students expect a greater utilisation of modern technologies in educational processes (Kennedy and Dunn 2018). This results from their easiness of use, convenience, availability as well as users' psychological readiness (Iqbal and Bhatti 2015, p. 96). A new competitive type of higher education institutions has appeared on the educational market—so-called virtual universities (Robins and Webster 2002). The implementation of new technologies contributes to more open management through assigning control and responsibility, increasing transparency, and standardising activities (Robins and Webster 2002; Agre 2000). However, it creates many problems as well. The most noticeable ones include the costs of implementing modern technologies, resistance from employees, or the necessity of restructuring a university's processes.

The development of a university is not linear and does not consist in a simple evolutionary movement from one model to another. Every university is different and a given school's management model is a conglomerate of various elements conditioned by the factors of the external and internal contexts (knowledge—its gathering and application, values and an organisational culture). What is also important is the simultaneous occurrence of various types of changes and connections created in consequence of their interactions.

At present it is possible to observe the process of clashes between the two competitive concepts of the role and place of the university in the economy and society: the traditional concept treating the university as a depositary of national culture and science, a centre of intellectual potential and knowledge creation and the modern concept in which the university becomes a subject on the market of educational and research services, a corporation specialising in the provision of a wide range of services. Such competition generates the following tensions:

- academic quality and excellence versus effectiveness and efficiency,
- compliance with the law and the requirements of rating agencies versus operational flexibility,
- integration and focus on pure science, discipline and the academic community versus networking of activities, participatory creation of science, and creation of socially useful science, and
- transparency of activities versus academic freedom and autonomy (Franz et al. 2012; Lucio-Villegas 2016, p. 6; Lacatus 2013, p. 424; Sułkowski 2016, pp. 28–29; Yorkstone 2016).

These tensions become a visible barrier to changes in management. Higher education institutions change slowly despite numerous reforms of the system introduced over the period of many years. It is indicated that created in the Middle Ages, the university's identity is extremely durable and resistant to changes despite the fact that it no longer fits the contemporary reality in which it has to function (Shaw and Lenartowicz 2016). This results also from the nature of knowledge itself and the manner in which it is created. Researchers try to explain why universities change so slowly, formulating arguments concerning the internal context in which universities function. Universities' lethargy, inertia, focus on self-recreation are explained as a conflict of values (Lenartowicz 2016), a strong organisational identity based on an autopoietic system (Sułkowski 2016), or the character of knowledge as a public good (it is uneconomical to produce goods which are available free of charge and whose value at the time of a market launch is zero) (Marginson 2015, p. 27). Researches conducted in the light of the institutional and neo-institutional theories (Santana et al. 2010, p. 325; Pawlak 2013, p. 91; Kwiek 2010, p. 83) indicate that the process of introducing changes in universities is dominated by compulsory isomorphism. The most important element forcing universities to change is the state's globally determined policy; the second and third places in the ranking are occupied by economic factors, and social and cultural factors (Sulaiman et al. 2013, p. 77; Prasad and Suri 2011). It is also emphasised that in some functional areas of universities, isomorphism may be connected more with inertia than change (an university's inertia consists in focusing on the fulfilment of minimum criteria, in consequence of which universities react very slowly to expectations of changes formulated by the surrounding world) (Santana et al. 2010, p. 333). Universities usually reject changes imposed from the outside or implement pseudo-changes in order to become more attractive for stakeholders (Alvesson 2013; Lenartowicz 2016). It is also noted that the university's uniqueness consists in its being an integrative organisation and unlike other purposive business organisations, such an organisation does not have one coherent objective (Temple 2012, p. 209), which also hinders the effective introduction of changes. Researchers also take into consideration whether a change is being implemented in accordance with the principles of procedural justice (democratic decision making) and distributive justice (equal rights and justice in access to the effects of changes) (By et al. 2008, p. 28).

Summing up, the conducted review of the literature on the subject indicates the following factors of the external context which determine the implementation of process management concepts:

- legal and political factors: transparency, accountability, formalisation, enterprise, professionalisation of management, global standardisation, participatory management, cooperation networks, orientation towards the future, sustainable development, improvement culture,
- social and cultural factors: society's educational aspirations, massification of education, demography, tensions among the state, the market and the academic oligarchy, the millennial generation,
- economic and market factors: economisation of activities, value for money, effectiveness, efficiency, student experience, quality of services, tuition fees, education as investment, brand building, rankings, competition, and
- technological factors: computerisation of universities, distance learning, e-learning, M-learning, globalisation, virtual university, network university.

The strength of the factors of the external context forced higher education institutions to implement many business management methods and techniques. Nevertheless, they did not adopt fully dominant business values. Such adoption is hindered by the external context of their functioning determined by their centuries-old traditions, values, goals, principles, functions, processes, structures, and dominant models of organisational cultures (collegial, bureaucratic, enterprising models). Therefore, in the light of the analysis conducted above, there appears a problem of the proper choice of approaches to as well as concepts and models of managing a university. On the one hand, they should make it possible to face challenges coming from the contemporary external environment, and on the other hand, they should take into consideration the demands of the academic community concerning the maintenance of the traditional academic values, principles, and functions. Contemporary higher education institutions will have to cope with the problem of looking for methods of improving their effectiveness and efficiency without losing their traditional social role and position. As Helbing stresses, *we won't solve new problems by means of old methods* (Helbing 2016, p. 3). In the author's opinion, this is the main and enormous challenge for managing contemporary universities. Inspirations for changes in university management are searched for in management methods and concepts based on the process approach and already verified in the manufacturing and service sectors. It is believed that their implementation will ensure the effectiveness and efficiency of activities conducted by a university and will result eventually in organisational excellence. It should eliminate or reduce tensions among the categories indicated above. One of the proposed ideas of changes which are becoming more and more popular in higher education institutions is the process approach-based concept of Lean Management.

2.3 The Process Approach in Managing Higher Education Institutions

2.3.1 The Development of the Concept of Process Management in Higher Education Institutions in the Light of the Literature on the Subject

The foundations of the process approach to managing organisations were laid already at the beginning of the twentieth century in the works of such forerunners of management as Frederic Taylor, Henry Ford (Davenport 2008, p. XIV), or Karol Adamiecki (Lisiecka and Maciąg 2007, pp. 87–91). Interest in BPM grew dramatically in the 1980s under the influence of works published by Michael Hammer and James Champy (1997). They put forward a concept of Business Process Reengineering (BPR) consisting in the radical redesigning of an organisation based on the process approach and modern technologies. During the course of the twentieth century process management from the operational level became a strategic organisational management concept which was also implemented effectively in public organisations and higher education institutions. Contemporary process management draws on the achievements of operational research and quality control (e.g. TQM, Statistical Process Control, Process Improvement Methods, Lean Management, Lean Six Sigma), process reengineering (e.g. Porter's concept of a value chain, BPR, Balance Scorecard, Activity Based Costing, Six Sigma, Outsourcing, Insourcing, Process Redesign/Reengineering

Methods) as well as information management technologies (e.g. ERP, CRM) (Harmon 2010; Lusk et al. 2005; Smith and Fingar 2007, p. 15). As Thomas H. Davenport (2008, p. XVI) emphasises, nowadays BPM has become a prerequisite for the effective and efficient functioning of an organisation in the twenty-first century.

A change in the management paradigm in public organisations in the spirit of NPM generated interest in using this concept in the restructuring of higher education institutions. In order to establish the temporal extent and the major issues addressed in the area of process management in universities, the author used the method of a systematic review of the related literature (Easterby-Smith et al. 2015, p. 15). In the conducted analysis, the author used the EBSCO database and accessorily the (Web of Sciences) service and Google Scholar. The databases were searched using the following keys: BPM and higher education. The search of the EBSCO database returned 14 records related to BPM and HE (subject terms) (Table 2.1). Only peer-reviewed articles were chosen for reviewing. Each of them was analysed, in consequence of which 5 articles were rejected as they did not constitute a description of the concept, concerned other sectors or the teaching of BPM.

The author noticed that the early phase of interest in process management in higher education institutions in the 1986s was dominated by articles on BPR and TQM (these concepts will be discussed in the further part of this chapter).

Table 2.1 The number of publications on BPM in higher education institutions according to EBSCO as at 21 October 2018

Criteria of searching	EBSCO—number of articles	The earliest indexed article
Key words: Business Process Management BPM, higher education (in abstract)	49 (24)	1986
Key words: Business Process Management BPM, higher education (subject terms)	14 (5)	2003
Key words: Business Process Management BPM, higher education (in title)	4 (2)	2000

Source The author's own work
( ) number of full text articles

The issues raised in the publications under analysis concerned the following:

- Using the Business Process Improvement (BPI) methodology to pursue an institution's strategic goals by focusing on service excellence and sustainable development (Ciancio 2018).
- Using BPM to understand flows and relations among processes in a university (Ismail and Abd El Aziz 2015).
- Assessing the possibility of using various BPM techniques in change management (Inês Dallavalle de Pádua et al. 2014).
- Implementing the concepts of IT solutions such as: Service Oriented Architecture (SOA) in public contract award procedures (Mircea 2010), using ICT to implement the process approach (Ismail and Abd El Aziz 2015), electronic resources management (ERM) (England et al. 2012).

The analysis of the number of publications in the particular years indicates that there has been a steady increase in the number of publications on BPM in universities. Most of the publications concern problems related to the implementation of ICT and information management systems, TQM, BPR, service management and service excellence, Lean Management and Lean Six Sigma. They usually have the form of a case study; there are few proposals relating to new concepts or theoretical approaches. The author notes the lack of studies on defining and characterising processes typical of higher education institutions as well as identifying conditions for implementing BPM taking into consideration the unique character as well as the external and internal contexts of the functioning of universities. The identified research gap allowed the author to set the main directions of her own research. The first of them is defining and describing the notion of process as well as criteria for classifying process, taking into consideration the specific character of management in higher education institutions. The other concerns identifying circumstances for the effective implementation of process-related concepts in universities in the light of the internal and external contexts of their functioning.

2.3.2 Processes in Higher Education Institutions

2.3.2.1 A Definition, Elements and Characterisation of Processes Taking Place in Higher Education Institutions

The theoretical foundations for these deliberations can be found in these publications (PN-EN ISO 9001:2015 2016a, p. 7; Grajewski 2007, p. 55; Bugdol and Jedynak 2012; Bugdol 2018; Dumas et al. 2013; Skrzypek and Hofman 2010; Bugdol and Szczepańska 2016). Broadly speaking, according to the terminology used in the ISO 9000:2015 standard, a process is a set of interrelated or interacting actions which transform input into output (PN-EN ISO 9001:2015 2016a, p. 7). A process can be defined as a logical arrangement of an organisation's material, financial, information and human resources as well as the courses of activities or operations which are oriented towards the achievement of results consistent with both internal and external customers' requirements and expectations (Grajewski 2007, p. 55). The essence and constituent elements of a process are presented in Fig. 2.1.

A process consists of the following elements (Dumas et al. 2013, p. 25; PN-EN ISO 9001:2015 2016a, p. 7):

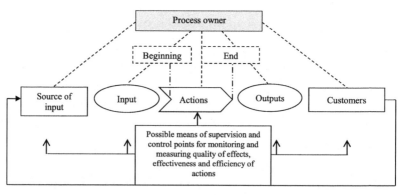

Fig. 2.1 The structure of a process (*Source* Prepared on the basis of PN-EN ISO 9001:2015 [2016, p. 7] and Dumas et al. [2013])

A. sources of input,
B. process input,
C. actions,
D. process output,
E. recipients of output,
F. feedback related to the assessment and improvement of the effectiveness and efficiency of a process, and
G. process owner.

Each of the listed elements of a process determines the quality of the final effect; therefore, it has to be controlled by means of appropriate methods and criteria. The aforementioned elements are described briefly below.

A. The sources of input into a process are processes taking place earlier and involving internal or external suppliers, customers, or other important interested parties (ISO 9001:2015 standard). In universities, the sources of input for many processes are actions performed by students (e.g. a correctly filled in application form, acceptance or approval in a system), external suppliers (e.g. an outsourced statistical analysis of conducted research),or employees within the scope of internal processes (e.g. an opinion on a purchase agreement prepared by a legal advisor or data coming from the student recruitment process entered into the studies management system). The theory of quality management refers to the concept of the internal customer. An internal customer can be a subsequent employee, process, or group of persons in the chain of creating quality and value in an organisation (Bugdol 2011b, p. 50). It is generally accepted that there is a relation between the satisfaction of an external customer and the satisfaction of an internal customer.

B. Process input should be understood as a set of the properties of resources necessary for the execution of a process and the achievement of a result in the form of the intended quality of a service or product. Input comprises tangible, financial, human and information resources owned (or controlled) by an organisation. Such resources should be adequate in terms of quantity and quality, and their quality should be assessed (e.g. assessment of suppliers, assessment of employees, assessment of the working environment, supervision over equipment, measuring instruments, etc.) (ISO 9001:2015). What also needs to be taken into consideration is the quality of resources provided by a customer (a customer's own contribution) or entities representing a customer (entities' contribution), e.g. information, documents, objects owned by the customers, powers of attorney. The more appropriately a university allocates its resources in the execution of its processes and the better it educates its customers with respect to providing optimum support for the execution of the processes, the higher their effectiveness and efficiency (Kłosowski 2012, p. 33 and subs.).

C. Processes consist of actions. They are purposefully and logically arranged sequences of deeds with a clearly defined beginning and end. A process may possess an extensive structure referred to as process architecture. It is created by the decomposition of a process, from its value chain, through its constituent business processes, their constituent processes, sub-processes, sub-sub-processes, actions, and steps (Hamrol 2007, p. 199). In praxeology, an action is defined as any deliberate and conscious behaviour of a human being who is the subject (originator) of an action causing the occurrence of particular events identified with established objectives related to a system of needs (Szafrański 2003, p. 23 and subs.). In a process-oriented organisation, actions are aimed at transforming input (materials, external services, and capital) into effects in the form of products fulfilling customers' needs and requirements (Miller et al. 2000, p. 2). As an organised activity, actions constitute the core of an organisation and are the essence of creating value for customers and other interested parties. Hence a process can be also understood as a chain of creating value (Rummler and Brache 2000, p. 75). The performance of actions requires the participation of many actors (human beings, organisations, information systems functioning on behalf or by order of human beings or organisations), tangible objects (equipment, materials, products, paper documents), and intangible ones (electronic documents or records) (Dumas et al. 2013, p. 25; PN-EN ISO 9001:2015 2016a, p. 7).

D. Process output or the result of a process is the effect of performed actions. In the case of higher education institutions, there are usually problems with indicating the result of carried out actions. The ISO standard defines result as all categories of output data (the effects of a process, i.e. equipment, software, services, processed materials, tangible products) (PN-EN ISO 9001:2015, Załącznik A.2, 2016b, s. 30). From the economic point of view, a university is a service organisation and the result of its actions is educational, research, organisational, cultural, sports, recreational, etc. services provided to students, employees, local communities, and other stakeholders. A service is any action consisting in exerting influence on a human being—customer or property in their possession (Hamrol and Mantura 2002, p. 174). In the ISO 9000:2015 standard, a service is defined as one of the types of an organisation's products, the result of processes executed in an organisation. Services provided by higher education institutions are characterised by intangibility, inseparability, the lack of ownership, intolerance of errors, changeability, heterogeneity, often seasonality and complexity (these qualities and their impact on managing universities will be discussed in the further part of the book). Intangibility and inseparability of services cause the customer assessing the results of a process to take into consideration all its elements and treat them as inseparable (an offer, service provision process, and result) (Daszkowska 1998, pp. 18–19). A characteristic feature of university processes is their execution in cooperation with the customer (it means that the customer is often a co-creator or participant of a process and their behaviour, knowledge experience and attitude may influence the quality and value of the final effect of a process, e.g. a more motivated student will achieve better results than others). Also, an assessment of process results is often impossible without the customer's participation because process results are often expressed in terms of a change which materialises in the customer or objects owned by them (e.g. a change consisting in increased knowledge and improved skills may be observed only by measuring relevant indexes such as speed of work, fewer errors, good examination results, etc.). Process results may be positive or negative (Dumas et al. 2013). The quality of process results may be assessed in terms of quantity or quality. In terms of quantity, the quality of results can be measured by means of indexes related to the quantity of provided services, their duration, timeliness, or defectibility (a number of defects). In terms of quality, the quality of process results can be measured by means of indexes related to the customer's or stakeholder's satisfaction, value, or loyalty.

E. Recipients of output are external customers, e.g. students, supervisory agencies, partners, and other interested parties as well as internal customers such as administration employees, lecturers, and researchers. All of them use process results to perform further actions in subsequent processes (e.g. subsequent stages of processing documents leading to the issue of a decision, the closing of a project, semester or course, or recruitment processes in an organisation where a student starts to work and submits their graduation diploma). Internal and external entities are interconnected and influence one another through a network of processes.

F. Feedback is a systemic feature of a process which allows its adaptation and continuous improvement on the basis of the results of its monitoring and final assessment. As it is emphasised in the ISO 9000:2015 standard, *improvement is essential for an organisation to maintain the current level of operational effects, the possibility of reacting to changes in internal and external conditions, as well as to create new opportunities* (PN-EN ISO 9000:2015 2016a, p. 10). Improvement activities are based on the PDCA method (Deming's wheel) (Deming 2012), which is a universal directive for improving the quality of services, processes, and organisational management systems.

Process quality is a category integrally related to process assessment. It can be defined as the ability of a process to achieve established quality objectives. Lisiecka indicates that the assessment of a process should be conducted in the context of its effectiveness, flexibility, and efficiency (Lisiecka 2002, p. 242). From the praxeological point of view, effectiveness, efficiency, and flexibility are the attributes of actions/processes which are productive, i.e. create value (Kotarbiński 1975, p. 104). The effectiveness of a process is measured by the degree of achieving an established objective (the degree to which planned actions are performed, and planned results are achieved) (ISO 9001:2015); efficiency is a measure showing a relation between achieved results and used resources, e.g. costs and time (ISO 9001:2015); flexibility is an organisation's ability to adjust to changes taking place in its environment. In the theory of organisation and management sciences, effectiveness and efficiency are combined in the category of productivity (Krzyżanowski 1985, p. 267). Productivity may be defined as maximising the degree of achieving an established goal (a planned effect) and simultaneously minimising the use of resources (expenditures).

G. In the concept of the process approach it is the so-called process owner that is responsible for process execution. The criterion for the selection of the process owner should be a range of control exercised over a process (Bugdol and Szczepańska 2016, p. 33). This does not have to be a manager of a particular unit, therefore, the skill of delegating authority is very important. In a university, the function of the process owner can be fulfilled for example by a deputy dean for education, a research project manager, a financial department manager, or an infrastructure department manager. According to the requirements of the ISO 9001 standard, if a process is to be manageable, it should be identified, defined, measured, monitored and assessed as well as improved, documented; it should have identified goals, risks and opportunities as well as allocated resources, persons responsible, and the owner; the principles of managing changes in a process should also be determined [ISO 9001]. These actions are included in the process management cycle (Dumas et al. 2013, p. 21). An important element of process identification in higher education institutions is determining the so-called process execution environment by identifying factors which can potentially influence their course as well as effectiveness and efficiency (Norma ISO 9001:2015; Bugdol 2018). Such factors comprise psychological factors (e.g. stress), social factors (e.g. relations within a group), and physical factors (e.g. temperature, lighting, ergonomy).

Process management in universities is influenced particularly by factors resulting from the specific character of a given organisation. On the basis of the definition of services (Daszkowska 1998, pp. 18–19) and their features (Lovelock and Patterson 2015) as well as the results of her own research, the author prepared a characterisation of processes executed in higher education institutions and resultant challenges for management. They are presented in Table 2.2.

The presented characterisation of processes allows their better understanding. It shows that not all of them will be subject to standardisation and in the case of some of them, standardisation will be difficult. There appears a dilemma concerning the categorisation of processes conducted in higher education institutions for the purposes of standardisation and the implementation of the process approach.

2.3.2.2 Process Categorisation in Higher Education Institutions

Categorisation makes it possible to divide processes into relatively homogeneous groups, which is important from the perspective of managing such processes. The literature on the subject indicates two main criteria according to which key processes in an organisation are identified: the ASQ (Bugdol 2011a, p. 83) criteria and the criteria included in the ISO 19011 standard (PN-EN ISO 19011:2003 2003). According to the rules of American Society for Quality (ASQ), key processes are those that concern more than one organisational unit (one department in an organisational structure), are directly important for an organisation's mission and quality goals, contribute to decision making, influence directly customer satisfaction, are connected with the production/provision of an organisation's basic products/services. This division of processes is used the most often in universities. Processes are divided into key processes, support processes, and management processes. A similar classification of processes is proposed by American Quality Productivity Center (APQC), which distinguishes operational processes, management processes, and service support processes (Process Classification Framework [PCF] Version 6.1.1.).

Key processes create the value of goods and services, are the source of revenue and profit for the university (e.g. a teaching process, a research

Table 2.2 A characterisation of processes carried out in higher education institutions

Features of processes performed in universities	Consequences for management	Challenges for managing universities
The lack of the possibility of tracking physically the course of processes	It is difficult to assess and control the very course of a process; the lack of the understanding of the scopes of actions performed within a process by employees (who does what and who is responsible for what); problems with identifying places where errors occur (errors are usually visible at the end of a process, sometimes many years later)	Using appropriate process mapping tools, which makes it possible to see what happens within a process
Products are partially intangible	It is possible to assess the products of processes, but simple quantitative indexes (time, costs, number of actions, compliance, etc.) and qualitative indexes (e.g. satisfaction) usually do not suffice. They do not reflect the specific character of a process and its products. Sometimes the lack of a product is also regarded as an important effect of a process (e.g. basic research). In educational processes, the graduate is a product carrier and assessment is postponed in time	Using an appropriate and flexible assessment system based on quantitative and qualitative indexes. Diversifying assessment methods; introducing observations, interviews, self-enquiry

(continued)

Table 2.2 (continued)

Features of processes performed in universities	Consequences for management	Challenges for managing universities
Inseparability between the service provision process and the consumption process	The performance of a process requires interaction with its recipient, e.g. a student, who often participates actively in a process. The required simultaneous presence of both a customer and a process executor (e.g. a teacher) causes a restriction in the scale of actions (at a given moment actions can be performed with respect to only one subject or object, e.g. a student). Interaction between a customer and a service provider is also an important factor in perceiving product quality. A customer is a supplier and a buyer of a service—a customer often provides basic information and documents necessary for performing a service, e.g. personal identification numbers, insurance policy numbers, etc. Process quality can be influenced by external and internal contexts (e.g. time of waiting perceived subjectively or objectively)	The necessity of involving a customer of a process in its assessment as well as proper preparation for the execution of a process (e.g. information); the standardisation and computerisation of processes (e.g. electronic systems of document processing, circulation, etc.)
The heterogeneity of processes resulting from their human dimension	Process quality can differ depending on a performer, an organisational context, an environment in which processes are carried out, and individual attitudes of employees (e.g. a physical and mental state). This results in problems with process standardisation, which makes it difficult to control quality—a quality standard depends to a considerable extent on a service provider and other independent factors, e.g. the reliability of an information system	The necessity of standardising typical and repeatable processes (e.g. personnel or financial processes, the settlement of project costs, the handling of student affairs). Supporting creative and innovative processes

Features of processes performed in universities	Consequences for management	Challenges for managing universities
The duration and complexity of process execution	Processes may differ with respect to the number of actions and the duration of their performance (sometimes processes last many years, e.g. teaching, carrying out a scientific project, preparing a doctoral dissertation). The same process may be performed on the basis of a number of legal regulations effective on the date of initiating a process (e.g. opening a doctoral dissertation defence process). Some actions or resources within a process may become outdated. There occur problems with controlling the course of a process in time and particular performed actions	It is necessary to appoint a process owner with a clearly specified scope of responsibility. Ensuring the continuity of the execution of processes through their standardisation. Monitoring the course of processes
The complexity and hierarchisation of processes	The complexity of processes is determined by legal regulations and the traditions of collegial management models. Processes are carried out in hierarchised and bureaucratic management structures, which results in a structure of dispersed responsibility as well as process looping, the necessity of multiple approvals, e.g. signing a contract with a service provider requires simultaneous approvals of a legal advisor, institute director, dean and bursar	A clear identification of the course of processes together with the allocation of resources and scopes of responsibility. A clear identification of the scope of centralisation/decentralisation of a university
The physical dispersion (because of various locations) of people carrying out processes	Particularly in universities with complex organisational structures and dispersed locations, the duration of process execution lengthens and flexibility in reacting to changes in the environment is reduced	Introducing an electronic document circulation system with a clear identification of document filing locations based on a process analysis

(continued)

Table 2.2 (continued)

Features of processes performed in universities	Consequences for management	Challenges for managing universities
Seasonality of processes	Problems with balancing workload; seasonal overwork of employees, e.g. in connection with student recruitment processes. Problems with reconciling family life (e.g. holidays) with duties at work	Identifying clearly the course of processes and ensuring adequate allocation of resources. Diagnosing employees' competences (matrices of competences). Flexible scope of duties and multi-tasking
Singularity, specificity, uniqueness. Processes related to innovativeness and creativity, creative processes requiring considerable freedom on the part of employees	A strong tradition concerning the manner of executing particular processes. Problems with standardisation or no possibility of standardisation. In certain situations, standardisation leads to increased inefficiency of performed processes (e.g. previously a process has been carried out in particular conditions, e.g. a time framework; imposing a strict schedule causes additional stress in students and lecturers as well as generates additional work for the administration—meeting deadlines). Rejecting by force a certain deeply rooted and well functioning custom may result in more damage than good	Becoming very well familiar with the history and conditions of executing a particular process (including traditions, customs, good practices, etc.). A precise assessment of a process as well as the possibilities and consequences of its standardisation
Intolerance of formal errors	Processes have to be carried out in accordance with the law; there is no margin for errors (legal regulations, accountability, official documents and certificates)	Introducing process execution procedures and solutions which make it impossible to make errors

Features of processes performed in universities	Consequences for management	Challenges for managing universities
Tolerance of economic inefficiency	Processes comprise actions which do not create value from the economic point of view, but are necessary in view of the law, a university's internal by-laws or traditions. Conflicts, the lack of consensus or accepting the point of view of just one group (e.g. academic oligarchy, managers, or students) may result in inefficiency in the course of processes	Defining clearly values, their dimensions and measures; involving stakeholders participating in a process and using its effects
Difficulties with establishing one obligatory standard for the correct course of a process. Insusceptibility to standardisation	This problem concerns teaching processes, academic and research processes, as well as certain organisational processes. In the case of research processes, a particular discipline-specific research methodology and methods apply and determine a correct course of actions. They undergo peer reviews. In educational processes, the logic of actions is determined, among other things, by the rules of academic didactics, the type of a teaching subject (programme), the level of a student group, interaction among students in class	Creating standards for the course of processes at a high level of generality; referring in such standards mainly to legal and organisational standards; moving the centre of gravity from documented operational procedures to training and environmental assessments

Source The author's own work

process, a process managing relations with the environment). At the input and output of these processes there is an external customer—a stakeholder (a student, candidate, parent, the state, businesses, local governments, and other entities with which the university cooperates) who formulates particular requirements and is ready to pay for process effects or incur other costs of obtaining such effects. The second group is support processes which accompany the key processes, provide data and information, or regulate their functioning; support processes usually do not create any added value. They include a purchasing process, a recruitment process, processes related to managing employees and the working environment, finances, infrastructure, knowledge and information, etc. Management processes are usually the responsibility of the university's authorities; they are of a regulatory and decision-making character. They include for example managing the university's strategy, analysing and improving the didactic process, managing the quality of research and implementation projects, and managing relations with the environment.

The criteria recommended by the ISO 19011 standard for process categorisation include distribution (Which processes are the most troublesome?), weight (Which processes have the greatest impact on the university's activities?), feasibility (Which process is the most susceptible to transformations?).

The author would like to note that there is a lack of another legal/compliance criterion for selecting key processes. Higher education institutions carry out processes involving many organisational units which do not create any added value for the customer. The necessity of executing such processes results exclusively from legal requirements (the reporting process is a case in point). In this case, the necessity of examining the expectations of external/internal stakeholders will not be taken into consideration.

On the basis of the aforementioned categories, a university should individually identify and define its processes. It is also possible to use available classifications, e.g. the classification developed by APQC or the PCF. The literature on the subject (Czubała et al. 2012, pp. 19–29; Sokołowicz and Srzednicki 2006, p. 89; Grajewski 2012, p. 46; Shostack 1984; Lovelock and Patterson 2015) indicates also many other criteria used to divided processes into groups, for example creating value for the customer of the process (Grajewski 2012; Czerska 2009), the level of direct contact between the customer and the service organisation (Czubała et al. 2012), the "visual availability" of the process for the customer (Shostack 1984), the function in the organisation (Bugdol and Szczepańska 2016), the degree of the customer's participation in the process (Lovelock and Patterson 2015). However, the aforementioned categorisations may not be sufficient for the arranging and defining processes carried out in higher education institutions for the purposes of their restructuring. On the basis of her own research and the existing normative division, the author would like to propose that descriptions of processes taking place in universities include the following other criteria:

- Repeatability of the process (how often the process is carried out).
- Mass character of the process (how many users are served).
- Significance of the process (how the process influences the functioning of the university).
- Level of errors (how many complaints are made, how many errors are detected in the process, what is their scale and importance with respect to the whole process).
- Scope of the process (the number of departments participating in performing the process).
- Susceptibility to standardisation determined by the necessary scope of employees' freedom (whether the process has a creative character).
- Necessity of standardisation (whether there is a requirement for standardisation).

Combining the criteria of susceptibility to standardisation and its necessity, it is possible to deepen the analysis of the structure of processes taking place in higher education institutions. The combination of the mentioned features makes it possible to distinguish the following four groups:

- Group I: Processes with a low level of susceptibility to standardisation and a low need of standardisation (e.g. creative or research processes, some educational processes).

- Group II: Processes with a low level of susceptibility to standardisation and a high need of standardisation (e.g. processes related to strategic management, planning, and decision making).
- Group III: Processes with a high level of susceptibility to standardisation and a high need of standardisation (e.g. administrative processes).
- Group IV: Processes with a high level of susceptibility to standardisation and a low need of standardisation (e.g. processes carried out on the basis of a university's traditions such as the organisation of meetings, ceremonies, inaugurations).

The above division indicates clearly which processes should first become the object of restructuring efforts for standardisation to improve the effectiveness and efficiency of their execution as well as the whole management system. This group of processes includes first of all repeatable, mass, interdepartmental processes with considerable influence on a university's functioning, a large number of errors, a high susceptibility to standardisation, and a high need of standardisation.

2.3.3 The Essence of Process Management in Universities

This sub-chapter defines the notion of process management, the internal context of implementing BPM, and the scope of actions to be taken by the university with a view to implementing this concept. The application of the concept of BPM in business organisations has been discussed extensively (Bugdol and Szczepańska 2016; Grajewski 2007; Jeston et al. 2008; Grajewski 2012; Dumas et al. 2013). Therefore, the author will focus on conditions for the implementation of this concept in higher education institutions.

In the process approach, an organisation is regarded as a dynamic system consisting of mutually related processes (material, financial, information relations) which are arranged hierarchically (Grajewski 2007, p. 55; PN-EN ISO 9000:2015 2015). The ISO 9001 standard emphasises that *coherent and foreseeable results are achieved more effectively and efficiently when actions are understood and managed as mutually related processes functioning as a coherent system* (PN-EN ISO 9000:2015 2015). BPM is achieving the organisation's goals by improving, managing, and controlling processes which constitute the foundation of its operations (Jeston et al. 2008, p. 11). In the broader perspective, process management consists in *shaping internal organisational relations with a view to achieving the effect of the system's dynamic functioning by optimizing its individual processes defined as a series of actions transforming the ideas and efforts of the organisation's members into an effect determined by the customer [...] this requires the rationalisation of the organisation's structural elements in order to achieve their optimum influence on creating the value of the final effect of such actions* (Grajewski 2012, p. 23). It is emphasised that *the understanding of the mechanism of the occurrence of effects in such a system will allow the organisation to optimise the system and the effects of its functioning* (PN-EN ISO 9000:2015 2015). Thus, process management can be analysed in a subjective dimension (the competences and responsibility of process owners and external customers), a functional dimension (actions, relations, transformation), and a resource dimension (a quantitative and qualitative structure of input and output of a process) (Bugdol and Szczepańska 2016, p. 33). It should be remembered that the logic of the process approach has its roots in business and manufacturing enterprises where operating principles, the specific character of management and performed processes are different from those of higher education institutions.

In order to define the internal context for implementing process changes in universities the author juxtaposed the characteristic features of a business organisation with those of a university. The output criteria adopted in the analysis are taken from a study by Walentynowicz (2013, pp. 83, 87) (he used these criteria to distinguish a traditional enterprise from a Lean enterprise). On the basis of the conducted review of the literature on the subject and her own research, the author adjusted the criteria so that they reflected the specificity of the internal context in which universities functioned. In the author's opinion, becoming aware of these differences is very important because they determine success in implementing management concepts based on the process approach in higher education institutions. A synthetic presentation of these differences is shown in Table 2.3.

The above analysis indicates that the university's internal context is unique and different from that of business enterprises. In the author's opinion, this poses two dilemmas. One of them concerns the extent to which the university can be restructured by means of the process approach without compromising its fundamental values. The other dilemma concerns the extent to which BPM can be modified in order to ensure its successful implementation but also not to lose the gist of this method. The author is of the opinion that in its essence and nature, the university is a process organisation because its functioning is based on the following two closely connected axes—processes: the process of development from a disciple to a master (the master-disciple relationship) and the process of creating knowledge (changing the unknown into the known) (Lenartowicz 2016). It constitutes a natural environment for implementing process management concepts. If this point of view is adopted, all other processes conducted in the university should be subordinate to the aforementioned main processes, i.e. the didactic process, the research process, and the shaping of relations with the environment. The concept of university management based on the process approach is presented in Fig. 2.2.

What constitutes a major barrier to changes is organisational cultures and traditional, hierarchical management models based on a strong structure. The implementation of the process approach requires a deep restructuring of university management systems, processes and structures through the following actions (Maciąg 2016):

- Translating the university's strategic goals into the goals of particular processes and communicating effectively the extent of their achievement (vertical and horizontal communication).
- Reviewing and adjusting the university's internal regulations from the point of view of a description of executed processes.
- Identifying and hierarchising the elements of processes; establishing parameters for assessing the quality of expenditures; identifying actions and activities within a process, their sequence and relations, together with documentation (instructions, regulations, procedures,

Table 2.3 A business organisation versus a university—the internal context of implementing management concepts based on the process approach

Criteria	Manufacturing or service providing business organisation	University—challenges for process management
Organisational model	A special-purpose organisation, a clearly determined business purpose	An integrative, multi-purpose organisation. A unitary model, a federated model, institutional autonomy
Governing bodies	Management board, supervisory board	Collegial and single-person, elected/appointed for terms of office
Responsibility	Precisely specified	Frequently dispersed responsibility
The basic mechanism ensuring action repeatability and organisational control	High standardisation of actions, processes, and their parameters	Norms and standards based on extensive regulations, resolutions, orders, administrative procedures, and traditions
Operational continuity	Losing customers means no work and bankruptcy (the customer is the main source of revenue for the organisation)	Frequently there is no direct relation between the number of customers and profitability. Numerous and change-able sources of financing. Continuity is ensured first of all by potential held by the university. Sometimes long periods of waiting for the effects of introduced changes
Products	Standardised and repeatable products with strictly specified properties. Possibility of establishing a level of (production) errors	The service is complex and requires the participation of highly qualified employees in the provision process. The participation of many people and entities in the service provision process causes difficulties with precise allocation of scopes of responsibility. Problems with quality standardisation and repeatability; failure to reach the expected result may also result from performed activities (e.g. in basic research); results may appear after a long time. In the teaching process, man is a carrier of values. Intolerance of errors

(continued)

Table 2.3 (continued)

Criteria	Manufacturing or service providing business organisation	University—challenges for process management
Approach to the customer	Clearly defined. The customer is a buyer (who pays for products). In principle, the customer is the employer, who is strongly involved in quality improvement	Many "customers" some of whom are not buyers. The student as an untypical customer who is not fully able to assess quality (time shift); in scientific research it is often difficult to define both results and a customer (e.g. the state is a customer)
Participation of the customer	The customer does not participate in manufacturing processes; the customer assesses quality and may reject a product; low buying risk; assessment to be first of all objective. Newer management concepts recommend that products be individualised and co-created with recipients	The customer is the subject and object of actions and cannot reject the services; high risk of losing time and resources; subjective assessment, often depending on other factors (e.g. the customer's experience, attitudes occurring within a process, etc.)
The customer's needs and satisfaction	The customer's satisfaction is the most important. Production quality can be assessed without the customer's participation. The customer is not a participant in production processes and cannot have direct influence on their course	The customer's needs are the most important. The customer's needs are often determined by experts, teachers, academics. The customer has limited influence on what they receive (e.g. the canon of knowledge). The customer participates in many processes, co-creates them; without the customer's participation, it is difficult to assess process quality

Criteria	Manufacturing or service providing business organisation	University—challenges for process management
Social system. Employees	Subordination to the enterprise's goals; integration with and loyalty towards the organisation. Corporate culture	Academic freedom, group structures with strongly distinguished dominant groups; extreme individualism. Liberal, collegial culture. Decisive advantage of very well educated employees. Interest groups. Increasing number of highly qualified specialists employed on a part-time basis, e.g. in connection with project execution. Projectsation
Expenditures, effects and performance metrics	Clear goals. Relations among expenditures, the process and effects are known and foreseeable. Results are usually measurable. Easiness of establishing performance metrics. Objective assessment: profit, costs, market share	Unclear goals. Frequently unclear relations among expenditures, processes, and results. Less control over expenditures, the process, and effects. Difficulty with measuring effects because of their multidimensional character. Subjective and relational assessment: compliance with procedures and legal regulations, place in rankings, parametric assessment

Source The author's own work

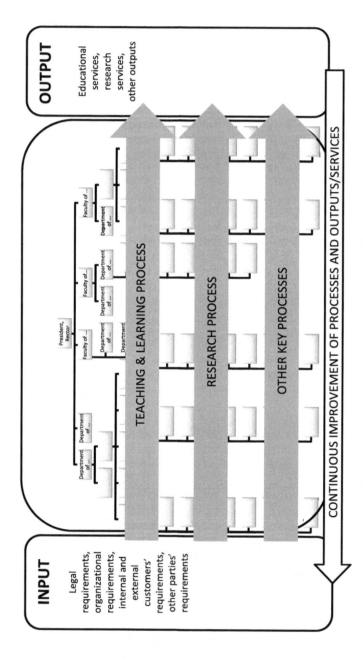

Fig. 2.2 The concept of university management based on the process approach (*Source* The author's own work)

etc.), establishing metrics for the assessment of process effectiveness and efficiency; identifying process effects/products, their recipients and quality assessment metrics.

- Configuring processes from the customer's point of view.
- Allocating responsibility and authority within processes (indicating process owners, responsibility, and decision-making rights) and identifying relations among processes, or a process architecture, in the university management system.
- Taking into consideration particular risks and opportunities in process execution (ISO 9001:2015) (risk management).
- Improving employees' knowledge and competences connected with process execution. Knowledge management in processes.
- Assessing and improving processes by implementing necessary changes in order to improve processes' potential to fulfil the customer's requirements and create value.

The aforementioned changes influence changes in the university's organisational culture.

The conducted analysis of the literature on the subject indicates that since the 1990s higher education institutions have been looking for effective concepts of changes based on the process approach. It shows the usefulness of the practical application of such management concepts and methods as TQM (including quality management methods and tools, e.g. ISO 9000 standards), BPR, Lean Management and Six Sigma in higher education institutions. They will be discussed in the subsequent parts of the book.

2.3.4 Process Management Concepts in Contemporary Higher Education Institutions

2.3.4.1 Total Quality Management

TQM is the most widely discussed concept concerning process management in higher education institutions. This subject was covered in management literature, among others, by Bonstingl (1995), Davies (2000),

Wawak (2011), Maciąg (2011a), Piasecka (2011), Tarí and Madeleine (2012), Chalaris et al. (2015), Tarí and Dick (2012), Manatos et al. (2017), Papanthymou and Darra (2017), and Psomas and Antony (2017). The first theoretical references to the possibility of using TQM in higher education institution appeared as early as 1991 (e.g. Sherr and Gregory Lozier 1991; Harvey and Knight 1996); since 2002 a number of articles have been published on the results on empirical researches conducted in this area in higher education institutions (e.g. Osseo-Asare and Longbottom 2002).

Researchers have been focused on the following three issues: conditions for the implementation of quality management; the models, techniques and tools of quality management, and the dimensions of quality management (Tarí and Dick 2012; Manatos et al. 2017; Papanthymou and Darra 2017). They indicate the usefulness of the following quality management models and concepts based on TQM: European Foundation for Quality Management (EFQM), Malcolm Baldrige National Quality Award (MBNQA), quality management systems based on the requirements of ISO 9000 series standards. They also emphasise that for the purposes of higher education institutions, dedicated TQM-based quality models are developed, e.g. The European Quality Improvement System (EQUIS), The European Network for Quality Assurance in Higher Education (ENQA), and national external education quality assurance systems, or existing systems are adapted to new requirements, e.g. Malcolm Baldrige Criteria for Performance Excellence for Education (Tarí and Madeleine 2012, p. 790).

The most important issues addressed in research include identifying and defining the dimensions of TQM as well as proposing and testing tools for measuring them. The key success factors in implementing TQM are the following: quality of leadership, vision, metrics and assessment, control and improvement of processes, development of programmes, quality improvement systems, employee commitment, appreciation and rewarding, education and training, focus on customers and stakeholders, availability of resources, quality culture maturity (Bayraktar et al. 2008, pp. 551–574; Wawak 2012, p. 81; Tarí and Madeleine 2012, p. 801). The TQM elements which are the most thoroughly adopted in higher education institutions include the following: student focus, leadership and top management commitment, strategic quality planning, process management, and teaching staff and employee involvement (Psomas and Antony 2017). Barriers for TQM implementation constitute another important research problem. Some of them are common for all organisations implementing this concept, however, managing universities generates unique limitations and barriers (Tarí and Dick 2012; Davies 2000, p. 13; Bonstingl 1995), for example: difficulties with measuring the core of learning processes; difficulties with controlling didactic processes in universities because of the diversity of products, places of delivery, manners of delivery, processes and personnel requiring control; the lack of managers' responsibility for quality; the lack of employees' empowerment to improve quality; the lack of standards reflecting customers' requirements; academic freedom; difficulties with identifying who is a customer; difficulties with identifying the university's product; irregular obligations to teach; and conflicts with research tasks.

Another research area is TQM effectiveness and efficiency assessment (Maciąg 2011b, 2013). It is recommended that assessment models focus more on efficiency, including financial criteria and metrics as well as effects for the university's stakeholders (Tarí and Dick 2012).

Research is also conducted on the use of the EFQM model in higher education institutions. The results of the research carried out by Tarí and Madeleine indicate that a self-assessment methodology based on EFQM has to be adjusted to the specificity and operational context of a given university. The culture of a particular country, including the promotion and tradition of a quality culture, and a low level of quality management maturity may constitute a barrier for implementing qualitative changes. The commitment of the management and resources are key success factors. Research shows that EFQM causes the following changes in higher education institutions: new vocabulary and a new system of notions, participatory management, improvement activities (Tarí and Madeleine 2012, p. 800).

A quality management system based on the requirements of the ISO 9001 standard can become a useful tool for implementing TQM in universities, although the standard is regarded, wrongly, as applicable to the manufacturing sector only. Therefore, attempts to introduce changes are met frequently with barriers of a cultural, social, technical, or organisational character (Wawak 2011; Maciąg 2011a; Piasecka 2011; Chalaris et al. 2015; Goranczewski 2011; Kasperavičiūtė-Černiauskienė and Serafinas 2018). It is indicated that success of a quality management system depends less on rigorism in implementing the requirements of the ISO 9001 standard and more on the active participation of stakeholders and their perception and interpretation of the system (Chalaris et al. 2015, p. 268).

In parallel with TQM and BPM, we can observe the development of the theory and practice of applying the concept of BPR in higher education institutions.

2.3.4.2 Business Process Reengineering

The first mentions about BPR come from 1999. The most important publications on this management concept include the following West (1999), Jeal (2005), Ahmad et al. (2007), and Abdous (2011). In the first study of reengineering in higher education institutions, the author uses this notion, describing the need to introduce market mechanisms into universities' activities with a view to implementing the corporate university model (Tsichritzis 1999). Various studies presented in the literature analyse the conditions for and effects of implementing BPR. It is emphasised that the application of reengineering may result in the centralising of administration and the breaking of barriers between the central administration and the departmental administration (West 1999). Attention is also drawn to such success factors as team work, quality culture, a quality management system, satisfactory rewards, effective change management, a less bureaucratic and more participatory information system, effective project management, and sufficient financial resources (Ahmad et al. 2007). The implementation of the reengineering concept faces various difficulties which result from complex organisational cultures, the requirements resulting from the implementation methodology (attention to detail and honesty), the necessity of properly planning communication and change management activities (Jeal 2005). A solution could be a general plan of implementing BPR in higher education institutions. Such a plan includes the following four phases (Abdous 2011): initiation (identifying, understanding the environment in which the process is to be carried out, documenting the process); analysis (analysing the process environment, mapping the process, identifying its strengths and weaknesses); process reengineering (restructuring the process, mapping a new process, communication, feedback); implementation and evaluation (a prototype of the new process, implementing the new process, assessment, and a report on achievements). Attention is paid to the context in which changes are to take place, i.e. organisational culture, leadership, and information technology. In the author's opinion, BPR offers a radical change strongly anchored in the information technology. This type of change frequently does not match a particular university's culture and is very expensive.

The analysis conducted above shows a growing interest in the implementation of process management concepts and methods in higher education institutions. However, researchers stress that a critically important determinant of successful changes in a management system of a university is the commitment of its managers and employees, changes in the organisational culture, as well as the allocation of adequate resources in support of undertaken process restructuring initiatives. The culture of audit and managerism, which start to dominate in universities, create an environment which encourages opportunistic behaviour such as favouritism, pursuing advantages, and the actions of organisational psychopaths (By, Diefenbach and Klarner 2008, p. 21). If change is implemented improperly, the result is wastage of resources, implementation for its own sake, further centralisation and bureaucratisation, formalisation, discouragement in employees, and short-term decision making. The lack of the holistic approach causes restructuring to be fragmentary and focusing first of all on didactic and research processes and does not strengthen the university's administrative core (which is a prerequisite for implementing the concept of an enterprising university) (Yokoyama 2006, p. 523). The lack of connections between the process approach and a change in an organisational culture decreases the permanence of the effects of restructuring and in the long term does not contribute to the improvement of processes in universities (Radnor et al. 2006).

Taking into consideration the results of the analysis of the literature on the subject and her own research, in the next sub-chapter the author will explain why process management concepts can become a useful approach to the restructuring of higher education institutions.

2.3.5 Process Management vs. the External and Internal Contexts of Higher Education Institutions

Because of the complexity, extent and multidimensionality of the issues raised in this book, the author wanted to concentrate on the most significant conditions of the university's external and internal contexts as well as the most persuasive arguments put forward in the discussion on the application of the process approach in the modernisation of the university. A relevant summary of these conditions and arguments is presented in Table 2.4.

An analysis of the arguments presented in the table indicates the correctness of the thesis on higher education institutions proposed by Peter H. Franz, Dr. Mathias Kirchmer, and Professor Michael Rosemann (2012). The researchers claim that the most important value associated with process management is transparency perceived as a deep understanding of processes taking place in an organisation. This is a basis for their continuous improvement. Process management makes it possible to combine such values as quality and effectiveness, flexibility and compliance, internal integration and networking. Particularly in higher education institutions, they are interpreted as contradictory and mutually exclusive. In the author's opinion, process management allows the university to create an environment in which consensus can be reached among the various requirements of the university's customers and stakeholders. This reduces tensions resulting from different historically conditioned management models, a large number of goals, the specificity of systems, structures and processes in higher education institutions. Strong emphasis is put on the necessity of changes in organisational cultures towards entrepreneurship and continuous improvement. Universities are looking for new methods of implementing deep and permanent changes. One of them is Lean Management.

Table 2.4 The factors of the external and internal contexts of managing higher education institutions vs. the process approach

Challenges for the contemporary management of universities	Justification for following the process approach
Legal and political factors. The age of transparency—honesty, transparency, disclosure, trust, accountability, formalisation	Transparency of actions and processes in organisations (actions are identified, described, and communicated). Formalisation builds also a culture of responsibility and discipline
Legal and political factors. Management reviews and inspections carried out within the process approach, e.g. education quality accreditation, parametric assessment of research activities, financial audits. Changes in the law	The process approach ensures control over processes performed in the organisation as well as the reduction of time necessary for preparations and dealing with (internal and external) controlling authorities. A clear process architecture allows the organisation to introduce changes made in the law and to follow their consequences
Market factors. Competition, networks, simultaneous cooperation and competition (coopetition)	Implementing the process approach facilitates the networking of activities. Clearly defined scopes of competence and responsibility in relations with external entities make it easier to function in coopetition conditions
Economic factors. Economisation of activities, value for money, effectiveness, efficiency, risk of higher education studies (time, costs, alternative costs)	Process analysis and redesigning make it possible to increase effectiveness and efficiency, and to decrease costs. Possibility of calculating process costs more accurately (Activity Based Costing)
Social factors. The millennial generation. A new type of students—*must have, must be*. Student experience. Numerous customers/stakeholders of the university	The customer, stakeholder and their expectations are the starting point for process development. Minimisation of bureaucracy, computerisation, transparency, and simplicity of operational procedures

(continued)

Table 2.4 (continued)

Challenges for the contemporary management of universities	Justification for following the process approach
Technological factors. Computerisation of universities, distance learning, e-learning, M-learning, globalisation, virtual university, network university	Implementing modern information solutions requires the application of the process approach. Information systems use zero-one logic based on processes. There are no exceptions
The internal context. Products and services created in networks of internal connections, increasingly complex character of work, necessity of cooperation with various entities within the scope of didactic, research, organisational, and project execution processes	Clearly defined scopes of competence and responsibility inside the organisation. Processes carried out above organisational (functional) divisions; the organisational structure is secondary with respect to processes (organisational units provide services for processes)
The internal context. Changing hierarchical structures based on control into a new world of networked institutions (heterarchy); changing the centre of power depending on the context and competences. Quality of leadership. Tensions between the models of a collegial university, a bureaucratic university, and an enterprising university	Process is a criterion for rearranging the organisation; process owners are appointed. The process approach increases responsibility for and control over processes without simultaneously reducing the organisation's flexibility. Delegation of powers. Professionalisation and strengthening of the quality of leadership
The internal context. Necessity of developing an organisational culture based on the organisation's sustainable development, quality, and entrepreneurship. The concept of a university as *living laboratories*	Quality, security, environment, social responsibility are values provided to stakeholders by the university; thus they constitute a starting point for designing processes. BPM ensures balancing of processes, effective allocation of resources
The internal context. Changeability of processes in the university. Many exceptions. Need of standardsation	Standardisation of processes (e.g. by means of information management systems, formalised instructions and procedures, statistical quality control). Deep understanding of processes through their categorisation

Challenges for the contemporary management of universities	Justification for following the process approach
The internal context. Organisational (collegial, bureaucratic) culture. Employees' resistance to changes	Commitment to change. Intra-organisational entrepreneurship. Creativity, initiative. Employee empowerment. All employees participate in the improvement process (Kaizen, employee suggestion schemes)
The internal context. Necessity of knowledge continuity management. Professionalisation of management. Employing academic personnel under short-term contracts for the duration of projects	Knowledge is recorded in the form of organisational documents (procedures, instructions, good practices, etc.) which describe the organisation's functioning and conducted processes. Putting the organisation's processes in order makes it possible to use employees' potential better by having them perform particular clearly defined tasks in the organisation (e.g. within didactic, research, and other processes). Increasing the possibility of replacing employees, e.g. in supporting processes without significant impact on the quality of executed processes
The internal context. The knowledge employee—improving the performance of knowledge employees	Improving the organisation's functioning results in increasing the amount of time which can be spent on creative and innovative activities oriented towards increasing value for the university's customer and stakeholder
The internal context. Implementing concepts based on process management, e.g. outsourcing, benchmarking, education quality assurance systems, shared service centres, knowledge management	Process identification allows the university to assess them and to compare itself with other schools. Knowledge of processes constitutes a basis for making economic and organisational decisions—fact-based decision making

Source Prepared on the basis of Grudzewski et al. (2010, pp. 14–15), Yokoyama (2006, pp. 523–555), Balzer (2010, p. 7), Goranczewski (2013), Leja (2013, pp. 63–69), and Kwiek (2015, pp. 12–47)

2.4   Lean Management as a Process Concept of Managing Higher Education Institutions—The Essence and Principles

2.4.1   The Development of the Concept of Lean Management in Higher Education in the Light of the Literature on the Subject

The works by Deming (1986) *Out of the Crisis*, Ohno (1988) *Toyota Production System: Beyond Large-Scale Production*, Womack et al. (1990) *The Machine That Changed the World: The Story of Lean Production*, Liker (2005) *The Toyota Way*, and Rother (2009) *Toyota Kata* are regarded as major breakthroughs in the development of Lean Management which systematised the foundations of this concept (Rother 2009). The rudiments of Lean Manufacturing created by Ford at the beginning of the twentieth century, based on Taylor's scientific management and enriched by Deming's quality control concept as well as the concepts of supermarkets and inventory management, were subsequently perfected in the Toyota Production System (TPS) (Liker 2005; Parkes 2017). They were discussed extensively in publications devoted to manufacturing enterprises (Womack and Jones 2001, 2010; Womack et al. 1990; Liker 2005). Over the years Lean Management evolved from the operational level into a philosophy of management used successfully also in service organisations and referred to as Lean Service (Locher 2016). Depending on a particular sector, Lean Management assumed such names as Lean Banking or Lean Education (Suárez-Barraza et al. 2012). The concept was also implemented and developed in public organisations (Radnor et al. 2006; Drotz 2014; Cole 2011; Bateman et al. 2018; Ludwiczak 2018).

First discussions on the application of Lean Management in education were initiated in the 1990s and at the beginning of the twenty-first century. They concerned the issue of leadership in TQM, the possibility of cost reduction by eliminating wastage in education institutions (Suárez-Barraza et al. 2012, p. 370), the implementation of TQM (Dahlgaard and Østergaard 2000) and the effectiveness of the Kaizen method, which is an integral part of Lean (Emiliani 2004, 2005). Interest in

Lean Management rose on the tide of scepticism about TQM (Balzer et al. 2016) and BPR. At present the Lean concept becomes an important issue addressed in the process of higher education reform, which is proved by the growing number of implementations all over the world (www1). In order to stress the specificity of the Lean concept in higher education the author proposes using such terms as LHE (Balzer 2010), Educational Lean (Waterbury 2011), Lean University (Emiliani 2015).

The growth of interest in the application of Lean Management in higher education can be analysed with respect to the quantity and types of publications and issues addressed in them. The most important books on this subject include the following: 2010—Lean Higher Education by William Balzer 2011—Educational Lean for Higher Education by Theresa Waterbury 2015—Lean University by Bob Emiliani. The analysis of the articles was based on the method of a systematic review of the related literature. In the conducted research, the author used the EBSCO database and accessorily the (WoS) service and Google Scholar. In the case of the EBSCO database, the author used the following key words: Lean Management and higher education (Table 2.5). Only peer-reviewed articles were chosen for reviewing.

In total, 29 items were selected (subject terms). On analysing the abstracts, the author rejected 14 publications (concerning hotels, other public administration units, consulting in the Lean area, hospitals, and teaching Lean). The analysis covered publications in the English language only. The search results show that the earliest indexed article comes from 2008. The topics of the selected articles are presented in Table 2.6.

Table 2.5 The number of publications on Lean Management in higher education institutions according to EBSCO as at 16 October 2018

Criteria of searching	EBSCO database—number of articles	The earliest indexed article
Key words: Lean Management, higher education (in abstract)	35 (16)	2005
Key words: Lean Management, higher education (subject terms)	29 (10)	2008
Key words: Lean Management, higher education (in title)	4 (2)	2014

Source The author's own work
( ) number of full text articles

Table 2.6 An analysis of articles on Lean Management in higher education

	Year of publication	Author	Type of article	Subject	Addressed issues and problems, results
1	2008	Kress, Nancy J.	Case study	Streamlining processes in a university library	Case study describes key principles of Lean thinking and how they have been implemented to improve shelving turnaround time. The conversion of the Department from a reactive model to Lean thinking has produced some dramatic performance improvements
2	2008	Hines, Peter; Lethbridge, Sarah	Conceptual framework	Experience of implementing Lean in universities	The academic environment is difficult to change, its structures do not favour quick changes; a lot of work is necessary to obtain commitment of all university employees
3	2013	Cristina, Dragomir; Felicia, Surugiu	Review (case study)	A review of Lean implementation models in higher education	Universities frequently resort to Lean in situations of crisis (e.g. budget cuts). Lean is a permanent and continuous change. A facilitator is necessary to ensure that implementation is correct. A review of the university's processes is necessary. It is necessary to establish an office and employ a manager to supervise the Lean implementation process. The results of changes should be communicated throughout the university
4	2014	Antony, Jiju	Conceptual framework	An assessment of readiness for LSS implementation	On the basis of an analysis of the literature on the subject, the author defines five groups of readiness factors: Leadership and vision; managers' commitment and resources, connections between LSS and the university's strategy, focus on the customer, selection of proper people for project execution

Year of publication	Author	Type of article	Subject	Addressed issues and problems, results
5	2015	Antony, Jiju	Conceptual framework	A presentation of challenges in the LSS implementation process in higher education	The challenges were defined in the organisational, technical, and individual dimensions. The problems are as follows: in the organisational dimension—the lack of proper leadership; in the technical dimension—difficulties with data collection; in the individual dimension—employee commitment, academic freedom and autonomy
6	2015	Vyas, Nick; Campbell, Mary	Review (literature)	The role of LSS in creating operation excellence	LSS practices reduce the cost associated with higher education administration by optimising resource allocations and increasing efficiency throughout educational systems
7	2015	Balzer, W. K.; Brodke, M. H.; Thomas Kizhakethalackal, E.	Review (literature)	Supporting LHE implementation through the concept of organisational change	The authors present LHE implementation models based on the achievements of the concept of organisational change. According to them, the most important factors determining successful change include the following: assessing and improving institutional readiness; enhancing leadership awareness, understanding, and support for LHE; strategic planning, Lean leadership, and getting help for LHE; facilitating an institution-wide transition to LHE
8	2015	Waterbury, T.	Research	An ocean of changes connected with Lean implementation	The identification of organisational and individual factors which influenced the reflection on Lean implementation in higher education. Lean coordinators and administrators participated in the research

(continued)

Table 2.6 (continued)

	Year of publication	Author	Type of article	Subject	Addressed issues and problems, results
9	2015	Svensson, Carsten; Antony, Jiju; Ba-Essa, Mohamed; Bakhsh, Majed; Albliwi, Saja	Case study	A presentation of an initiative in the area of LSS	The conducted programme allowed the university to improve its processes. The challenges included impatience with waiting for effects, the lack of full understanding of the system and introduced improvements. The importance of the role of the LSS specialist
10	2015	Douglas, Jacqueline Ann; Antony, Jiju; Douglas, Alexander	Research	The identification of eight types of wastage in the university	The identification of wastage in accordance with the developed classification, the indication of typical examples, the presentation of specimen wastage identification methods, i.e. Value Stream Mapping, 5S, Point of use storage (POUS)
11	2015	Thomas, Andrew J.; Antony, Jiju; Francis, Mark; Fisher, Ron	Review (case study)	A review of the approaches to Lean implementation in higher education in the UK	The study results indicate the maturity levels of various elements of the Lean concept. A tendency to reduce wastage rather than to support the function, isolating Lean initiatives, a weak connection between the Lean strategy and the university's strategy, local strategies, employee empowerment, self-organising Lean teams, more focus on revenue than on effectiveness and improvement
12	2016	Balzer, William K.; Francis, David E.; Krehbiel, Timothy C.; Shea, Nicholas	Review (literature)	A summary and an indication of further research directions	Further research directions: the formalisation of the LHE definition, the development of metrics measuring the influence of LHE on the university, further support for LHE development based on good databases, the promotion of LHE with a view to ensuring that the concept is understood by the university's employees and stakeholders

	Year of publication	Author	Type of article	Subject	Addressed issues and problems, results
13	2017	Lu, Jing; Laux, Chad; Antony, Jiju	Conceptual framework	A model of leadership in LSS	The model uses various forms of leadership and combines them with knowledge and skills related to LSS. LSS leadership creates an organisation based on continuous change through empowering employees to identify opportunities for change and improvement
14	2017	Tay, Huay Ling; Low, Stephen Wee Kiat	Case study	The use of Lean in resource digitalisation for teaching purposes	The case study indicates the most important determinants for Lean implementation in the university: common vision, top management support and leadership, timely information sharing, and relationship management with key stakeholders in the transformation processes
15	2017	Billings, L.; Llamas, N. A.; Snyder, B. E.; Sung, Y.	Case study	The use of Lean in improving library processes	The identification of workflows in a library: acquisitions/receiving, cataloguing, and cataloguing maintenance. A description of process execution and related challenges

Source Prepared on the basis of Kress (2008), Hines and Lethbridge (2008), Antony (2014, 2015), Dragomir and Surugiu (2013), Vyas and Campbell (2015), Balzer et al. (2015), Waterbury (2015), Svensson et al. (2015), Douglas et al. (2015), Thomas et al. (2015), Balzer et al. (2016), Lu et al. (2017), and Billings et al. (2017)

Comparing the analysis results to those concerning process management, it is possible to notice that interest in BPM decreases, while that in Lean Management is on the rise. Lean Management initiatives are undertaken at the levels of processes, organisational units, and whole universities. There is strong development in the area of Lean Six Sigma applications. Academic publications are dominated by topics connected with operational conditions for Lean implementation as well as related organisational, technical, and economic issues. It should be noted that academic publications were preceded by works of a practical, guiding, or—less frequently—conceptual character. They were case studies describing Lean Management implementation processes in particular universities (e.g. Robinson and Yorkstone 2014; Moore et al. 2007) or conceptual papers (e.g. Yorkstone 2016). The first documented cases of Lean implementations in higher education come from the beginning of the twentieth century (e.g. Dragomir and Surugiu 2013); formal initiatives in this area in British universities date back to 2006 (Radnor and Bucci 2011). In 2011 Radnor and Bucci carried out a review of Lean Management initiatives in the British higher education sector (Radnor and Bucci 2011). The first comprehensive review of the literature on the subject was published in 2015 (Balzer et al. 2016).

The performed analysis of the literature on the subject shows that the number and quality of publications have been changing over time. There are more and more surveys and conceptual papers formulating challenges in the area of Lean implementation. Creating a coherent theoretical framework for Lean Management appears to be a considerable challenge.

2.4.2   The Essence of Lean Management

2.4.2.1 Defining Lean Management

Attempts to define the notion of Lean Management in higher education have been undertaken, among others, by Balzer (2010), Maciąg (2016), Emiliani (2004), Robinson and Yorkstone (2014), and Waterbury (2011). In the literature on the subject, it is difficult to fine one dominant definition of the concept. Lean is defined as a management philosophy, system, approach, management method, set of techniques and tools, behaviours and attitudes.

In the literature, the notion of Lean itself is explained narrowly as making slim or slimming down, and more broadly as flexibility (the ability to adjust to changes quickly), resilience (the speed and dynamics of reacting to changes) (Czerska 2009, pp. 1–16), or agility (ability to survive and thrive in unforeseeable conditions) (Bednarek 2007, p. 33). The author's own research shows that in many languages, e.g. Polish, Norwegian, or Dutch, there is no good equivalent of the word lean, therefore the name of the concept is often left untranslated into a particular national language.

Lean Management in higher education is defined multidimensionally as: a system designed in such a way as to ensure that it addresses the needs of people in the organisation and allows the provision of better effects for key stakeholders: customers, investors, associations, communities, suppliers (Emiliani 2004); a methodology which uses the power of collective knowledge, the scientific method and understanding of values in order to redesign the administrative and academic function so that they function from the point of view of the student's interests (Waterbury 2011, p. 31); a central improvement strategy (Francis 2014), a comprehensive approach to organisational change and improvement (Balzer 2010, p. 15); an approach to process improvement at the workplace (Robinson and Yorkstone 2014).

The author proposes that the definition of Lean Management in higher education be systematised in the following sections:

- From a behavioural perspective, Lean Management means a set of various behaviours of organisation members who participate in Lean implementation (social standards, situational and personal factors, etc.). In the broad meaning, it can be identified with Lean Culture.
- In the attributive context, Lean Management is a set of features assigned to a process, organisational unit, university, etc. (e.g. slimness, agility, speed, adaptability, excellence, etc.). It can apply to a Lean maturity level at which a process or organisation is at a given time.

• From a functional point of view, Lean Management is a methodology of implementing the Lean Principles (strategy, programme, system, structure, methods, techniques, tools for making the organisation lean, managing change, projects, strategies, etc.).

The proposed classification may be used to pursue various research objectives. It is identical with research approaches.

At present Lean cannot be reduced to simple solutions in the area of the university's operations. It constitutes a holistic management concept oriented towards bringing about required changes in the social, technical, organisational, and economic systems. In the author's opinion, the essence of the Lean Management concept in higher education includes basic assumptions (Lean Thinking philosophy, Lean Values, and Lean Principles), a Lean Management system (an organisational structure, programme, procedures, resources), as well as Lean methods and tools. All these elements are indispensable, interact with each other, and condition the maturity of a Lean Culture (Fig. 2.3). They will be elaborated on in the subsequent parts of the book.

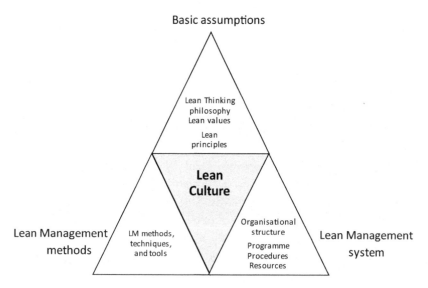

Fig. 2.3 The essence of the Lean Management concept (*Source* The author's own work)

The Lean Thinking philosophy focuses first of all on acting economically, i.e. improving the efficiency of actions by eliminating or minimising waste and controlling the flow of added value (Hamrol et al. 2015, p. 99; Walentynowicz 2013). The concept of Lean Management is founded on the two most important values: respect for people and continuous improvement (Robinson and Yorkstone 2014; Emiliani 2015). A Lean strategy can be defined as a comprehensive plan for achieving goals in the area of improving the university's functioning on the basis of the Lean Principles (Collis 2016). A Lean strategy should be connected closely with and interpenetrate the university's development strategy. The Lean Principles reflect the fundamental assumptions of this concept: value, value stream, pull, flow, improvement (which will be discussed in the further part of the chapter). A Lean Management system is defined by the author as a tool for implementing the fundamental assumptions and Lean programme (these issues will be discussed in Chapter 4). A model of such a system can comprise the following elements:

- An organisational structure created for the purpose of implementing a Lean programme (teams, units, networks).
- Procedures (appointing people responsible for concept implementation, selecting appropriate techniques and tools, effectiveness and efficiency indexes, monitoring and improvement methods).
- Resources (human, material, financial, information resources; time).

The last constituent element is Lean methods and tools (presented in the further part of this chapter and discussed in Chapter 4). It is emphasised that the prerequisite for success is creating an organisational culture supporting efforts towards continuous improvement. According to Liker, "lean thinking" requires a thorough cultural transformation (Liker 2005, p. 40). Lean Culture can be defined as an organisational culture which is the result of learning together how to solve problems in the process of external adaptation and internal integration based on the continuous pursuit of excellence and respect for people (Maciąg 2018) (issues related to Lean Culture will be discussed in Chapter 3).

The key elements of Lean Thinking are the notions of added value created for the customer and wastage.

2.4.2.2 Defining Value in Higher Education Processes

The literature on the subject contains many definitions of value as perceived in the process approach. According to Lean Lexicon, the value of a product from the point of view of the customer is reflected in its price and market demand (*Lean Lexicon* 2010). Value is benefits expressed by means of a monetary measure which the customer receives in return for the paid price (for services or products, economic or social values) (Orzen 2014, p. 214). Customer value can be defined as the surplus of benefits perceived subjectively by the customer (such benefits are related to the needs which the customer wants to satisfy) over the subjectively perceived costs related to buying and using a product (Szymura-Tyc 2012, pp. 50–51). Value is also defined as a set of tangible and intangible benefits which meet stakeholders' needs in a timely, effective, and efficient manner (Makkar et al. 2008, p. 183).

The author proposes the adoption of the following three perspectives in defining value: a subjective perspective (who is value created for), an objective perspective (what is a carrier of value), and a resultant perspective (how value can be measured). In the subjective approach, value is defined from the point of view of the university's internal and external customers (Geryk 2010, pp. 40–54; Reavill 1998, p. 55; Stoller 2015, p. 312). The basic problem is indicating the beneficiary of the process, their requirements and expected benefits. In the objective approach, added value is created by technical elements (tangible infrastructure, including technical and technological one), economic elements (costs incurred for studies, tuition fees, financial support), service elements (services supporting students and other entities, organisation), social elements (access to information) (Orzen 2014, p. 216). In the resultant approach, value can be defined in terms of quality, satisfaction, compliance, as well as cost and time metrics. The selection of added value metrics is determined by the requirements and expectations of the customer of the process, as well as the specificity of the process and provided service. With respect to the student, Botas defines values expected by them as functional (the usefulness of education from the perspective of employment), social (contacts, friendships, life in a group, trust in others), emotional (consistence among study subjects, interests, and preferences), creative (innovativeness, intellectual development), and resulting from the obtainment of new professional qualifications (Botas 2011, p. 2). Value created in the educational process can be also defined and assessed in the didactic aspect (metrics related to learning outcomes), the marketing aspect (the level of satisfaction of students, graduates, and other stakeholders, etc.), the economic aspect (the metrics of the benefits and costs of processes), and the organisational aspect (metrics related to process organisation) (Maciąg 2011a). Employee value can be defined based on indexes concerning satisfaction, relational trust, and quality of life in the workplace (Bugdol 2011b) Customer value is created within a value stream. A value stream comprises all activities (both those which add value and those which do not) necessary in a product creation process (Rother and Shooka 1999, p. 49). There are two basic types of value streams: product development value streams and operational (product creation and delivery) streams (*Lean Lexicon* 2010; Locher 2016, p. 25; Czerska 2009, p. 21). The idea of value is strongly connected with the idea of wastage.

2.4.2.3 Wastage in Higher Education

According to the Lean concept, wastage is every action which uses resources, but does not add value for the customer (from the Japanese *muda*) (*Lean Lexicon* 2010). Among the sources of wastage, we can distinguish two categories of actions: actions which do not create value, but are indispensable for the proper provision of a service (e.g. actions required under the law or the university's internal regulations, customs, or traditions) and actions which do not create value and are redundant from the point of view of the organisation's external and internal customers. Proposed by Ohno, the classical division of the sources of wastage comprises the following categories (Ohno 1988): overproduction, waiting, unnecessary transport, excessive or improper processing, excessive inventories, unnecessary movements, defects (e.g. data entry mistakes, incorrect timetables). Additionally, the eighth category is recognised, i.e. employees' unused creativity (Douglas et al. 2013, p. 22, 2015). The above categories are also referred to by means of the abbreviation TIMWOOD. The analysis of the literature on the subject indicates that classifications of waste sources cannot be unquestioningly transferred from production enterprises to the service sector, and in particular to higher education institutions. Balzer proposes the division of wastage sources in higher education into the following categories (Balzer 2010): wastage in human resources (the inability to use fully the knowledge, skills and talents of employees and employee groups), wastage in processes (the result of shortcomings in process design and implementation), wastage of information (information processes do not support the university's processes), wastage of assets—the improper use of the university's human, infrastructural, and service provision resources. On the basis of researches conducted in British universities, the following wastage categories were proposed: delay, duplication, unnecessary movement, unclear communication, incorrect inventory, opportunity lost, errors, people (Radnor et al. 2006). The author's own research allowed her to identify the following wastage sources:

- the lack of process automation (certain actions are performed manually, which takes more time and is the source of errors, employees are not able to utilise fully the possibilities offered by software already available in the university, e.g. excel),
- wrongly assigned scopes of responsibility and competences, which lengthens the authorisation process (many persons have to sign a given document; frequently such persons are not competent in a given respect and put their signature only because of a position held in a hierarchy or, because of the number of documents to sign, they are not able to become thoroughly familiar with each of them),
- the lack of an assessment of the consequences of implemented changes and made decisions (the lack of a holistic and systemic

approach; the lack of an implemented process approach makes it difficult to assess the consequences of made decisions),

- unnecessary process standardisation (these processes which function well on the basis of good practices or academic traditions are subject matter of changes and regulations),
- the lack of connections among processes, the so-called black holes (the lack of information, the lack of joints among actions in a given process if it is executed by a few different departments and employee, e.g. a researcher, is such a connecting element, provides documents, information, etc.),
- meetings (long ineffective meetings of excessively large teams do not favour solving problems and are oriented towards procrastination), and
- legal regulations and their changeability (unadjusted to the specificity of the university, e.g. labour law, tax law, public procurement law).

In the author's opinion, the aforementioned examples prove that the sources of wastage in organisations are first of all badly designed, badly implemented and unimproved management processes and systems in higher education. Deming claimed that managers were responsible for 80% of problems occurring in organisations. They consume the organisation's resources without creating value for its customers, employees, and stakeholders, and first of all they waste human capital, which is the basis for the university's functioning. They are the reason for the lack of satisfaction, low commitment and morale, general disaffection, which translates into relations in employee teams, students, superiors, and other stakeholders of the university.

2.4.2.4 The Lean Principles in Higher Education

The five principles of Lean Management constitute another part of the foundations of the Lean concept. The principles and the tools for their implementation are described in Table 2.7. The basic barriers to their complete implementation are also identified.

Table 2.7 The Lean Principles in higher education—essence, application barrier, implementation techniques, and tools

Lean Management principles	Essence of Lean in higher education	Problems	Lean Management tools (some tools may be relevant for more than one principle)
Determining precisely the value of a particular product/service	Defining value to be provided by processes from the point of view of the university's all (internal and external) customers	Large number and changeability of stakeholders. The student is not a typical customer. The lack of consensus about what value is. Partial unpredictability of effects	Customer opinion surveys, quality function deployment, stakeholder analysis, voice of customer
Identifying a value stream for each product	Identifying the course of the process from the perspective of the customer and the organisation; assessing the constituent activities and actions from the point of view of value creation	The lack of holistic thinking about processes taking place in the university. Poor communication among the departments during the course of the process. High autonomisation of the particular units. Specificity of processes. Difficulties with following this principle in certain operating areas of the university, e.g. preparing a timetable	Value Stream Mapping, SIPOC, block diagrams
Ensuring an undisturbed flow of value	Eliminating wastage sources. Process reorganisation through the use of bottom-up creativity and employee commitment; the management's competences and commitment are of primary importance	Tolerance of inefficiency constitutes an integral part of the institution's specificity. Changeability of processes. Creative processes. Diffused responsibility	Training, Kaizen, 5S, standardisation of activities and processes, standard operating procedures, visualisation CRM, Pareto principle, Ishikawa diagram

Lean Management principles	Essence of Lean in higher education	Problems	Lean Management tools (some tools may be relevant for more than one principle)
Creating value when it is expected by the customer	Making processes free from any disturbances or down-time and performing only actions required by the customer (a pull system)	The university has to maintain its potential, which is used for achieving different goals. The permanence of this potential is the basis for creating didactic and research excellence	Andon, process automation and computerisation, Kanban, FIFO delivery systems
Pursuing continuous improvement	Continuous improvement through the commitment of the university's employees and management in accordance with the PDCA cycle	There may occur contradictions between excellence in the individual dimension and the process or institutional dimension	Kaizen, appropriate motivational system, empowerment, learning organisation concept, knowledge management, project management, change management, Hoshin Kanrii, strategic balanced scorecard, Six Sigma, institutionalisation of organisational solutions, standardisation

Source The author's own work based on Dahlgaard and Østergaard (2000), Robinson and Yorkstone (2014), Balzer (2010, p. 7), Maciąg (2016), Emiliani (2000), and Rich et al. (2006)

Lean Management in higher education uses an extensive range of techniques and tools developed within BPM, BPR, TQM, and Six Sigma. The aim is to carry out effective changes in all sub-systems of the university, at the strategic and operational levels. Nevertheless, they have to be modified and adjusted to the specific character of academic processes and the university as an organisation (Balzer et al. 2016).

The explanation of the essence of the Lean Management concept in higher education provides the author with a theoretical framework for determining the characteristic features of the Lean University.

2.4.3 The Lean University—Proposed Assumptions

The implementation of the Lean Management concept in higher education is a strategic decision which requires full commitment on the part of the management and employees as well as deep changes in the organisation's operating principles. On the basis of her own analysis of the literature on the subject and research, the author identified the main areas which need to undergo change in the Lean implementation process. The result is a characterisation of the Lean University (Table 2.8).

The analysis presented in Table 2.8 indicates clearly that success in Lean implementation not only requires changes in the university's organisational and technical spheres but is also connected with a deep change in its social sphere and organisational culture.

Successful Lean implementation can generate numerous benefits for the university. In the light of the conducted research, the most important of them are the following:

- The integration of the diversified and multi-purpose organisation. Successful Lean implementation makes it possible to utilise better energy resulting from synergy based on the culture of continuous improvement.
- The strengthening of institutional autonomy.

Table 2.8 The Lean University—a characterisation

Areas of change	The Lean University—a characterisation
University model	A university is a set of main and auxiliary processes subordinated to the common goal of fulfilling the needs of the internal customer and the external customer. Cooperation based on partnership, trust and team work. Factual institutional autonomy
Operational goals	Quality, excellence, flexibility, individualisation, satisfaction, value, wastage minimisation. Long-term perspective
Values	Respect and continuous improvement
Organisational structure model	Process structure model. Slimmed and flattened organisational structure. Organisational units focused on processes and sub-processes, configurable, multi-specialist, with a considerable range of independence. Temporary interdisciplinary project teams appointed to solve problems in the area of continuous improvement. Strengthening the role of the professional manager (e.g. the chancellor), decreasing the number of people in collegial bodies. Professionalisation
Social system	Integration around the university's values, missions, strategies, and goals. Relationships have an open character, are based on respect, dialogue and information sharing. Partnership cooperation relationships and full empowerment. Mutual recognition of competences and responsibilities
Ensuring the repeatability, control and continuity of the university's activities	Standardisation of activities, processes, and their parameters; continuation of the university's traditions and good practices taking into consideration the specific character of the university's processes. Precisely described standards easy to understand for the addressee, frequently prepared in a visual form. Monitoring and improving the standards in response to changes in the environment. Standards are the basis for audits of the university's functioning. Systematic approach to data collection. Strong management systems ensure sustainable development and operational continuity
Organising the service provision process	Focus on processes and provided value. Implementing a pull system, taking into consideration the specific character of processes. Flexibility. Wide range of ICT and Internet applications. Implementing the five Lean Principles

(continued)

Table 2.8 (continued)

Areas of change	The Lean University—a characterisation
Approach to costs	Identifying and categorising wastage sources. Cost reduction based on the thorough understanding of the activities creating value and the elimination of wastage sources
Internal and external communication	Domination of horizontal communication along value streams and in multi-functional teams dealing with value streams. De-formalised communication based on trust. An efficient communication network improves information flows, facilitates their accurate interpretations, and accelerates reactions. Cooperation with external partners with respect to knowledge sharing, benchmarking, a community of practitioners
Approach to the external customer	The customer is a partner, recipient of value. Quality is an autotelic goal; the university competes first of all with itself without ignoring its competitors
Leadership	Leadership oriented towards delegating tasks and powers, and obtaining employee commitment. Making decisions on the basis of facts, in a responsible manner, participation in operating activities (e.g. Kaizen, gemba), standardising managerial tasks, eliminating wastage sources, focus on problem solving. Power based on personal authority. Responsibility. A development path for leaders in the university
People	The university's most important resource and development potential. Creativity and commitment to the improvement process. Bottom-up changes—employees create changes. Continuous training. Empowerment. Appreciating and rewarding. Emphasis on preventive actions. Continuous improvement is a part of everyday work. A sense of loyalty and responsibility for work
An approach to change implementation	Change management. Following simultaneously bottom-up and top-down approaches. The characteristic features of a process of changes based on the Lean concept include certain predictability and an evolutionary character
Success metrics	Customer satisfaction, effectiveness, efficiency, quality—assessments made first of all by stakeholders, including employees. A certain degree of tolerance for inefficiency (understood in a business context)

Source The author's own work

- Greater stability and ensured operational continuity in the changing environment. Minimised risks related to the external context of the university's activities.
- A greater transparency of the university's activities for its internal and external stakeholders. Sorting out the documentation and ensuring it is managed properly.
- The increasingly effective utilisation of the university's tangible, financial, information, and human resources.
- Freeing academics and administration employees from redundant bureaucracy by "slimming processes and procedures". Recovered time and resources allow greater involvement in activities creating value (fund acquisition, projects, teaching, cooperation with the environment). The effects include greater job satisfaction, less boredom and routine, better prospects for development.
- Smaller resistance to a greater acceptance for organisational, technical and social changes. Employees' and managers' involvement in the process of changes. They are the creators of changes. The bottom-up approach.
- Low implementation costs—Lean is usually introduced based on an organisation's own resources as its major objective is to change the organisational culture.

The greatest challenges for implementing the Lean concept in higher education are connected with overcoming organisational, technical, and cultural barriers. Among the organisational and technical barriers, we can distinguish the lack of a holistic approach (only selected processes or units are improved; a local character of changes; particular individual and group interests are protected) (Balzer et al. 2016), the lack of balance between the top-down and bottom-up approaches (Hines and Lethbridge 2008), the lack of a proper understanding of the concept of a process approach, excessive radicalism and immature support (Dumas et al. 2013), adjustment to the specificity of creative, academic, and teaching processes (Balzer et al. 2016). The cultural barriers include leadership models in higher education (Lu et al. 2017), the lack of a Lean implementation maturity assessment (Antony 2014; Balzer et al. 2016; Maciąg 2018), improper adjustment to the university's specific organisational culture (Balzer et al. 2016; Maciąg 2018). Researchers indicate that there is still no conceptual framework connecting Lean Management to organisational learning, change management, project management, or organisational development of the university. There is consensus that the greatest challenge is the proper shaping of the university's organisational culture. The Lean Culture is a guarantor of the permanence and continuity of changes. There is a research gap in this respect. There is a lack of a theoretical framework comprising definitions of the Lean Culture, its dimensions, methods and tools for diagnosing its maturity and measuring its development towards continuous improvement. This was the subject of the author's further in-depth research. Its results are presented in the subsequent chapters.

2.5   Chapter Summary

For a very long time universities functioned in a stable and predictable environment. They were assigned important culture-forming and social functions of creators and carriers of intergenerational knowledge, as well as depositaries of national culture. Changes in the external management context resulted in new requirements in the areas of economisation, improved effectiveness, efficiency, and flexibility of undertaken activities, as well as the quality of achieved effects. Universities found themselves in a difficult situation, becoming institutions full of tensions, stretched between the traditional models of functioning (determined by law, culture, history, mentality) and the challenges formulated by the financing entities, i.e. the state, students, and other stakeholders. Traditional collegial and bureaucratic university management models exhausted their potential for development. Created in a different external and internal context, they became a visible barrier for development in new conditions.

On the tide of NPM, higher education institutions implement solutions already proven in the business and manufacturing sectors, as well as process-based concepts and methods. It is expected that their implementation will be as successful as it was in the case of business enterprises; it will improve universities' productivity and eliminate or reduce the tensions mentioned above. Lean Management is one of such concepts.

The objective of this chapter was to identify the internal and external contexts of the functioning of the modern university and to determine their influence on the university's ability to implement effectively process-based management concepts such as Lean Management. The conducted analysis of the literature on the subject and the results of the author's own research allowed her to conclude that Lean Management is an effective method of changing management models in higher education. Confirmations were also obtained for the formulated thesis according to which:

- Process management concepts and Lean Management allow for a holistic and systemic change in the university's management model, taking into consideration its mission, goals, and context of functioning.
- The processes carried out in higher education institutions have specific qualities and division criteria, which requires the adoption of a new approach to a model presentation of the university in the Lean Management concept.

As was shown by the analysis conducted in this chapter, more and more universities introduce organisational changes based on process-based concepts such as BPM, BPR, TQM, Lean Management, and Lean Six Sigma. However, experts are still of the opinion that universities change too slowly, long-lasting reforms of higher education fail on a regular basis, and universities tend to resort to pseudo-changes in order to become more attractive in the eyes of their stakeholders. Universities manifest resistance to changes, but the main reason for this state of affairs has not been identified yet. Is it a misunderstanding of the essence of process management? A bad selection of methods and improper implementation of changes? A misunderstanding of the essence of the processes taking place in higher education or an inadequate modification of the methods of process management in higher education? Are people the carriers of resistance or does it result more from the nature of the university determined by the autotelic character of knowledge and the combination of teaching and research? These issues certainly require in-depth research.

The university is a specific organisation. But it has many qualities such as self-government, institutional autonomy, openness and tolerance for different opinions, discussion, pursuit of consensus, focus on processes which facilitate process-based concepts such as Lean Management. It is important that organisational and technical changes be combined simultaneously with a deliberate change in the organisational culture. Only such an approach can ensure the continuity and permanence of changes. The conducted analysis shows that universities turn away from TQM, BPM, and BPR, opting for Lean Management as a concept more strongly oriented towards changes in the organisational culture. However, the issue of cultural conditions for implementing Lean Management in higher education has not been discussed sufficiently enough. There is a lack of definitions, theoretical models, concepts, methodologies of building a Lean Culture and assessing its maturity as a dimension of the university's organisational culture. It is important because despite contradictory meanings and challenges, the university itself should determine which values and principles constitute its organisational culture and consciously manage changes in this culture. Many universities face such questions as "Who are we?", "Who do we want to be?", "How do we perceive our role in the environment?", "Where do we want to shape our academic, didactic, and organisational excellence?" Universities look for their identity and organisational cultures connect and unite employees through their behavioural dimension. Therefore, organisational cultures are worth investing in. A Lean Culture, developing its definition, theoretical model, dimensions, concepts, and methods of assessing its maturity and structure as an element of an organisational culture in higher education is the goal of the following chapter.

References

Abdous, M. H. (2011). Towards a framework for business process reengineering in higher education. *Journal of Higher Education Policy and Management, 33*(4), 427–433.

Agre, P. E. (2000). Infrastructure and institutional change in the networked university. *Information, Communication & Society, 3*(4), 494–507.

Ahmad, H., Francis, A., & Zairi, M. (2007). Business process reengineering: Critical success factors in higher education. *Business Process Management Journal, 13*(3), 451–469.

Altbach, P. G., Reisberg, L., & Rumbley, L. E. (2009). *Trends in global higher education: Tracking an academic revolution.* A Report Prepared for the UNESCO 2009 World Conference on Higher Education.

Alvesson, M. (2013). *The triumph of emptiness: Consumption, higher education, and work organization.* Oxford: Oxford University Press.

Anders-Morawska, J., & Rudolf, W. (2015). *Orientacja rynkowa we współzarządzaniu miastem* [A market orientation in municipal co-management]. Łódź: Wyd. Uniwersytetu Łódzkiego.

Antonowicz, D. (2005). *Uniwersytet przyszłości. Wyzwania i modele polityki* [The university of the future. Challenges and policy models]. Warszawa: Wydawnictwo ISP.

Antonowicz, D. (2015). *Między siłą globalnych procesów a lokalną tradycją. Polskie szkolnictwo wyższe w dobie przemian* [Between the power of global processes and the local tradition. Poland's higher education in the period of changes]. Toruń: Wydawnictwo Naukowe Uniwersytetu Mikołaja Kopernika.

Antony, J. (2014). Readiness factors for the Lean Six Sigma journey in the higher education sector. *International Journal of Productivity and Performance Management, 63*(2), 257–264.

Antony, J. (2015). Challenges in the deployment of LSS in the higher education sector: Viewpoints from leading academics and practitioners. *International Journal of Productivity and Performance Management, 64*(6), 893–899.

Balzer, K. (2010). *Lean higher education.* New York: CRC Press, Taylor & Francis.

Balzer, W. K., Brodke, M. H., & Kizhakethalackal, T. E. (2015). Lean higher education: Successes, challenges, and realizing potential. *International Journal of Quality & Reliability Management, 32*(9), 924–933.

Balzer, W. K., Francis, D. E., Krehbiel, T. C., & Shea, N. (2016). A review and perspective on Lean in higher education. *Quality Assurance in Education, 24*(4), 442–462.

Bateman, N., Radnor, Z., & Glennon, R. (2018). The landscape of Lean across public services. *Public Money & Management, 38*(1), 1–4.

Bay, D., & Daniel, H. (2001). The student is not the customer—An alternative perspective. *Journal of Marketing for Higher Education, 11*(1), 1–19.

Bayraktar, E., Tatoglu, E., & Zaim, S. (2008). An instrument for measuring the critical factors of TQM in Turkish higher education. *Total Quality Management, 19*(6), 551–574.

Bednarek, M. (2007). *Doskonalenie systemów zarządzania. Nowa droga do przedsiębiorstwa Lean* [Improving management systems. A new way towards a Lean enterprise]. Warszawa: Difin.

Billings, L., Llamas, N. A., Snyder, B. E., & Sung, Y. (2017). Many languages, many workflows: Mapping and analyzing technical services processes for East Asian and international studies materials. *Cataloging & Classification Quarterly, 55*(7–8), 606–629.

Blöndal, S., Field, S., & Girouard, N. (2002). *Investment in human capital through post-compulsory education and training: Selected efficiency and equity aspects* (No. 333). Paris: OECD.

Bloom, A. (1997). *Umysł zamknięty. O tym, jak amerykańskie szkolnictwo wyższe zawiodło demokrację i zubożyło dusze dzisiejszych studentów* [The closing of the American mind: How higher education has failed democracy and impoverished the souls of today's students]. Poznań: Wydawnictwo Zysk i S-ka.

Bonstingl, J. J. (1995). *Szkoły Jakości. Wprowadzenie do TQM w edukacji* [Schools of quality. An introduction to TQM in education]. Warszawa: Wydawnictwa CODN.

Botas, P. (2011). The consumption values of and empowerment of student as customer in higher education and its implications for higher education policy. In *Positive Futures for Higher Education: Connections, Communities and Criticality Conference Papers Society for Research into Higher Education.* Newport, Great Britain.

Bowden, J. L. H. (2011). Engaging the student as a customer: A relationship marketing approach. *Marketing Education Review, 21*(3), 211–228.

Budd, R. (2017). Undergraduate orientations towards higher education in Germany and England: Problematizing the notion of 'student as customer'. *Higher Education, 73*(1), 23–37.

Bugdol, M. (2011a). *Zarzadzanie jakością w urzędach administracji publicznej* [Quality management in public administration offices]. Warszawa: Difin.

Bugdol, M. (2011b). *Zarządzanie pracownikami-klientami wewnętrznymi w organizacjach projakościowych* [Managing employees or internal customers in pro-quality organizations]. Warszawa: Difin.

Bugdol, M. (2018). *System zarządzania jakością według normy ISO 9001:2015* [Quality management systems based on the ISO 9001:2015 standard]. Gliwice: One Press.

Bugdol, M., & Jedynak, P. (2012). *Współczesne systemy zarządzania: jakość, bezpieczeństwo, ryzyko* [Contemporary management systems: Quality, security, risk]. Gliwice: Wydawnictwo Helion.

Bugdol, M., & Szczepańska, K. (2016). *Podstawy zarządzania procesami* [Rudiments of process management]. Warszawa: Difin.

By, R. T., Diefenbach, T., & Klarner, P. (2008). Getting organizational change right in public services: The case of European higher education. *Journal of Change Management, 8*(1), 21–35.

Chalaris, I., Chalaris, M., Gritzalis, S., & Belsis, P. (2015). Process' standardization and change management in higher education. The case of TEI of Athens. In *AIP Conference Proceedings* (Vol. 1644, No. 1, pp. 263–270). Shing: AIP.

Chapman R. G. (1986). Toward a theory of college selection: A model of college search and choice behaviour. In R. J. Lutz (Ed.), *Advances in consumer research* (Vol. 13). Provo, UT: Association for Consumer Research.

Charta, M. (1988). *The Magna Charta Universitatum*. Rectors of European Universities.

Ciancio, S. (2018). The prevalence of service excellence and the use of business process improvement methodologies in Australian universities. *Journal of Higher Education Policy and Management, 40*(2), 121–139.

Clark, B. R. (1986). *The higher education system: Academic organization in cross-national perspective*. Berkeley: University of California Press.

Cole, B. (2011). *Lean-Six Sigma for the public sector* (p. 496). Milwaukee: ASQ Quality.

Collis, D. (2016, March). Lean strategy. *Harvard Business Review*. Downloaded from: https://hbr.org/2016/03/lean-strategy. Accessed 15 May 2018.

Council, B. (2017). *Trends: Transformative changes in higher education*. London, UK: British Council.

Crosier, D., Dalferth, S., Kerpanova, V., & Parveva, T. (2011). *Modernisation of higher education in Europe: Funding and the social dimension*. Brussels: Education, Audiovisual and Culture Executive Agency, European Commission. Available from EU Bookshop.

Cyfert, S., & Kochalski, C. (Ed.). (2011). *Projektowanie i wdrażanie strategii rozwoju w publicznych szkołach wyższych w Polsce: aspekty teoretyczne i praktyczne* [Designing and implementing development strategies in public higher education institutions]. Poznań: Wydawnictwo Uniwersytetu Ekonomicznego w Poznaniu.

Czerska, J. (2009). *Doskonalenie strumienia wartości* [The improvement of value streams]. Warszawa: Difin.

Czubała, A., Jonas, A., Smoleń, T., & Wiktor, J. W. (2012). *Marketing usług* [The marketing of services]. Warszawa: Oficyna Wolters Kluwer Business.

Dahlgaard, J. J., & Østergaard, P. (2000). TQM and Lean thinking in higher education. *The Best on Quality: Targets, Improvements, Systems, 11,* 203–226.

Daszkowska, M. (1998). *Usługi. Produkcja, rynek, marketing* [Services. Production, market, marketing]. Warszawa: PWN.

Davenport, T. H. (2008). Foreword. In J. Jetson & J. Nelis (Ed.), *Business process management. Practical guidelines to successful implementation.* Oxford: Elsevier.

Davies, J. (2000). Cultural change in universities in the context of strategic and quality initiatives. In P. Tabatoni, J. Davies, & A. Barblan (Eds.), *Strategic management and universities' institutional development* (pp. 12–23). www.eau.

Deming, W. E. (1986). *Out of the crisis* (Vol. 510, pp. 419–425). Cambridge, MA: Center for Advanced Engineering Study, Massachusetts Institute of Technology.

Deming, W. E. (2012). *Wyjście z kryzysu: Out of the crisis.* OpExBooks.pl.

Denhardt, R. B. (2011). *Theories of public organization.* Boston: Wadsworth Cengage Learning.

Douglas, A., Douglas, J., & Antony, J. (2013, June 24–25). Gold in the mine: Recognising waste in UK HEIs using Lean thinking. In *Proceedings of First International Conference on Lean Six Sigma for Higher Education.* Glasgow, Scotland, UK (electronic material). *Enhancing Process Efficiency and Effectiveness in Higher Education Using Lean Six Sigma.*

Douglas, J., Antony, J., & Douglas, A. (2015). Waste identification and elimination in HEIs: The role of Lean thinking. *International Journal of Quality & Reliability Management, 32*(9), 970–981.

Dragomir, C., & Surugiu, F. (2013). Implementing Lean in a higher education university. *Constanta Maritime University: Constanta, Romania, XIII, 18,* 279–282.

Drotz, E. (2014). *Lean in the public sector possibilities and limitations.* Linköping, Sweden: Department of Management and Engineering, Linköping University.

Dumas, M., La Rosa, M., Mendling, J., & Reijers, H. A. (2013). Introduction to business process management. In *Fundamentals of business process management* (pp. 1–31). Berlin and Heidelberg: Springer.

Easterby-Smith, M., Thorpe, R., & Jackson, P. R. (2015). *Management and business research.* London: Sage.

Emiliani, M. L. (2000). Cracking the code of business. *Management Decision, 38*(2), 60–79.

Emiliani, M. L. (2004). Improving business school courses by applying Lean principles and practices. *Quality Assurance in Education, 12*(4), 175–187.

Emiliani, M. L. (2005). Using kaizen to improve graduate business school degree programs. *Quality Assurance in Education, 13*(1), 37–52.

Emiliani, B. (2015). *Lean university: A guide to renewal and prosperity.* Wethersfield: CLBM, LLC.

England, L., Fu, L., & Miller, S. (2012). Optimizing your ERM: The application of business process management to operations. *Technical Services Quarterly, 29*(4), 265–279.

Ernest Osseo-Asare, A. E., & Longbottom, D. (2002). The need for education and training in the use of the EFQM model for quality management in UK higher education institutions. *Quality Assurance in Education, 10*(1), 26–36.

Etzkowitz, H., Webster, A., Gebhardt, C., & Terra, B. R. C. (2000). The future of the university and the university of the future: Evolution of ivory tower to entrepreneurial paradigm. *Research Policy, 29*(2), 313–330.

Francis, D. E. (2014, April 28). Lean and the learning organization in higher education. *Canadian Journal of Educational Administration and Policy* (157), 1–23.

Francis, D. E., Krehbiel, T. C., & Balzer, W. K. (2017). *Lean applications in higher education.* Downloaded from: https://the-lmj.com/2017/03/.

Franz, P. H., Kirchmer, M., & Rosemann, M. (2012). *Value-driven business process management impact and benefits.* Accenture. Downloaded from: https://www.accenture.com/mx-es/~/media/Accenture/Conversion-Assets/DotCom/Documents/Local/es-la/PDF2/Accenture-Value-Driven-Business-Process-Management.pdf. Accessed 25 May 2018.

Geppert, M., & Hollinshead, G. (2017). Signs of dystopia and demoralization in global academia: Reflections on the precarious and destructive effects of the colonization of the Lebenswelt. *Critical Perspectives on International Business, 13*(2), 136–150.

Geryk, M. (2010). *Społeczna odpowiedzialność uczelni w percepcji jej interesariuszy* [A university's social responsibility as perceived by its stakeholders]. Warszawa: Oficyna Wydawnicza SGH.

Gibb, A., Haskins, G., & Robertson, I. (2012). Leading the entrepreneurial university: Meeting the entrepreneurial development needs of higher education institutions. In A. Altmann & B. Ebersberger (Eds.), *Universities in change* (pp. 9–45). New York, NY: Springer.

Goranczewski, B. (2011). Zarządzanie jakością w uczelni wyższej: ujęcie holistyczne [Quality management in higher education: A holistic approach]. *Prace Naukowe Wyższej Szkoły Bankowej w Gdańsku, 14,* 339–357.

Goranczewski, B. (2013). Standaryzacja jako podstawowa determinanta jakości usługi edukacyjnej [Standardization as a basic determinant of educational service quality]. In J. Dworak (Ed.), *Zarządzanie szkołą wyższą* (pp. 161–178). Gdańsk: Prace Naukowe Wyższej Szkoły Bankowej w Gdańsku no. 24.

Graczyk, P. (2015). *Embedding a living lab approach at the University of Edinburgh*. Edinburgh: University of Edinburgh.

Grajewski, P. (2007). *Organizacja procesowa. Projektowanie i konfiguracja* [A process organization. Designing and configuration]. Warszawa: PWE.

Grajewski, P. (2012). *Procesowe zarządzanie organizacją* [Process management in organizations]. Warszawa: PWE.

Grudzewski, W. M., Hejduk, I. K., Sankowska, A., & Wańtuchowicz, M. (2010). *Sustainability w biznesie czyli przedsiębiorstwo przyszłości. Zmiany paradygmatów i koncepcji zarządzania* [Sustainability in business or the enterprise of the future. Changes in management concepts and paradigms]. Warszawa: Wyd. POLTEX.

Hammer, M., & Champy, J. (1997). *Reengineering the corporation: A manifesto for business revolution*. London: Nicholas Brealey Publishing.

Hamrol, A. (2007). *Zarządzanie jakością z przykładami* [Quality Management on Examples]. Warsaw: WN PWN.

Hamrol, A., & Mantura, W. (2002). *Zarządzanie jakością. Teoria i praktyka* [Quality management. Theory and practice]. Warszawa-Poznań: WP PWN.

Hamrol, A., Gawlik, J., & Skołud, B. (2015). *Strategie i praktyki sprawnego działania: Lean, Six Sigma i inne* [Strategies and practices of efficient operation: Lean, Six Sigma, and others]. Warszawa: Wydawnictwo Naukowe PWN.

Hansson, F., & Mønsted, M. (2008). Research leadership as entrepreneurial organizing for research. *Higher Education, 55*(6), 651–670.

Harmon, P. (2010). *Business process change: A guide for business managers and BPM and Six Sigma professionals*. Amsterdam: Elsevier.

Harvey, L., & Knight, P. T. (1996). *Transforming higher education*. Bristol: Open University Press and Taylor & Francis.

Helbing, D. (2016). *Innovation accelerator: Why our innovation system is failing—And how to change this working paper*. Downloaded from: https://www.researchgate.net/publication/305969593.

Hines, P., & Lethbridge, S. (2008). New development: Creating a Lean University. *Public Money and Management, 28*(1), 53–56.

Inês Dallavalle de Pádua, S., Mascarenhas Hornos da Costa, J., Segatto, M., Aparecido de Souza Júnior, M., & José Chiappetta Jabbour, C. (2014). BPM for change management: Two process diagnosis techniques. *Business Process Management Journal, 20*(2), 247–271.

Iqbal, S., & Bhatti, Z. A. (2015). An investigation of university student readiness towards m-learning using technology acceptance model. *The*

International Review of Research in Open and Distributed Learning, 16(4), 83–103.

Ismail, R. F., & Abd El Aziz, R. (2015). Using ICT to improve the Egyptian higher education business processes: A case study. *Journal of Organisational Studies and Innovation, 2*(3), 25–38.

Jeal, Y. (2005). Re-engineering customer services: University of Salford information services division. *New Library World, 106*(7/8), 352–362.

Jeston, J., Nelis, J., & Davenport, T. (2008). *Business process management: Practical guidelines to successful implementations.* Las Vegas, NV: Elsevier.

Kasperavičiūtė-Černiauskienė, R., & Serafinas, D. (2018). The adoption of ISO 9001 standard within higher education institutions in Lithuania: Innovation diffusion approach. *Total Quality Management & Business Excellence, 29*(1–2), 74–93.

Kennedy, M., & Dunn, T. J. (2018). Improving the use of technology enhanced learning environments in higher education in the UK: A qualitative visualization of students' views. *Contemporary Educational Technology, 9*(1), 76–89.

Kłosowski, A. (2012). Produktywność i jakość usług a produktywność firmy [Service productivity and quality versus business productivity]. *Problemy Jakości, 44*(2), 32–34.

Kotarbiński, T. (1975). *Traktat o dobrej robocie* [Praxiology. An introduction to the science of efficient action]. Wrocław: Wydawnictwo Zakład Narodowy im. Ossolińskich.

Koźmiński, A. K. (1999). Misje i strategie szkół wyższych [Missions and strategies of higher education institutions]. In J. Woźnicki (Ed.), *Model zarządzania publiczną instytucją akademicką.* Warszawa: JSP.

Kress, N. J. (2008). Lean thinking in libraries: A case study on improving shelving turnaround. *Journal of Access Services, 5*(1–2), 159–172.

Krzyżanowski, L. (1985). *Podstawy nauki zarządzania* [Rudiments of management science]. Warszawa: PWN.

Kwiek, M. (2010). *Transformacje uniwersytetu. Zmiany instytucjonalne i ewolucje polityki edukacyjnej w Europie* [Transformations in universities. Institutional changes and evolutions of educational policies in Europe]. Poznań: Wydawnictwo Naukowe UAM.

Kwiek, M. (2015). *Uniwersytet w dobie przemian* [The university in the period of changes]. Warszawa: PWN.

Lacatus, M. L. (2013). Organizational culture in contemporary university. *Procedia-Social and Behavioral Sciences, 76,* 421–425.

Lambert, R., & Butler, N. (2006, June 1). *The future of European universities. Renaissance or decay?* Report Published by the Centre for European Reform (CER), London.

Lean Lexicon (2010). Wrocław: Wydawnictwo Lean Enterprise Institute Polska.

Leja, K. (2013). *Zarządzanie uczelnią. Koncepcje i współczesne wyzwania* [University management. Concepts and contemporary challenges]. Warszawa: Oficyna a Wolters Kluwer Business.

Lenartowicz, M. (2016). *Natura oporu Uniwersytet jako samowytwarzający się system społeczny* [The nature of resistance. The university as a self-creating social system]. Poznań: CSPP UAM.

Liker, J. K. (2005). *The Toyota Way.* Warsaw: Esensi.

Lisiecka, K. (2002). *Kreowanie jakości* [Creation of quality]. Katowice: Wydawnictwo Akademii Ekonomicznej w Katowicach.

Lisiecka, K., & Maciąg, J. (2007). Karol Adamiecki współtwórcą podstaw nauki organizacji i zarządzania procesem kształtowania jakości produktów [Karol Adamiecki as a co-creator of the rudiments of the science of organizing and managing the product quality shaping process]. In E. Skrzypek (Ed.), *Wielcy twórcy jakości w Polsce i na świecie.* Lublin: Wyd. Uniwersytet M. Curie-Skłodowskiej w Lublinie.

Locher, D. A. (2016). *Lean office and service simplified: The definitive how-to guide.* New York: Productivity Press.

Lovelock, C., & Patterson, P. (2015). *Services marketing.* Frenchs Forest: Pearson Australia.

Lu, J., Laux, C., & Antony, J. (2017). Lean Six Sigma leadership in higher education institutions. *International Journal of Productivity and Performance Management, 66*(5), 638–650.

Lucio-Villegas, E. (2016). Building knowledge democracy from the university: A case study in Spain. *Action Research, 14*(1), 3–18.

Ludwiczak, A. (2018). *Zarządzanie procesami w administracji samorządowej. Doskonalenie z wykorzystaniem lean government* [Process management in local government administration. Improvement based on Lean government]. Warszawa: Difin.

Lusk, S., Paley, S., & Spanyi, A. (2005). The evolution of business process management as a professional discipline. *BP Trends, 20,* 1–9.

Maciąg, J. (2011a). Wieloaspektowa ocena jakości usług edukacyjnych (na przykładzie AWF im. Jerzego Kukuczki w Katowicach) [A multi-aspect evaluation of the quality of educational services (as exemplified by the Jerzy Kukuczka Academy of Physical Education in Katowice)]. *Nauka i Szkolnictwo Wyższe, 2*(38), 123–138.

Maciąg, J. (2011b). *Ocena systemu zapewnienia jakości kształcenia w szkole wyższej* [An evaluation of a quality assurance system in a university]. Katowice: Wyd. AWF w Katowicach.

Maciąg, J. (2013, June 24–25). Methods of quality management system efficiency measurement in HEIs. FICL6σ. In *Proceedings of First International Conference on Lean Six Sigma for Higher Education*. Glasgow, Scotland, UK (electronic material). Enhancing Process Efficiency and Effectiveness in Higher Education Using Lean Six Sigma.

Maciąg, J. (2016). Uwarunkowania wdrożenia koncepcji Lean Service w polskich szkołach wyższych [The conditions of implementing the Lean service concept in Polish higher education institutions]. *Zarządzanie Publiczne, 1*(33), 51–64.

Maciąg, J. (2018). Kultura Lean Management w polskich szkołach wyższych (wyniki badań pilotażowych) [The Lean management culture in Polish higher education institutions (pilot studies results)]. *Nauka i Szkolnictwo Wyższe, 1*(51), 69–95.

Maciąg, J., & Prawelska-Skrzypek, G. (2017). Główne nurty krytyki ewaluacji polityki naukowej i innowacyjnej oraz sposoby jej doskonalenia na przykładzie wybranych krajów [The main trends in the critique of evaluating academic and innovation policies as well as the methods of their improvement as exemplified by selected countries]. In G. Prawelska-Skrzypek (Ed.), *Ewaluacja w procesie tworzenia polityki naukowej i innowacyjnej*. Warszawa: Wyd. PAN.

Makkar, U., Gabriel, E., & Tripathi, S. K. (2008, February). Value chain for higher education sector-case studies of India and Tanzania. *Journal of Services Research, 8*(Special Issue), 183–200.

Manatos, M. J., Sarrico, C. S., & Rosa, M. J. (2017). The integration of quality management in higher education institutions: A systematic literature review. *Total Quality Management & Business Excellence, 28*(1–2), 159–175.

Marginson, S. (2015). O niemożliwości zaistnienia kapitalistycznych rynków w szkolnictwie wyższym [On the impossibility of the occurrence of capitalist markets in higher education]. *Nauka i Szkolnictwo Wyższe, 1*(45), 11–37.

Mause, K. (2009). Too much competition in higher education? Some conceptual remarks on the excessive-signaling hypothesis. *American Journal of Economics and Sociology, 68*(5), 1107–1133.

Miller, J. A., Pniewski, K., & Polakowski, M. (2000). *Zarządzanie kosztami działań* [Operating cost management]. Warszawa: WIG Press.

Mircea, M. (2010). Adapt business processes to service oriented environment to achieve business agility. *Journal of Applied Quantitative Methods, 5*(4), 679–691.

Moore, M., Nash, M., & Henderson, K. (2007). *Becoming a Lean University. Best Practices of Southern Association of College and University Business Officers (SACUBO).*

Neave, G., & Van Vught, F. A. (1991). *Prometheus bound: The changing relationship between government and higher education in Western Europe.* Oxford: Pergamon Press.

Norma PN-EN ISO 9000:2015. (2015). PKN Warszawa 2015.

Nowaczyk, G., & Kolasiński, M. (2004). *Marketing szkół wyższych* [The marketing of higher education institutions]. Poznań: Wydawnictwo Wyższej Szkoły Bankowej.

Nowaczyk, G., & Lisiecki, P. (2006). *Marketingowe zarządzanie szkołą wyższą* [Marketing management in higher education institutions]. Poznań: Wydawnictwo Wyższej Szkoły Bankowej.

OECD Science. (2016). *OECD Science, Technology and Innovation Outlook.* Paris: OECD. Downloaded from: http://www.keepeek.com/Digital-Asset-Management/oecd/science-and-technology/oecd-science-technology-and-innovation-outlook-2016_sti_in_outlook-2016-en#.

Ohno, T. (1988). *Toyota production system: Beyond large-scale production.* New York: CRC Press.

Orzen, M. (2014). Connecting with the customer to create greater value. In T. Koch (Ed.), *XV Międzynarodowa Konferencja Lean Management, Materiały konferencyjne.* Wrocław: Polska.

Papanthymou, A., & Darra, M. (2017). Quality management in higher education: Review and perspectives. *Higher Education Studies, 7*(3), 132–147.

Parkes, A. (2017). *Kulturowe uwarunkowania Lean Management* [The cultural conditions of Lean management]. Warszawa: Difin.

Pawlak, M. (2013). *Organizacyjna reakcja na nowe zjawisko: Szkoły i instytucje pomocowe wobec uchodźców w Polsce po 2004 r* [Organizational reactions to a new phenomenon: Schools and support institutions in the face of refugees in Poland after 2004]. Warszawa: IPSiR UW.

Peter, H. F., Kirchmer, M., & Rosemann, M. (2012). *Value-driven business process management impact and benefits.* Downloaded from: https://www.accenture.com/mx-es/~/media/Accenture/Conversion-Assets/DotCom/Documents/Local/es-la/PDF2/Accenture-Value-Driven-Business-Process-Management.pdf.

Piasecka, A. (2011). *Wybrane aspekty zarządzania jakością w szkole wyższej* [The selected aspects of quality management in higher education institutions]. Lublin: Wydawnictwo Uniwersytetu Marii Curie-Skłodowskiej.

Pluta-Olearnik, M. (2009). *Przedsiębiorcza uczelnia i jej relacje z otoczeniem* [The enterprising university and its relations with the environment]. Warszawa: Difin.

PN-EN ISO 19011:2003. (2003). *Wytyczne dotyczące auditowania systemów zarządzania jakością i/lub zarządzania środowiskowego* [PN-EN ISO 19011:2003 guidelines for auditing quality management and/or environment management systems]. PKN Warszawa 2003.

PN-EN ISO 9001:2015. (2016a). *Systemy zarządzania jakością—Wymagania* [PN-EN ISO 9001:2015 Quality management systems—Requirements]. Warszawa: PKN.

PN-EN ISO 9001:2015. (2016b). *Systemy zarządzania jakością—Wymagania, Załącznik A.2 Wyroby i usługi* [PN-EN ISO 9001:2015 Quality management systems—Requirements, Annex A.2 products and services]. Warszawa: PKN.

Prasad, U. C., & Suri, R. K. (2011). Modeling of continuity and change forces in private higher technical education using total interpretive structural modeling (TISM). *Global Journal of Flexible Systems Management, 12*(3–4), 31–39.

Process Classification Framework Version 6.1.1. American Quality Productivity Center. Downloaded from: http://www.apqc.org/knowledgebase/download/313690/K05162_PCF_Ver_6%201_1.pdf. Accessed 7 February 2015.

Psomas, E., & Antony, J. (2017). Total quality management elements and results in higher education institutions: The Greek case. *Quality Assurance in Education, 25*(2), 206–223.

Radnor, Z., & Bucci, G. (2011). *Analysis of Lean implementation in UK business schools and universities.* London: Association of Business Schools.

Radnor, Z., Walley, P., Stephens, A., & Bucci, G. (2006). Evaluation of the Lean approach to business management and its use in the public sector. *Scottish Executive Social Research, 20.*

Reavill, L. R. (1998). Quality assessment, total quality management and the stakeholders in the UK higher education system. *Managing Service Quality: An International Journal, 8*(1), 55–63.

Rich, N., Bateman, N., Esain, A., Massey, L., & Samuel, D. (2006). *Lean evolution: Lessons from the workplace.* Cambridge: Cambridge University Press.

Robins, K., & Webster, F. (Eds.). (2002). *The virtual university? Knowledge, markets, and management.* Oxford: University Press.

Robinson, M., & Yorkstone, S. (2014). Becoming a Lean University: The case of the University of St Andrews. *Leadership and Governance in Higher Education, 1,* 42–72.

Rother, M. (2009). *Toyota kata.* New York: McGraw-Hill.

Rother M., & Shooka J. (1999). Learning to see. Lean Enterprise Institute [after:]. Mapowanie strumienia wartości—narzędzie analizy i projektowania szczupłych systemów produkcyjnych [The mapping of a value stream—A tool to analyse and design Lean production systems]. In L. Kornicki (Ed.), *Praktyczne aspekty jakości i produktywności*. TQM-SOFT.cs.

Rudolph, D. W., & Steffens, U. (2012). Strategic management for growing business schools. In *Universities in change* (pp. 171–199). New York, NY: Springer.

Rummler, G. A., & Brache, A. P. (2000). *Podnoszenie efektywności organizacji* [Improving performance]. Warszawa: PWE.

Rybkowski, R. (2015). Autonomia a rozliczalność–polskie wyzwania [Autonomy versus accountability—Polish challenges]. *Nauka i Szkolnictwo Wyższe, 1*(45), 95–115.

Santana, S., Moreira, C., Roberto, T., & Azambuja, F. (2010). Fighting for excellence: The case of the Federal University of Pelotas. *Higher Education, 60*(3), 321–341.

Santiago, P., Tremblay, K., Basri, E., & Arnal, E. (2008). *Tertiary education for the knowledge society* (Vol. 1). Paris: OECD.

Scrabec, Q., Jr. (2000). A quality education is not customer driven. *Journal of Education for Business, 75*(5), 298–300.

Shaw, M. A., & Lenartowicz, M. (2016). Humboldt is (not) dead: A social systems perspective on reforming European universities. In J. Leemann Regula, Ch. Imdorf, J. W. Powell, & M. Sertl (Eds.), *Die Organisation von Bildung: Soziologische Analysen zu Schule, Berufsbildung, Hochschule und Weiterbildung*. Weinheim and Basel: Beltz Verlag.

Shek, D. T., & Hollister, R. M. (2017). *University social responsibility and quality of life*. Singapore: Springer.

Sherr, L. A., & Gregory Lozier, G. (1991). Total quality management in higher education. *New Directions for Institutional Research, 1991*(71), 3–11.

Shostack, G. L. (1984). Designing services that delivered. *Harvard Business Review, 62*(1), 133–139.

Skrzypek, E., & Hofman, M. (2010). *Zarządzanie procesami w przedsiębiorstwie: identyfikowanie, pomiar, usprawnianie* [Process management in a business enterprise: Identification, measurement, improvement]. Warszawa: Oficyna a Wolters Kluwer Business.

Slaughter, S. (2001). *Reflections on students as consumers and students as captive markets: Complexities and contradictions in academic capitalism*. Tucson: The Center for the Study of Higher Education, University of Arizona.

Slaughter, S., & Rhoades, G. (2004). *Academic capitalism and the new economy: Markets, state, and higher education*. Baltimore: JHU Press.
Smith, H., & Fingar, P. (2007). *Business process management: The third wave* (Vol. 1). Tampa: Meghan-Kiffer Press.
Sokołowicz, W., & Srzednicki, A. (2006). *ISO System zarządzania jakością oraz inne systemy oparte na normach* [The ISO quality management system and other systems based on standards]. Warszawa: CH Beck Warszawa.
Sowa, K. Z. (2009). *Gdy myślę uniwersytet…* [When I think of a university…]. Kraków: Wydawnictwo Uniwersytetu Jagiellońskiego.
Stoller, J. (2015). *Lean CEO: w drodze do doskonałości* [The Lean CEO: Leading the way to world-class excellence]. Warszawa: MT Biznes.
Suárez-Barraza, M. F., Smith, T., & Dahlgaard-Park, S. M. (2012). Lean service: A literature analysis and classification. *Total Quality Management & Business Excellence, 23*(3–4), 359–380.
Sulaiman, N. F., Manochehri, N. N., & Al-Esmail, R. A. (2013). Level of total quality management adoption in Qatari educational institutions: Private and semi-government sector. *Journal of Education for Business, 88*(2), 76–87.
Sułkowski, Ł. (2016). *Kultura akademicka. Koniec utopii?* [The academic culture. The end of a utopia?] Warszawa: Wydawnictwo Naukowe PWN.
Svensson, C., Antony, J., Ba-Essa, M., Bakhsh, M., & Albliwi, S. (2015). A Lean Six Sigma program in higher education. *International Journal of Quality & Reliability Management, 32*(9), 951–969.
Szadkowski, K. (2015). *Poza uniwersytet-fabrykę. Warunki funkcjonowania „transnarodowego stowarzyszenia kapitałów" w szkolnictwie wyższym* [Beyond a university-factory. The conditions of the functioning of a "transnational association of capital" in higher education]. *Nauka i Szkolnictwo Wyższe, 1*(45), 235–267.
Szafrański, A. (2003). Skuteczność działania [Operational effectiveness]. *Problemy Jakości*, nr 3.
Szczepański, M., & Śliz, A. (2015). Idea i powinności uniwersytetu: próba uogólnionej refleksji historyczno-socjologicznej [The idea and obligations of the university: An attempt to present a generalized historical-sociological reflection]. In M. Szczepański, K. Szafraniec, & A. Śliz (Eds.), *Szkolnictwo wyższe, uniwersytet, kształcenie akademickie w obliczu koniecznej zmiany* (pp. 19–39). Warszawa: KS PAN.
Sześciło, D. (2015). *Samoobsługowe państwo dobrobytu* [A self-service welfare state]. Warszawa: Wyd. nauk. Scholar.

Szymura-Tyc, M. (2012). Współczesne procesy innowacyjne w kształtowaniu produktów systemowych [Contemporary innovative processes in the shaping of systemic products]. In L. Żabiński (Ed.), *Marketing produktów systemowych*. Warsaw: PWE.

Tarí, J. J., & Dick, G. P. M. (2012). A review of quality management research in higher education institutions. In *BAM 2012 Cardiff Conference Proceedings*.

Tarí, J. J., & Madeleine, C. (2012). Introducing management models in service organisations in developed and developing countries. *The Service Industries Journal, 32*(5), 789–806.

Temple, P. (2012). Effective universities: Some considerations of funding, governance and management. In M. Kwiek & A. Kurkiewicz (Eds.), *The modernisation of European universities: Cross-national academic perspectives* (Vol. 1, p. 199). New York: Peter Lang.

Thieme, J. K. (2009). *Szkolnictwo wyższe. Wyzwania XXI wieku. Polska. Europa. USA* [Higher education. The challenges of the 21st century. Poland. Europe. The USA]. Warszawa: Difin.

Thomas, A., Antony, J., Francis, M., & Fisher, R. (2015). A comparative study of Lean implementation in higher and further education institutions in the UK. *International Journal of Quality & Reliability Management, 32*(9), 982–996.

Tsichritzis, D. (1999). Reengineering the university. *Communications of the ACM, 42*(6), 93–100.

Vaira, M. (2004). Globalization and higher education organizational change: A framework for analysis. *Higher Education, 48*(4), 483–510.

Vyas, N., & Campbell, M. (2015). Industry in crisis. *Six Sigma Forum Magazine, 15*(1), 18–22.

Walentynowicz, P. (2013). *Uwarunkowania skuteczności wdrażania Lean management w przedsiębiorstwach produkcyjnych w Polsce* [The conditions for the effective implementation of Lean management in production enterprises in Poland]. Gdańsk: Wydawnictwo Uniwersytetu Gdańskiego.

Waterbury, T. (2011). *Educational Lean for higher education: Theory and practice*. Lulu.com.

Waterbury, T. (2015). Learning from the pioneers: A multiple-case analysis of implementing Lean in higher education. *International Journal of Quality & Reliability Management, 32*(9), 934–950.

Wawak, T. (2011). *Wyzwania zarządzania jakością w szkołach wyższych* [The challenges of quality management in higher education institutions]. Kraków: Wyd. UJ w Krakowie.

Wawak, T. (2012). *Jakość zarządzania w szkołach wyższych* [The quality of management in higher education institutions]. Kraków: Wyd. UJ w Krakowie.

Webber, K. L., & Calderon, A. J. (2015). Institutional research and planning: Its role in higher education decision support and policy development. In *The Palgrave international handbook of higher education policy and governance* (pp. 192–208). London: Palgrave Macmillan.

West, A. (1999). 'Re-engineering' student administration—A practical case-study. *Perspectives: Policy & Practice in Higher Education, 3*(4), 114–117.

Womack, J. P., & Jones, D. T. (2001). *Odchudzanie firm: eliminacja marnotrawstwa-kluczem do sukcesu* [Towards Lean businesses: The elimination of wastage as a key to success]. Warsaw: Centrum Informacji Menedżera.

Womack, J. P., & Jones, D. T. (2010). *Szczupłe rozwiązania czyli Jak przedsiębiorstwa i ich klienci mogą pomnażać korzyści ze wzajemnej współpracy stosując zasady Lean Mangement* [Lean solutions or how enterprises and their customers can multiply benefits resulting from mutual cooperation using the Lean management principles]. Wrocław: Wydawnictwo Lean Enterprise Institute Polska.

Womack, J. P., Jones, D. T., & Roos, D. (1990). *The machine that changed the world: The story of Lean production* (p. 85). New York: Rawson Associates.

Woźnicki, J. (2000). Dylematy modelowe w kształtowaniu systemu szkolnictwa wyższego u progu XXI wieku [Model dilemmas in the shaping of a higher education system on the eve of the 21st century]. *Nauka, 4,* 55–56.

Yokoyama, K. (2006). Entrepreneurialism in Japanese and UK universities: Governance, management, leadership, and funding. *Higher Education, 52*(3), 523–555.

Yorkstone, S. (2016). Lean Universities. In T. Netland & D. J. Powell (Eds.), *The Routledge companion to Lean management.* Abingdon: Taylor & Francis (Routledge).

Zeller, P. (2011). Specyfika zarządzania szkołami wyższymi w świetle literatury [The specific character of managing higher education institutions in the light of the literature on the subject]. In C. Kochalski (Ed.), *Model projektowania i wdrażania strategii rozwoju w publicznych szkołach wyższych w Polsce.* Poznań: Wyd. UE w Poznaniu.

(www1) http://www.leanhehub.ac.uk.

(www2) https://en.oxforddictionaries.com/definition/university.

(www3) https://www.oecd.org/innovation/policyplatform/48373782.pdf.

3

Lean Culture in Higher Education—A Model Approach

3.1 Introduction

The use of the Lean Management concept in higher education is an increasingly popular subject of research studies. Their results indicate that the Lean concept generates positive effects in the organisational and technical system, but there are doubts about the permanence of such results (Radnor and Bucci 2011). Little emphasis is put on the development of Lean Culture (Francis et al. 2017). A preliminary review of the literature on the subject proves that the traditional constitutive academic values do not stand in opposition to the Lean Values (Maciąg 2016b; Emiliani 2005). However, in the functionalist paradigm used to assess the effects of changes, which is based on superficial "production-oriented" measures, it is impossible to understand fully the essence and maturity of the university for the implementation of Lean. Such an ontological and epistemological attitude hampers a complete and deep cognition and understanding of changes as well as providing them with meaning (Kostera 2005; Hatch 2002; Weick 2016). Therefore many authors propose supplementing the research perspective with a humanistic approach based on the interpretative-symbolic

© The Author(s) 2019
J. Maciąg, *Lean Culture in Higher Education*,
https://doi.org/10.1007/978-3-030-05686-5_3

paradigm (Hatch 2002; Kostera 2005; Alvesson 2009; Czarniawska 2010; Sułkowski 2012; Zawadzki 2014; Weick 2016). In this approach, Lean Culture is defined as an epistemological metaphor of an organisation (Kostera 2005). It is considered at the level of people's relationships and personal experiences (Sikorski 2009, p. 13). Researchers have dealt with the particular dimensions of Lean Culture such as leadership, employees and team work, methods and tools of change, organisational climate, internal conditions for the implementation of the Lean Management concept, readiness for the implementation of Lean Six Sigma (Balzer 2010; Emiliani 2015; Waterbury 2011; Antony 2014, 2017; Hines and Lethbridge 2008; Balzer et al. 2016; Radnor and Bucci 2011; Yorkstone 2016; Allan and Sinha 2013). They have emphasised its importance as a condition for the effective implementation of the concept of Lean Management in higher education, but have not studied it comprehensively as an organisational culture of the university. The applied research methodology makes it possible to classify the aforementioned research studies as representing the research perspective typical of the functionalist paradigm.

The conducted analysis of the literature on the subject allowed the author to indicate the following research gaps:

• There is a lack of research on the external and internal context for the building of the maturity of Lean Culture in higher education institutions.
• There is a lack of research and studies proposing a comprehensive and holistic approach to Lean Culture in universities as their organisational culture (there is a lack of definitions, research approaches, and systematics of elements). There is no model presentation of Lean Culture in higher education which would identify its dimensions and the most important descriptors constructing such dimensions.
• There is a lack of research on organisational culture with respect to Lean Management implementation conducted from research perspectives extended beyond the functionalist paradigm to include the interpretative-symbolic paradigm.
• So far there has been no comprehensive research aimed at showing how manufacturing concepts such as Lean Management introduced

in educational or public organisations change their definitions, meanings, ways of understanding and implementing.

The objective of this chapter is to present the author's proposal of a model of Lean Culture maturity in higher education as well as conditions necessary for the building of such maturity. The specific goals of this chapter are the following:

- To identify the external and internal contexts for the building of a Lean Culture in higher education institutions.
- To define the notion of Lean Culture and to create a model of the maturity of a Lean Culture in higher education (Lean Culture Maturity Model in HE) as well as to determine its dimensions and descriptors.
- To identify interdependences, contradictions, and gaps in higher education organisational culture and Lean Culture.
- To determine the extent to which the Lean Management concept changes during the course of its implementation in higher education.

For this purpose, the chapter includes the following specific research questions:

- What factors condition the effective building of a mature Lean Culture in higher education?
- Will the application of the point of view of the relations definition of organisational culture based on the interpretative-symbolic paradigm in research on organisational culture in higher education institutions reveal anything new that could not be seen in the functionalist approaches to the definition and modelling of Lean Culture?
- Will the broadening of the research perspective with the interpretative-symbolic paradigm make it possible to identify interdependences, contradictions, and gaps in higher education organisational culture and Lean Culture.
- Does the Lean Management concept change its definitions, meanings, ways of understanding and implementing in higher education institutions?

In order to answer the question, the following theses were advanced:

- Lean Culture is strongly influenced by factors resulting from traditions, the models of organisational culture in higher education, and the national culture of a particular country.
- The application of the relational definition of organisational culture based on the interpretative-symbolic paradigm in research on Lean Culture allows the identification of new, previously undefined dimensions and descriptors of organisational culture as well as their prioritisation with respect to importance.
- The interpretative-symbolic perspective makes it possible to capture the fundamental premises of organisational culture in higher education and to identify interdependences, contradictions, and gaps in Lean Culture.
- The external and internal contexts of higher education institutions, including their organisational culture, cause changes in the understanding of the essence of Lean Management as compared to business organisations.

In order to find arguments supporting the correctness of the premises, the following research methods were used: analysing the literature on the subject, analysing internal documents of the surveyed universities, conducting interviews in higher education institutions in Poland and abroad, carrying out observations, analysing the results of the qualitative research (the open coding method), applying the method of incomplete enumerative induction at the stage of generalising the results of the interviews and observations and creating a model (a detailed description of the research methodology is included in Chapter 1 and Section 3.3.4 of this chapter).

This chapter discusses issues related to organisational culture in higher education, defines the notion of Lean Culture and approaches to research on Lean Culture, and describes the external context for the shaping of the maturity of Lean Culture, as well as the dimensions and descriptors of Lean Culture in higher education. The deliberations presented in this chapter are summarised in the author's proposal for a Lean Culture model in higher education. The model is based on the following three pillars: theoretical research (analysis of literature), practical research (conducted in higher education institutions), and the author's experience gained during the execution of various Lean projects. The model has become a basis for building a research tool to diagnose Lean Culture maturity in higher education (it is presented in Chapter 4).

3.2 Organisational Culture in Higher Education

3.2.1 Organisational Culture—Research Approaches, Definitions, and Typologies

As an introduction into issues related to research on organisational culture in higher education, the author conducted a review of basic notions, research approaches, typologies, and functions of organisational culture. Important works on this subject include (Schein 2004; Ott 1989; Kotter and Haskett 1992; Hofstede et al. 2011; Cameron and Quinn 2015; Hatch 2002; Sułkowski 2012; Sikorski 2009; Czerska 2003; Smircich 1983).

At the beginning, research on organisational culture was connected first of all with anthropological studies on national culture (Hofstede et al. 2011, p. 31). It was only in the twentieth century that it became a subject matter of sociological, psychological, and management research. It appeared initially as an element of human relations concerning mainly organisational climate (Sułkowski 2012, p. 56; Ott 1989, p. 145). In the 1980s organisational culture became a separate trend within management science (Smircich 1983). Issues related to culture were also addressed in research on Total Quality Management (TQM), Business Process Reengineering (BRR), and Human Resources Management (HRM) (Willmott 2003). According to researchers, the main reason for the growing interest in organisational culture is the fact that the methods used previously turned out to be insufficient for explaining the complexity of organisations and changes taking place in them (Ott 1989, p. 8; Cardona and Rey 2009, p. 33). Organisations were treated rationally and mechanically; the understanding of their behaviour was based on a structural and systemic approach as well as research on their goals, structures, and decision making processes. Therefore, descriptions of organisations started to include a number of categories connected with the intangible and imperceptible aspects of their functioning (Cameron and Quinn 2015, p. 28). As Schein emphasises, it is these invisible elements, lying, as it were, under the surface of an organisation, that play the essential role in the shaping of attitudes, relations, and functioning of a whole organisation (Schein 2004, p. 8). Kotter and Heskett indicated that in the future organisational culture can become the most important factor determining the success of organisations (Kotter and Haskett 1992, p. 11).

The literature on the subject presents many approaches to how organisational culture should be defined. This results from a large number of ontological premises and epistemological attitudes. The consequence is the lack of univocal definitions, models, and research methods applicable to organisational culture. In developing a scientific theory of research on organisational culture, researchers indicate the possibility of using the four basic paradigms of social sciences proposed by Burell and Morgan (2005). They are based on ontological premises (concerning the very existence of organisational culture) and epistemological premises (concerning the methods of obtaining knowledge of organisational culture) (Hatch 2002, p. 204; Kostera 2005, pp. 15, 31; Sułkowski 2012, p. 38; Sułkowski 2016, p. 181). These paradigms are as follows:

- The functionalist paradigm. It dominates in research on organisational culture. Culture is a sub-system of the organisational systems; an external (connected with national culture) or internal variable which can be managed and controlled, which influences the organisation's efficiency—organisational culture is an instrument of management, a tool for achieving values determined by its leaders. Organisational culture is a model of conducting activities developed by the organisation, based on common and accepted premises. Schein emphasises that such an approach can be dangerous because it implies the existence of one correct organisational culture (culture can be assessed as being good or bad) (Schein 2004, p. 8).

The research methods are of an objectivising and quantitative character; survey research dominates (Sułkowski 2014, p. 13). Organisational culture changes through designing and implementing development and optimisation changes. The most important representatives are Schein (2004), Hofstede et al. (2011), and Cameron and Quinn (2015).

• The interpretative-symbolic paradigm. Organisational culture constitutes a community of meanings characteristic of members of a given organisation; its components are subcultures and organisational identity. It is an amorphous being which is difficult to control. Culture is defined as a root metaphor and studied as a form of human expression in an organisation (Smircich 1983). Culture is an epistemological metaphor of an organisation; an organisation is culture (Kostera 2005). Research on organisational culture is based on qualitative methods, with the dominant role played by organisational anthropology and ethnography. Changes in organisational culture are based on creating and developing new meanings (Sułkowski 2014, p. 13). The most important representatives are Morgan and Wiankowska-Ładyka (2013), Smircich (1983), Van Maanen (2011), Hatch (2002), Kostera (2005, p. 10), and Czarniawska (2010).

• The (critical) paradigm of radical structuralism. Organisational culture is a tool for exercising organisational power; it is based on symbolic violence and indoctrination. Culture is studied by revealing instrumental and manipulative organisational practices. Organisational culture is a tool for translating organisational values such as quality, efficiency, value into individual values of the employee (Willmott 2003) Culture changes in consequence of the criticism of its oppressiveness and the implementation of emancipatory changes such as empowerment, the actions of change leaders and agents (Sułkowski 2014, p. 16). The most important representatives are Willmott (2003), Alvesson and Willmott (1992).

• The post-modernist paradigm focuses on identifying the continuous changeability of organisational cultures, their inconsistency and ambiguity, as well as a large number of subcultures. Value judgements are avoided. In this paradigm, an anti-methodological approach is adopted and there are no research methods. Metaphors are used, for example, ones referring to rhizomes or happenings (Sułkowski 2014). The most important representative is Joanne Martin (2001).

Adopting a particular research paradigm translates consistently into defining organisational culture, methods used in its examination, and a change implementation methodology.

Organisational culture is also defined from the dynamic and static points of view. From the dynamic point of view, organisational culture is defined as a social process, social structure, and continuous restructuring (Ott 1989, p. 51). Such an approach is close to social constructivism (Czarniawska 2010). From the static point of view, what dominates is enumerative definitions which indicate a set of elements creating an organisational culture. Such elements can include language, customs, traditions, rituals, standards, held values, philosophy, game rules, climate, metaphors, means of communication, stories, narratives, myths, symbols, routines, subcultures, stereotypes, heroes, taboo, and artefacts (e.g. Ott distinguished 73 individual terms and phrases describing organisational culture; Schein proposed 11 complex categories) (Ott 1989, p. 53; Schein 2004, pp. 12–13; Sułkowski 2017a, p. 284). The aforementioned elements of organisational culture are not regarded as equivalent or of equal importance. The literature contains numerous models arranging these elements of organisational culture on the basis of various criteria. For example:

- susceptibility to change, e.g. Hofstede's onion diagram (elements of culture are divided into these that constitute its core—permanent values—and these that constitute the so-called envelope, i.e. practices which may undergo change) (Hofstede et al. 2011, p. 23), or
- a level of awareness and research possibilities, e.g. Schein's model of organisational culture (culture consists of basic premises/fundamental values—invisible and usually unconscious, standards and values—partly visible, partly unconscious, artefacts and cultural products—visible, but frequently incomprehensible and requiring interpretation) (Schein 2004, p. 26).

Taking into consideration the methods of conducting research, the process of defining organisational culture can be based on an inductive approach or a deductive approach (Ott 1989, p. 49). In the inductive approach, a general theory is built through individual experience, preferences, and premises. In the deductive approach, the researcher moves from a general theory through case studies to modifications of the theory based on acquired research results.

Organisational culture can be also defined with respect to functions fulfilled in the organisation (Ott 1989, p. 68). Organisational culture:

- Provides a shared model of cognitive interpretation or perception, hence organisation members know how they are expected to act and think.
- Provides a shared model of interaction, an emotional sense of involvement and commitment to comply with organisational values and moral codes—things worth working for and believing in, organisation members know what values they should hold and how they are expected to feel.
- Defines and maintains identification borders determining who is an organisation member and who is not.
- Functions as an organisational system of control, commands, and prohibitions aimed at restricting certain forms of behaviour.
- May influence the organisation's operational results (Kotter and Heskett conducted research in this respect and proved the existence of a relationship between an organisational culture and an organisation's long-term financial results) (Kotter and Hesket 1992, p. 11).

Although organisational culture is a complex, multidimensional and abstract notion, it becomes a useful concept in thinking about organisations and explaining the principles of their functioning.

One of the most popular models describing organisational culture is that proposed by Schein. The criterion for distinguishing the elements of culture is their visibility for the observer and permanence (resistance to change). According to Schein, differences in organisational culture are easier to notice for an outsider who appears in the organisation or at the time when two separate organisations decide to cooperate or merge.

Table 3.1 The elements of organisational culture according to Schein, as developed by Ott

Elements of culture	Examples
Artefacts	Organisational anecdotes, art, celebrations, ceremonies, communication patterns, heroes, historical traces, jargon, language, metaphors and rituals, tangible objects, myths, spatial arrangement, scripts, organisational stories, symbols, tradition, translating myths into actions and relations
Artefacts—behaviour patterns	Attitudes, rules of behaviour, customs, manners of performing actions, shared expectations, routines, relationships patterns, metaphors and rituals, management practices, ways of being, standards, rituals, ritualistic practices, informal system of rules, styles, tradition
Held values and beliefs	Attitudes, existence, beliefs, shared beliefs, cognitive process, commitment to excellence, consensus level, core, ethics, ethos, feelings, identity, ideologies, assessment of behaviour, knowledge, meaning patterns, meanings, intersubjective meanings, way of thinking, philosophy, practical syllogisms, goals, sentiments, sources of standards, customs, attitudes, principles and roles, understanding, values, core or fundamental values, shared values, visions, manner, world view
Fundamental assumptions	Assumptions people live by, assumptions—basic patterns, shared assumptions, existence, core, constitutive assumptions, adhesive holding the organisation together, identity, way of thinking, philosophy, organisational scripts, organisational spirit, manner, world view

Source The author's own work based on Ott (1989, pp. 63–64)

Schein distinguished the following three levels of organisational culture (Schein 2004):

• The visible level—artefacts (visible organisational structures and processes). Artefacts may be of a tangible, linguistic, or behavioural character.
• The partly visible level—held values, beliefs, and standards (strategies, goals, philosophy, justification for existence). Values govern people's behaviour and constitute a basis for the shaping of the aforementioned level of artefacts. Values cannot be observed directly; they

can be inferred from interviews with an organisation's key members or from official documents such as statutes.

- The invisible level—fundamental assumptions (unconscious and taken for granted, perception, thinking, and feelings, the basic source of values and actions). According to Schein, fundamental values functioned earlier as values. And because values manifest themselves in behaviour and behaviour starts to bring about a solution to a problem, a value becomes a learned reaction to a given problem, an assumption concerning the character of reality and indicating how one should behave.

Analysing publications on organisational culture, Ott (1989) distinguished elements which make up the particular categories identified by Schein (Table 3.1).

Conducted for many years, research on organisational culture made it possible to distinguish its many models and types based on various criteria. Special recognition among management specialists was achieved by models proposed by the following researchers:

- Goffee and Jones (1998), who, based on the concepts of sociability and solidarity, identified four forms of organisational cultures (i.e. networked, mercenary, fragmented, and communal) (Goffee and Jones 1998).
- Cameron and Quinn (2015), who put forward a model of competing values. The criteria for distinguishing organisational cultures are the following: flexibility and operating freedom versus stability and control, orientation towards internal matters and integration versus orientation towards a place in the environment and diversity. They distinguished the following four types of cultures: clan, adhortation, hierarchy, market.
- Wallach (1983), who suggested that there were three main types of organisational cultures (i.e. bureaucratic, supportive and innovative). As a distinguishing criterion, he proposes individual motivation, personality versus organisational culture.
- Kotter and Heskett (1992; Cardona and Rey 2009, p. 27), who, using a criterion of unity and profit, distinguished the following four

types of organisational cultures: paternalistic, bureaucratic, aggressive, and competency-related.

The literature on the subject addresses also the issue of defining the strength of organisational culture, relations between organisational culture and organisational climate, subcultures, and organisational identity.

Kotter and Hesket define a strong organisational culture as one in which all leaders share a system of value and operating methods, and new employees accept such a system (Kotter and Hesket 1992, p. 15). Cardona and Rey define the strength of organisational culture as the intensity of employees' commitment to the organisation's mission, the coherence of values, and the organisation's ability to function and pursue its mission (Cardona and Rey 2009, p. 56). A strong organisational culture makes it possible for the organisation's employees to achieve a higher level of consensus (Martin 2001). It is difficult for new leaders to change a strong organisational culture.

An important area of scholarly exploration is relations between the concepts of organisational culture and organisational climate. Organisational climate has many different definitions. It can be defined as the perception of formal and informal organisational policies, procedures, and practices (Ostroff et al. 2003, p. 569). Ott defines organisational climate as a separate phenomenon which is not an element of organisational culture. In his opinion, it is a combination of feelings or a transitory organisational mood. (Ott 1989, p. 47). Wallace, Hunt, Richards, and Holloway emphasise that organisational climate is strongly connected with organisational culture; nevertheless, organisational culture is a broader concept because it is based on common and shared premises, while organisational climate is based on common shared perception (Wallace et al. 1999; Holloway 2012). Jones and James distinguish the following elements making up organisational climate: leadership and support provided by leaders; cooperation within work teams, kindliness and warmth; conflict and ambiguity; professional and organisational spirit; work-related challenges, meaning and diversity; as well as mutual understanding (Jones and James 1979; Wallace et al. 1999). Generally speaking, particular qualities are more permanent in organisational culture than in organisational climate. Organisational climate may be changeable and contextual, strongly determined, e.g. by a workplace (department, team) (Zohar and Hofmann 2012). In spite of this, organisational climate is more susceptible to measuring and examination than organisational culture (Balzer 2010, p. 122).

Another issue discussed in research on organisational culture are subcultures. Organisations are not monoliths. They are extremely complex and diversified, which translates also into their organisational cultures. An organisation can have one dominant culture based on common values and principles as well as many subcultures, which determines its multiculturalism (Hofstede et al. 2011, p. 316; Ott 1989, p. 45; Schein 2004, p. 22). Subcultures may occur in very different horizontal or vertical arrangements. Their borders may be determined by social factors (e.g. groups, teams), organisational factors (departments, schools, faculties), material factors (offices, storeys in a building), positions in an organisation (e.g. academics, administration workers, central or departmental administration workers), functions in an organisation (superiors, subordinates), professions (e.g. accountants, project specialists, public procurement, process or Lean Management, etc.), nationality, ethical, or religious attitudes (Ott 1989, p. 45; Schein 2004, p. 22). Subcultures intertwine and overlap, but sometimes they can be in conflict with one another (Ott 1989, p. 46; Hofstede et al. 2011, p. 316). Schein indicates that the existence of subcultures poses the question whether it is possible to talk about one common culture in a given organisation (Schein 2004, p. 20). Taking into consideration forces influencing dominant values in an organisation, Siehl and Martin (1984) distinguished the following three types of subcultures: enhancing subcultures, orthogonal subcultures (orthogonal cultures accept common values and premises, but they also have their own ones), and countercultures (countercultures are in conflict with the dominant culture). The existence of subcultures may influence research premises and approaches applied to organisational culture. Martin proposed that a research approach to organisational culture (Martin 1992, p. 13) be characterised by the following qualities: integration (the premise: an organisation has one homogeneous culture), differentiation (the premise: instead of one homogeneous culture, there are subcultures with consensus among them), and fragmentation (the premise: there is no one homogeneous culture, there are even no subcultures; there is a large number of separate points of view; culture in an individualised construct of reality).

Another problem studied in the literature is the relationship between organisational culture and organisational identity. According to Sułkowski, organisational identity is a symbolic and collective interpretation of people making up an organisation concerning what their organisation is and what it would like to be. In stable conditions, identity is a subject matter of collective and often default consensus (Sułkowski 2008). Organisational identity is set in organisational culture which can be perceived as an internal and symbolic context for the development and maintenance of organisational identity (Jo Hatch and Schultz 1997). The issue of organisational identity becomes particularly important in contemporary organisations, where boundaries between their inside and outside spaces become blurred (e.g. in consequence of the networking of activities). Organisational identity should meet the following conditions: reflecting the core values on which the consensus of organisation members is based and allowing the organisation to distinguish itself effectively from other organisations. Through identity, organisation members determine their organisation's boundaries. Thanks to its timeless character, identity is a carrier of the continuity of the organisation's activities (Gioia et al. 2000; Sułkowski 2008). It is emphasised that if the organisation wants to keep its identity, paradoxically, it has to change (Gioia et al. 2000).

The above review of the literature shows that research on organisational culture develops continuously. Many questions are posed about the principles of selecting proper paradigms, approaches (inductive or deductive), and research methods. There is more in-depth research into relationships between organisational culture and organisational climate, into subcultures and organisational identity. It is of particular importance in the case of higher education institutions whose organisational cultures are strongly established in the historical, legal, cultural, and mental dimensions.

3.2.2 Organisational Culture in Higher Education

Organisational culture in higher education is of a unique character determined by the university's centuries-old tradition and mission. Modifying the division put forward by Ott (1989, p. 75), the author proposes that the main factors determining the unique organisational culture of the university include the following:

- University tradition.
- The culture of a society in which the university functions.
- The nature of the university's activities (teaching, research, social mission) and environment.
- The beliefs, values and basic premises of the university's founders and leaders.

University Tradition

The organisational culture of the university was traditionally determined by such values as truth, knowledge, autonomy, independence, freedom, transnationality, communitarianism, and the master–disciple relationship (Woźnicki 2000, p. 59). Referring to Czarniawska's proposal (Czarniawska 2010, p. 34) explaining how institutions come into being, it is possible to state that the university is the result of the institutionalisation of a repeatable model of collective activities based on traditional values and academic principles. Since the beginnings of the university, its mission has been connected with the uncompromising pursuit of cognition, truth, and knowledge as autotelic values. The organisational culture of the collegial university created an environment favourable for its accomplishment. In the successive centuries the mission of the university underwent changes under the influence of the following factors (Leja 2013; Sułkowski 2016; Lacatus 2013):

- cultural trends (the Humboldt trend based on academic freedom, pure knowledge, and the integration of research and teaching; the Newman trend emphasising teaching, pragmaticism, and autonomy),

- political trends (liberal, etatist, neoliberal),
- trends in public organisation management (administrative, scientific, bureaucratic, New Public Management, good governance, networking of activities).

At present, the mission of the university takes into consideration the expectations of many of its stakeholders (the academic community, the state, students, employees, etc.). This has caused transformations in the university organisational culture. It has become more complex, combining in itself the elements of the traditional collegial culture with the elements of the bureaucratic, corporate and enterprising cultures. Such an organisational culture creates a challenging environment in which the university is to pursue its mission.

The Culture of a Society in Which the University Functions

The influence of national culture on organisational culture was proved in the research conducted by Hofstede et al. (2011). The author notes that organisational culture is not a being restricted in its existence to the minds of the members of a given organisation as it is rooted in the consciousness of its stakeholders. In the case of the university, stakeholders include the academic community, employees, students, employers, trade organisations, the state, local communities, taxpayers. With respect to the university, the society formulates concrete expectations. For example, parents who finance the educational system expect that their children will receive good services and develop their competences. Taxpayers expect the university to be managed efficiently. Employees expect continuity of employment, good salaries, and stability. The development of universities' organisational cultures is also influenced by their internationalisation. A problem appears in the case of universities with local branches in many countries (Hofstede's research); such branches create their own subcultures dominated by particular national values.

The Nature of Universities' Activities

Despite their considerable diversification, particular universities' organisational cultures are similar to one another. Similarities among university organisational cultures can be explained as follows (Ott 1989, p. 80):

- Universities are dominated by similar professional cultures of academics, teachers of various disciplines and specialisations, therefore a university organisational culture can be compared to a professional culture (Hofstede et al. 2011, p. 321).
- The nature of conducted activities defines in advance with whom the university enters into relationships, e.g. agencies which finance research, controlling authorities, students and their organisations, trade organisations, research networks, publishing houses, etc. Such relationships can generate tensions which are the result of differences among the organisational cultures of particular institutions, e.g. enterprises financing research and universities. The character of such tensions can be ethical (e.g. in the case of public procurement procedures), moral (sponsoring and financing versus corruption), and organisational (business enterprises operate faster than public organisations, etc.).
- Special attention is paid to the following two market factors diversifying organisational cultures: the risk level and the speed with which an organisation receives feedback on the effectiveness of its decisions and strategy. The university is still an organisation focused more on its potential and duration, with a relatively low-risk level and a low speed of feedback.

The author is of the opinion that state policies are also an important factor unifying organisational cultures of higher education institutions in a particular country. Such policies determine the legal framework for the functioning of universities, influencing their collegiality levels, authorities and organisational structures, decision making processes, etc.

The Beliefs, Values and Basic Premises of the University's Founders and Leaders

Keeping in mind the complexity of the organisational models of higher education institutions, we should, first of all, determine who fulfils the functions of university founders and dominant leaders. In the legal dimension, this is governed by applicable regulations. These are chancellors, rectors, presidents, etc. In the organisational dimension, these are people who look for and attract others, who share the same views, values, beliefs and assumptions, who are able to shape culture thanks to the power of their personalities (Ott 1989, p. 81). They tend to attract people who share their visions. In a university, such functions can be performed by charismatic change leaders, heroes, outstanding scholars, teachers, thinkers or researchers.

The analysis conducted above shows that university organisational culture is diversified at the level of particular countries or universities. On the other hand, however, it is relatively homogeneous because of traditions, historical conditions, and the nature of academic activities. It makes it possible to develop common conceptual and theoretical frameworks in research on organisational culture.

The first research works on organisational culture in higher education were published as early as the 1960s and concerned student culture. The subsequent years witnessed an intensive development of research in this area. The addressed topics included the following: the types of organisational culture in higher education (Bergquist 1992; Bergquist and Pawlak 2008; Clark 1972), the applicable research methods (Masland 1985), the importance of various elements of organisational culture, e.g. organisational sagas (Clark 1972), the significance of time, space, and communication in the individual and organisational dimensions of particular cultures (Tierney 1988), research on relationships between the strength of organisational culture and the university's effectiveness (Smart and St. John 1996), research on the influence of organisational culture on the process of changes in the university (Kezar and Eckel 2002) as well as research on the impact of organisational culture on the university's brand (Toma et al. 2005). Research on organisational culture was conducted on the basis of the adopted functionalist paradigm. Among other tools, researchers used the model of competing values proposed by Cameron and Quinn (Smart and St. John 1996; Beytekđn et al. 2010). Based on this model, McNay and Lacatus distinguished four types of organisational culture in higher education. For the purpose of categorisation, they adopted the following two criteria: ability to create culture and the scope of control over policy implementation in higher education (McNay 2006; Lacatus 2013, p. 424). The researchers distinguished a collegial culture, a bureaucratic culture, a corporate culture, and an enterprising culture. Meanwhile, Bergquist (1992), using various theories in the areas of history, anthropology, architecture, sociology, and business, identified the following four models of organisational culture in higher education: collegial culture, managerial culture, developmental culture, and negotiating culture. The further research bore fruit in the form of two more models: the virtual model and the tangible model (Bergquist and Pawlak 2008). Few researchers use the interpretative-symbolic paradigm in their studies on organisational culture in higher education. It is researched by means of ethnographic tools (Kezar and Eckel 2002). Issues related to organisational culture are also raised in the critical trend of management studies. The subject matter of studies are changes in organisational culture, especially under the influence of New Public Management (NPM) and the managerisation of higher education. Researchers emphasise that the traditional organisational culture is supplemented with numerous values regarded as culturally foreign. These are effectiveness, efficiency, saving, productivity (Jabłecka 2000, p. 9). The organisational culture based on trust and ethos is replaced by a culture of proof, audit, control, and assessment (Sułkowski 2016, p. 25). The feminist trend in critical management studies raises the issue of contradiction between new management methods and management culture favoured by women (Deem 1998). The analysis of the literature on the subject shows an insufficient number of theoretical and empirical works on organisational culture in higher education. Conducted research is based mainly on the functionalist paradigm, hence organisational culture is treated as a tool for implementing changes in the spirit of NPM, as well as building the university's brand and market position.

The objective of the analysis conducted by the author in Chapter 3.2 was to create a theoretical framework necessary for defining new notions connected with Lean Culture in higher education, as well as identifying approaches to research on Lean Culture, its dimensions, and the internal and external contexts for building its maturity. The results of the author's own research are presented in the subsequent parts of this chapter.

3.3   Lean Culture in Higher Education

3.3.1 The Status of Research on Lean Culture in the Light of the Literature on the Subject

In order to present the status of research on Lean Culture and issues related to it, the author conducted a review of the literature on the subject. The most important works include Deming (2012), Bicheno, Holweg (2000), Liker (2005), Balzer (2010), Angelis et al. (2011), Mann (2014), Parkes (2017), Womack et al. (1990), and Hoseus and Liker (2008).

In the analysis, the author followed the method of a systematic review of the literature. The conducted research was based on the EBSCO database and, accessorily, the Web of Science and Google Scholar services. Searching the databases, the author used the following key phrases: Lean Culture and HEI (as appearing in abstracts, subject terms, and titles). The application of key words returned no records from the EBSCO database. The conducted systematic review of the literature on Lean Culture showed that in comparison to the total number of publications on Lean Management, articles dedicated to Lean Culture constituted a small minority. When the words "Lean" and "organisational culture" were used as keys, the EBSCO database returned: 123 records containing the key words in abstracts (23 full-length articles; the first reviewed academic publications come from 2001), no records containing the key words in subject terms, 9 records containing the key words in titles (6 full-length articles; the first reviewed academic publications come from 2015). The EBSCO database was additionally searched using the phrase "culture of continuous improvement" (as appearing in titles). The search returned 25 records, including 4 records concerning higher education. Indexed in the EBSCO database, the first publications on a culture of continuous improvement date back to 1994 and are connected with the implementation of the TQM concept in corporations (Sinclair and Arthur 1994). As far as higher education is concerned, this issue is raised in the context of building a culture of evidence (besides accreditation and accountability, continuous improvement is considered as one of the tools for building such a culture) (Morest 2009), improving an electronic document circulation system in a university library (Charles Bruno 2013), improving educational processes in a multicultural student environment (Lindahl and Fanelli 2002). The conducted analysis of the literature on the subject shows that the ideological premises on which Lean Culture is based were already formulated by Deming in the TQM concept in the form of 14 points for managers presented in his *Out of the Crisis* (2012). Another important work is *The Toyota Way* by Liker (2005). Liker defines the Toyota culture through a set of 14 principles divided into the following four dimensions: a general concept (far-reaching thinking), a process (elimination of wastage), people and partners (respect, creating challenges, education), and solving problems (continuous improvement and learning). He observes that changes in an organisational culture result from the implementation of the Lean Management concept and mentions difficulties in changing an organisational culture as well as differences in particular national cultures which condition the effective implementation of Lean Management. These problems are studied further in the work entitled *Toyota Culture* (Hoseus and Liker 2008). The authors emphasised that Lean Culture is oriented towards achieving results. Another important contribution to research on Lean Culture is David Mann's *Creating a Lean Culture: Tools to Sustain Lean Conversions* (2014). The author analyses in detail the methods and tools for carrying out a cultural change in an organisation. He also emphasises that one of the characteristic features of organisational culture is its enormous inertia and resistance to change. He observes that organisational and technical changes alone do not suffice; the key to building a Lean Culture is a change of habits (Mann 2014, p. 18).

The publications on Lean Culture discussed below address first of all the issues of defining success factors in the building of a Lean Culture, the impact of a national culture on a Lean Culture, and approaches to changes in a Lean Culture.

Defining a Lean Culture, the authors most frequently refer to the definition of organisational culture put forward by Schein (Parkes 2017, p. 64; Hoseus and Liker 2008). The most important factors of the internal context for the building of a Lean Culture include the following: allowing employees to participate in improvement-oriented projects (Angelis et al. 2011), supporting employees by superiors in task execution (Angelis et al. 2011), if necessary, ensuring assistance in the proper application of production standards (Angelis et al. 2011), applying job rotation (Angelis et al. 2011), informing employees of work results and related deviations (Zarbo 2012; Angelis et al. 2011), team work (Zarbo 2012), employee empowerment (Zarbo 2012), using the scientific method of data-driven plan-do-check-act (PDCA) (Zarbo 2012), identifying defects and sources of wastage (Zarbo 2012), accepting changes (Taherimashhadi and Ribas 2018). Emphasis is placed on the huge role of leaders in building a Lean Culture. They are responsible for implementing the Lean concept and creating an appropriate working environment (Mann 2014; Liker 2005; Van der Merwe et al. 2014; Zarbo 2012; Mann 2009). Authors stress that Lean Culture is based on trained employees who continuously increase their competence. They are the greatest value in a Lean Culture (Mann 2014; Liker 2005; Zarbo 2012). Researchers also draw attention to the external context determining the shaping of a Lean Culture, and first of all to a national culture (Deming 2012; Liker and Convis 2012; Taherimashhadi and Ribas 2018; Parkes 2017; Liker 2005; Pakdil and Leonard 2017; Erthal and Marques 2018; Womack et al. 1990; Hoseus and Liker 2008; Parkes 2015). They emphasise differences between Japanese culture and other national cultures. Parkes notes that a variety of national cultures creates a variety of organisational cultures which may be incompatible with Lean Culture. Lean Culture is an organisational culture which comes into being on the basis of a national culture, a culture of a given business sector or a culture of a particular organisation; its elements are functional and professional subcultures, cliques, and fractions (Hoseus and Liker 2008).

A cultural change takes a long time, which can be frustrating. It requires the building of structures and processes which will strengthen and accelerate the process of continuous improvement in the organisation (Taherimashhadi and Ribas 2018; Zarbo 2012). Implementing the Lean concept, decision makers often forget about its culture-creating dimension (Radnor and Bucci 2011) and put emphasis first of all on organisational, technical, and economic aspects. Therefore, the literature on the subject contains numerous recommendations concerning the methods of changing an organisational culture into a Lean Culture (Van der Merwe et al. 2014). The recommended actions include justifying the necessity of changes, creating a vision, achieving the first success, building a structure, team work, training, assessment, awareness, commitment, consistency, and accountability. The processes which combine the aforementioned categories of actions are communication and coordination.

In view of the fact that the conducted searches did not return any publications directly concerning Lean Culture in higher education, the author conducted a critical analysis of publications dealing with Lean Management in higher education. Its results are presented in Table 3.2.

The above analysis shows that the earliest works dedicated to Lean Culture were published in 2008. Researchers started to use the notion of Lean Culture itself in 2011, treating it as equivalent to the notion of a culture of continuous improvement. In the author's opinion, this is not quite right because culture of continuous improvement is also associated with TQM, BPM, BPR and other process management concepts. Therefore, it is proposed to use the term "Lean Culture" to differentiate it from other concepts.

The literature stresses that higher education is characterised by a unique culture, structure, and processes. In the context of Lean Management implementation, a university's organisational culture is referred to as a silo culture (Kamp 2017), a blame culture (Kamp 2017), a culture of apathy (Kamp 2017), a culture of no change (Radnor and Bucci 2011). The problem of relations between the existing organisational culture of a university and Lean Culture is addressed in most publications. Various issues are raised. It is noted that the direct adaptation of Lean methods used in the business and manufacturing sectors to changes in a university's organisational culture is rather risky and may end in failure (a school is not a factory) (Lu et al. 2017, p. 647). Change has to take place first of all in university leaders, whom authors describe as "bottlenecks" (Lu et al. 2017, p. 647; Emiliani 2015, p. 43). The existing organisational culture of a university may limit possibilities of an open approach to improvement actions proposed by employees, who frequently do not consider themselves to be a part of their organisation (Thomas et al. 2013, p. 138). Understanding the essence of Lean,

Table 3.2 A review of approaches to Lean Culture in higher education—the results of an analysis of the literature on the subject

#	Year of publication	Author	Designation of Lean Culture	Issues related to Lean Culture
1	2008	Hines, Peter; Lethbridge, Sarah	None	The authors indicate that an effective strategy and consensus can be achieved only through strong leadership which, in turn, will be exercised successfully only in a positive organisational culture open to learning and improvement. A true change in an organisational culture in the spirit of Lean is possible only through top-down thinking
2	2010	Balzer	Workplace climate	The author uses the notion of organisational climate as an element influencing the university's readiness for Lean concept implementation. He identifies the following types of climate important from the Lean perspective: a climate of standards, a climate of support, a climate of commitment. The author also analyses relations between the practices of leaders and an organisational climate
3	2011	Radnor, Z. and Bucci, G.	Lean Culture, culture of continuous improvement	The development of a Lean Culture is not emphasised. The implementation approach is based more on projects which are not developed further. Changes in an organisational culture are the result of the continuous improvement process. Managers should learn how to support a Lean Culture in a positive manner. The character of changes should be holistic, and not insular
4	2013	Cristina, Dragomir; Felicia, Surugiu	Culture of continuous improvement	The implementation of Lean Principles influences the building of a change culture in a university. Lean is analysed rather as a cultural change in behaviour and attitudes. Managers should learn how to provide positive support for a culture of continuous improvement. Changing the organisational culture is a priority in Lean implementation

#	Year of publication	Author	Designation of Lean Culture	Issues related to Lean Culture
5	2013	Robert Ross Allan, Tammi Sinha	Culture of continuous improvement, Lean Culture	The authors emphasise the importance of employee commitment and motivation in the building of a Lean Culture. Required levels of commitment and motivation can be achieved through training, support, and structured Lean implementation in the univeristy
6	2013	Carsten Svensson, Mohamed Ba-Essa, Majed Bakhsh	Culture of continuous improvement	Changing the organisational culture is of fundamental importance in Lean implementation. A culture of continuous improvement should be tended in a structured manner
7	2013	Andrew Thomas, Mark Francis, Ron Fisher, Kevin Chilton	Culture of continuous improvement, culture of Lean	The authors emphasise that a lack of commitment and support from senior executive teams makes it difficult to foster a culture of continuous improvement. The existing organisational culture may restrict the possibilities of implementing the Lean concept. Organisational culture and employee empowerment are important factors in university development
8	2014	Antony, Jiju	None	The author analyses the factors of readiness for change, using Lean Six Sigma. He observes that they can accelerate changes in a university organisational culture
9	2015	Bob Emiliani	None	The author proposes using the Lean Transformation Model. It is based on process improvement, commitment, consistent leadership, and talent development

(Continued)

Table 3.2 (Continued)

#	Year of publication	Author	Designation of Lean Culture	Issues related to Lean Culture
10	2015	Svensson, Carsten; Antony, Jiju; Ba-Essa, Mohamed; Bakhsh, Majed; Albliwi, Saja	culture of CI (continuous improvement)	The authors analyse a CI culture in the context of LSS implementation
11	2015	Douglas, Jacqueline Ann; Antony, Jiju; Douglas, Alexander	Continuous improvement culture	The authors emphasise that embedding such a culture in a culture of a public organisation is not a simple task. Creating a proper organisational culture can constitute a considerable challenge, particularly with respect to identifying sources of wastage
12	2015	Thomas, Andrew J.; Antony, Jiju; Francis, Mark; Fisher, Ron	Culture of continuous improvement, culture of Lean	The objective of the conducted research was to gain an understanding of the methods and dynamics of Lean implementation in higher education. The authors note that a lack of commitment and support from senior executive teams hinders the development of a culture of continuous improvement. Researches conducted in British universities show that they have started to develop a Lean Culture, but in the past four years, they did not do anything which could have any significant impact. The author's conclusions are based on interviews and the results of a questionnaire survey of organisational learning (30 questions, assessment based on a five-point Likert scale)

#	Year of publication	Author	Designation of Lean Culture	Issues related to Lean Culture
13	2015	Lawrence H. Cairns N.	Culture of continuous improvement	Lean implementation changes a culture towards transparency in data collection and recording. Measuring effectiveness is a key tool for building a culture of continuous improvement. It allows the presentation of the effects of changes achieved in a long period of time
14	2016	Balzer, William K.; Francis, David E.; Krehbiel, Timothy C.; Shea, Nicholas	None	On the basis of the reviewed literature, the authors emphasise that a university's organisational culture strongly conditions its success in implementing the Lean higher education concept
15	2016	Cano, M., Moyes, D.,, and Kobi, A.	Culture of continuous improvement	An organisational culture may influence the success or failure of a Lean programme. Executed projects indicate that Lean implementation has a positive impact on the building of a culture of continuous improvement in higher education.
16	2017	Lu, Jing; Laux, Chad; Antony, Jiju	Lean Six Sigma Culture	The authors emphasise that an LSS culture could aid the growth of data-driven decision making

(Continued)

Table 3.2 (Continued)

#	Year of publication	Author	Designation of Lean Culture	Issues related to Lean Culture
17	2017	Kamp, P. M.	Culture of continuous improvement Lean Culture, Lean team's culture	A Lean Culture is considered from the point of view of its shaping in Lean teams. It is noted that a Lean strategy has to be compatible with a university organisational culture. A silo mentality and a blame culture hinder the building of a Lean Culture. In a Lean Culture, employees realise that Lean does not threat their jobs, while academics realize that Lean does not threaten their academic freedom. Lean is not capable of changing the culture on its own
18	2016	Yorkstone Stephen	Lean Culture	The author analyses the impact of a Lean implementation method in a university on changes in its organisational culture (event-driven Lean, advocate-led Lean, tool-led Lean)

Source Prepared on the basis of: (Hines and Lethbridge 2008; Antony 2014; Dragomir and Surugiu 2013; Allan and Sinha 2013; Svensson et al. 2013; Thomas et al. 2013; Vyas and Campbell 2015; Svensson et al. 2015; Douglas et al. 2015; Thomas et al. 2015; Balzer et al. 2016; Lu and Laux Antony 2017; Billings et al. 2017; Kamp 2017; Cano et al. 2016; Langer 2011; Radnor and Bucci 2011; Yorkstone 2016) empowering employees, and providing them with adequate tools bring about positive changes in a university's organisational culture (Thomas et al. 2013, p. 138). The literature stresses that Lean is not able to change a university's organisational culture by itself, but it can be used as a tool for cultural transformation (Kamp 2017, p. 34).

Defining Lean in higher education, authors use such notions as a culture of continuous improvement and based on respect for people (Radnor and Bucci 2011), a culture of entrepreneurship (Lu et al. 2017, p. 647), a culture of collecting relevant data (Antony 2014, p. 259), a culture of openness, trust and acceptance (Kamp 2017, p. 23), a non-blaming culture (Kamp 2017, p. 23), a culture of innovation (Francis 2014). Conducting the review of various theories and research results, the author concludes that the factors determining the shaping of a Lean Culture in higher education include the following: Lean leadership, team work, employee commitment, employee empowerment, and fact-based decision making. Some authors regard these factors as separate from, existing, as it were, beside, or being equivalent to, a Lean Culture or as constitutive elements of such a culture.

The author is of the opinion that the presented approach to Lean Culture is located within the functionalist paradigm. Discussed issues include the shaping of Lean Culture in higher education, investments in Lean Culture, its constituent elements, and success factors. Therefore, in the ontological perspective, it is assumed that Lean Culture exists as a university phenomenon or process which can be shaped. Characteristically for the functionalist paradigm, an instrumental approach to Lean Culture is also presented. In the epistemological perspective, the authors of the reviewed publications do not refer directly to the issue of measuring the maturity of Lean Culture, but draw attention, for example, to the necessity of measuring readiness for Lean concept implementation.

The above analysis of the literature on the subject allows the author to indicate gaps in research on Lean Culture in higher education. The major research gaps are the following:

- The lack of a definition of Lean Culture in higher education.
- The lack of a theoretical framework systematising and describing the dimensions of Lean Culture in higher education.

- The lack of standardised and reliable tools to diagnose Lean Culture maturity.
- The lack of indication which of the obvious conditions for organisational change implementation are unique for Lean Culture.

The identified research gaps were the reason for the author to undertake her own research in this area.

3.3.2 Defining Lean Culture in Higher Education

A definition of Lean Culture in higher education has a multidimensional character, and is the effect of interpenetrating approaches to defining organisational culture, organisational culture in higher education, and Lean Culture. Its final shape is determined by the external and internal contexts in which a university functions. The literature on the subject presents various attempts to define Lean Culture, but there is still a lack of an unequivocal definition. Researchers use such terms as Lean Culture change (Atkinson and Nicholls 2013), culture of a lean organisation (Walentynowicz 2013, p. 82; Mann 2014, p. 190), culture of continuous improvement and change (Zarbo 2012; Miller 2011), culture of performance improvement (Kusy et al. 2015).

In order to put the approaches to Lean Culture in order the author proposes that the following approaches and perspectives be introduced:

- A philosophical perspective. Lean Culture is referred to as an organisation's operating philosophy—Lean thinking. It focuses first of all on economical functioning, i.e. improving the efficiency of activities by eliminating wastage, minimising wastefulness, and controlling the flow of added value (Hamrol 2015, p. 99). It is a specific philosophy of performing the particular functions of an organisation (Czerska 2003, p. 13). Lean Culture in higher education is defined as an operating philosophy whose essence is the quality of relations among people, common forms of behaviour, and a work culture (Yorkstone 2016). The literature also defines Lean as a philosophy of value-driven continuous improvement (Van der Merwe et al. 2014).

Lean Culture is defined in terms of such values as continuous improvement and respect for people (Robinson and Yorkstone 2014, p. 47), *a sustained commitment to drive continuous and never-ending improvement* (Atkinson and Nicholls 2013, p. 10). As Sikorski emphasises (Sikorski 2009, p. 13), organisational culture understood as philosophy has a double meaning. Paraphrasing the author, it can be said that Lean Culture concerns both a particular university (it is its organisational culture) and organisations which are implementing the Lean concept (Lean Culture is a phenomenon characteristic of all organisations implementing this concept).

- Enumerative definitions. Such definitions result from enumerating the elements/layers making up Lean Culture. A case in point is the definition proposed by Parkes (2017, p. 64). According to that author, Lean Culture consists of such layers as—an operating philosophy,—principles, attitudes, convictions, values, thinking and acting oriented towards creation of value and elimination of wastage,—linguistic, behavioural and physical artefacts,—standards and rules, as well as methods, techniques and tools.

- Normative definitions. Lean Culture is defined in terms of organisational and social rules and standards regulating the behaviour of organisation members. An example is the concept introduced by Liker. According to Liker, Lean Management constitutes a holistic concept of management based on the 14 principles developed by Toyota (Liker 2005, p. 43) and successfully adapted also to the service sector (Liker and Morgan 2006, pp. 5–20). Their implementation allows an effective implementation of the Lean concept in the strategic and operational spheres of organisational management as well as a change of organisational culture towards employee commitment and continuous improvement. On the basis of a conducted analysis, Pakdil and Leonard (2017, p. 703) formulate the following principles constituting the foundation of Lean Culture: employee involvement, creativity, problem-solving processes, and decentralisation, control, standardisation and predictable performance outcomes, efficiency, productivity, continuous quality improvement, and long-term philosophy (Pakdil and Leonard 2017).

- Psychological definitions. They emphasise the role of people in an organisation and their attitude towards change. Mann indicates, among other things, the necessity of suppressing and/or changing employees' habits and customs (Mann 2014, p. 24). Some researchers raise the issue of the proper motivation of employees in a Lean environment (Jakubik et al. 2012, p. 87). With respect to higher education, Balzer draws attention to the factors of organisational climate which influence employees' behaviour and attitudes and how they understand and perceive their roles in the organisation (Balzer 2010, p. 96).
- Definitions based on a cultural gap. A cultural gap may be defined at the level of an organisation or an individual. At the level of an organisation, Lean Culture is defined by juxtaposing a culture of a traditional organisation with a culture of a Lean organisation. Such a definition of Lean Culture is proposed by Mann (2014, p. 19), who compares the qualities of a mass production culture to those of a Lean production culture or the traditional approach to the Lean Management approach (Walentynowicz 2013, p. 87), the traditional university to the Lean University (Maciąg 2016a). A cultural gap may be analysed at the level of individual experiences of people in an organisation. As Sikorski emphasises, in such an approach, an organisational culture is a set of an employee's conviction about the qualities of their organisation (Sikorski 2009, p. 9). Such convictions are relatively permanent, go beyond an organisation's borders, have their sources in families, groups, schools, communities, and other organisations (Schein 2004, p. 8). It is possible to talk about a so-called individual organisational culture. Every employee perceives and assesses various aspects of organisational reality. In such an approach, a cultural gap may appear between how an employee factually perceives organisational culture and what their expectations in this respect are.

Lean Management is defined as a cultural change, and Lean Culture is simultaneously a factor influencing the implementation of the concept of Lean Management and its effect (Radnor et al. 2006, p. 62). There is consensus among authors that Lean Culture is an essential success factor of Lean Management in organisations (Starbird 2017; Emiliani 1998).

Researchers stress that the values and standards lying at the foundations of Lean processes may cause conflicts with the culture already existing in the organisation, which may delay the implementation of this concept (Pakdil and Leonard 2015). The analysis of the literature on the subject shows that research on Lean Culture and its connections with organisational culture and national culture acquires more and more importance. Researchers and practitioners more and more appreciate its significance, observing that technical and organisational changes are decidedly simpler to introduce (Hines et al. 2004), but their success and permanence depend on the building of a proper Lean Culture.

3.3.3 The Concepts of Lean Culture— A Multiparadigmatic Approach

For the purpose of arranging the perspectives used in research on Lean Culture, the author used the classification of paradigms proposed by Burell and Morgan (Burell and Morgan 2005), and developed by (Hatch 2002, p. 204; Kostera 2005, p. 15; Sułkowski 2012, p. 38; Sułkowski 2016, p. 181). Taking into consideration the adopted ontological and epistemological premises, the author carried out a classification of research on Lean Culture according to the dominant paradigm on the basis of which research was conducted. The results of the analysis are presented below.

• Lean Culture in the light of the functional-systemic paradigm.

This is a dominant approach in research on Lean Culture in organisations (Mann 2014; Pakdil and Leonard 2017; Erthal and Marques 2018; Paro and Gerolamo 2017; Losonci et al. 2017; Pakdil and Leonard 2015). It is based on a positivist premise that thanks to systematic, structured, and repeatable scientific observations, it is possible to discover objective knowledge (Kawalec 2017, p. 22). Perceived in this way, Lean Culture is a tool to improve the operational effectiveness and efficiency of the university. It is an instrument used by leaders to implement the fundamental principles of Lean Management. Lean Culture is assessed with respect to the context in which the organisation functions.

Researchers studying Lean Culture used the concept of Hofstede (Pakdil and Leonard 2017; Erthal and Marques 2018) as well as the competing values model proposed by Cameron and Quin (Paro and Gerolamo 2017; Losonci et al. 2017; Pakdil and Leonard 2015). The maturity of Lean Culture is also studied in the functionalist paradigm (Shah and Ward 2007; Urban 2015; Doolen and Hacker 2005; AL-Najem et al. 2012; Caffyn 1999; Jørgensen et al. 2007). In this case, the deductive approach dominates.

• Lean Culture from the perspective of the interpretative-symbolic paradigm.

In this approach, Lean Culture is defined as a theoretical epistemological metaphor of the university (the university is culture) (Kostera 2005). It is defined as an obligation and commitment, an employee's attitude, their personal way of living and solving problems in the organisation. Lean Culture is a community of meanings characteristic of the university's employees (Sułkowski 2012, p. 41). The author emphasises that perceived in this way, culture is difficult to control, consists of subcultures and organisational identity. In research on Lean Culture, this paradigm was used, among others, by Langer (2011). He used the functionalist and interpretative-symbolic approaches to formulate a concept of implementing Lean Management in higher education. He stressed that universities unquestioningly followed various management methods because they appeared to be modern, effective and efficient for university stakeholders, which ensured the legitimacy of introduced changes. In this type of research on Lean Culture, the inductive approach dominates.

• Lean Culture from the perspective of the critical paradigm.

Lean Culture is interpreted as oppression, violence, and domination. This approach to Lean Culture belongs to the trend of critical management. This research perspective is often adopted in the literature with respect to higher education. Lean Culture may be perceived as oppressive in either the individual dimension or the dimension of the university. Employees perceive it as hostile if its elements (values, beliefs, principles, methods) are at variance with their expectations. In the organisational dimension, Lean Culture may be at variance with the university's organisational culture. This may lead to conflicts of values (e.g. if business definitions of values based on economic metrics are used as a starting point for the restructuring of processes in the university) or conflicts about Lean Principles (e.g. the university's strong hierarchisation does not create an open space for discussions, expression of opinions, or changes). In such circumstances, Lean Culture is regarded as some kind of violence, interference at a primeval level. This approach is explained, for example, by the concept of autopoiesis, which was described extensively by M. Lenartowicz (2016). Cultural changes in the university may occur only through empowerment, denaturalisation (undermining the existing status quo), self-reflection.

- Lean Culture in the postmodernist paradigm.

Lean Culture is an indigenous metaphor, an inseparable part of the organisation or a part of a wider cultural formation. Taking into consideration the ontological and epistemological attitude characteristic of postmodernism, it is possible to define Lean Culture as a paradox, a situation in which the university should not find itself. In this approach, Lean Culture is a discourse only and exists within a language only. It is a great illusion (Sułkowski 2012, p. 51). Through rationalisation and instrumentalisation, it acts against man (Sułowski 2012, p. 51).

All attempts to categorise Lean Culture according to criteria established beforehand have a conventional character. They arrange a section of organisational reality in order to get to know and understand it better. Conducted by the author, the paradigmatic analysis of Lean Culture shows how differently it can be perceived and studied in the higher education context. Analysing the qualities of Lean in the spirit of each of the paradigms, it is possible to find many themes raised in current discussions. As it has been noted earlier, research on Lean Culture is conducted mainly in the functionalist paradigm, using the deductive method. In the author's opinion, this is insufficient because it does not provide the possibility of explaining and understanding the phenomenon of Lean Culture in higher education. Especially if the university's unique character as an organisation is taken into consideration. With respect to the manner of shaping relations among employees and organising work, the university differs considerably from manufacturing enterprises or service providing organisations (which was discussed in Chapter 2). The university is a place dominated by a culture of individualism where people usually work in a small project or research teams, or administrative departments. It is characterised by a strong division of labour, specialisation, and a high degree of autonomy in the execution of key academic, didactic and administrative tasks and processes. Such tasks or processes are often executed by one person or a small group of specialists. Interpersonal relations are not built in the same way as in business organisations. Therefore, the author proposes the broadening of the functionalist perspective in her own research on Lean Culture, which will be described in the following section.

3.3.4 The Paradigmatic Premises for the Author's Own Research on Lean Culture in Higher Education

The objective of the research conducted by the author was to define the notion and maturity of Lean Culture in higher education institutions as well as to determine its key dimensions and descriptors in the light of the adopted ontological and epistemological premises. The cognitive objective of the research was formulated as defining the notion of Lean Culture as well as the dimensions and descriptors of its maturity; the methodological objective was formulated as developing and testing the author's original model of assessing the maturity of Lean Culture in higher education (Lean Culture Maturity Model in Higher Education—LCMMHE) and tools for testing the maturity of Lean Culture (Lean Culture Maturity Questionnaire—LCMQ), as well as determining conditions for their implementation. The research methodology and procedure were discussed in Chapter 1. In this part, the author intends to present the way of constructing the research paradigm adopted in her research on Lean Culture in higher education. As is emphasised by Sułkowski, a researcher undertaking studies on Lean Culture in higher education should, first of all, determine their research attitude and propose or adopt a definition of organisational culture. This will translate subsequently into an applied research approach (Sułkowski 2012, p. 51).

Taking into consideration the conducted analysis of the literature on the subject, the author adopted the following ontological and epistemological premises. In this perspective and referring to the functionalist paradigm, the author formulates the following premises:

- Lean Culture exists as a part of organisational culture of higher education;
- Lean Culture is a tool to manage organisational behaviour. It is an organisational mechanism of control, informally approving or restricting certain models of behaviour depending on their compliance with the philosophy, values, and principles of Lean Management.

Keeping in mind restrictions resulting from basing her research on Lean Culture on the functionalist paradigm only, the author supplemented it with the relational approach to defining Lean Culture. In the relational perspective, Lean Culture is analysed at the level of people's individual experiences in the organisation. As Sikorski observes, the relational approach is close to the interpretative-symbolic approach (Sikorski 2009, p. 13). He notes that, *in the relational perspective, subjective relations between a person and various aspects of the organization do not rule out objective, and hence independent of such relations, qualities of the organizational system [..] the symbolic sphere does not replace the material sphere.* Adopting such an approach allows the author to broaden the ontological perspective of the research with the following premise:

- Lean Culture is a construct created by the behaviour and the attitudes of the university's employees.

The adoption of this ontological attitude provides the research with the humanistic perspective. Man becomes a point of interest, and Lean Culture is created in the networks of various relations and meanings, in people's interpretations. Such ontological premises are characteristic of the constructivist approach (Czarniawska 2010, p. 16). It means that the structure of Lean Culture is created through people's behaviour and emanations.

The adopted ontological premises consistently translate into the epistemological premises adopted in the research on Lean Culture. Formulating the epistemological premises, the author adopted the position of epistemological pluralism (Sułkowski 2012, p. 51; Kawalec 2017, p. 22). The following premises were adopted:

- Lean Culture is monolithic at the level of a theoretical framework (it is a harmonised, consistent and coherent whole);
- Lean Culture provides university employees with a way of understanding and giving sense to events and symbols related to the implementation of a Lean Strategy;
- Lean Culture constitutes a basis for ensuring the permanence of continuous improvement;
- Lean Culture is the result of learning processes in the individual and organisational dimensions;
- Lean Culture in higher education is unique because its shape is influenced by the organisational culture of a particular university as well as the external and internal context of its functioning.

Taking into consideration the adopted ontological and epistemological premises and on the basis of the inductive approach, the author proposes the following definition of Lean Culture in higher education:

> Lean Culture in higher education is a harmonised, consistent and coherent model of behaviour which is the result of common learning in the process of organisational improvement based on the fundamental premises, system, and methods of Lean Management.

In the author's opinion, Lean Culture has an important universal and humanistic dimension because its centre is occupied by the human being. Referring to Schein's concept (2004), it is expressed through (behavioural, linguistic, tangible) artefacts, values and principles held by employees, as well as underlying assumptions based on such values and principles. Lean Culture manifests itself through employees' actions and behaviour, opinions, attitudes, held values and principles; the manner of shaping relations within teams between employees and superiors, language, customs, rituals, applied technical, organisational, and visual solutions.

Such a research attitude determined the adoption of a strategy based on mixed methods in the research on Lean Culture (Kawalec 2017; Creswell 2013, p. 37; Ott 1989, p. 103). It manifests itself in the applied qualitative research methods (categorised interview, in-depth interview, participatory or non-participatory open observation, analysis of documents made available by the surveyed universities, analysis of audio-visual materials). The qualitative material collected during interviews was transcribed by the author. Simultaneously with the transcribing process, the author was carrying out a preliminary analysis of the gathered material. Its objective was to detect regularities indicating theoretical explanations concerning dimensions in which Lean Culture in higher education manifested itself. Analysing the interviews, the author used the open coding process (Babbie 2013, p. 430; Creswell 2013, p. 202). Lean Culture was the key notion in the analysis of the content of the interviews. In the further analysis, important notions/aspects related to Lean Culture were identified. It happened during the data analysis process. They were referred to as codes. The codes corresponded to the dimensions of Lean Culture. The subsequent detailed analysis covered employees' actions and behaviour described in the conducted interviews and manifesting themselves in their opinions, attitudes, held values and principles, the manner of shaping relations in teams between employees and superiors as well as language, customs, rituals, technical, organisational, and visual solutions. On the basis of the analysis, the author divided the research material into separate parts corresponding to the previously established codes, i.e. dimensions of Lean Culture in higher education. The analysis of the data in the dimensions of Lean Culture allowed their further exploration and detection of its most important descriptors. Consequently, the author obtained a set of higher education specific descriptors describing the particular dimensions of Lean Culture. The application of many qualitative research methods allowed the triangulation of data sources. The author also used notes taken during observations conducted in the visited universities. This contributed to the creation of foundations for the coherent Lean Culture Model in higher education, which is presented at the end of this chapter. In order to ensure the accuracy, reliability, and credibility of the qualitative research results the author applied the following procedures as recommended in the literature (Creswell 2013; Kvale 2010; Babbie 2013; Charmaz 2009):

• Preparing an interview questionnaire in accordance with guidelines included in the literature, holding consultations with specialists and performing tests of the interview questionnaire.
• Preparing a full transcript of the interviews ensuring a comprehensive and detailed description.
• Creating codes in accordance with the coding principles (Creswell 2013, p. 202).
• Conducting the triangulation of data sources.
• Self-reflection and self-correction at all stages of the qualitative research.

The author wishes to emphasise that the conducted research did not include a comprehensive review of the organisational cultures of the selected universities; instead, it focused on the manifestations of organisational cultures connected with the implementation of the Lean concept. In the subsequent parts of the chapter, the author presents the results of her research on Lean Culture in higher education and the proposed Lean Culture Model. In each of the subsections the following structure of the argument was adopted: First of all the author presented the results of her research, strengthening them with selected anonymised quotations from the interviews. Each quotation was described by means of the following categories: the number of years' experience in implementing the Lean concept, the presently held position in the Lean system, the source of the first experience in Lean—a university, another organisation. In the next step, the author elaborated on the research results and conclusions from the review of the literature on the implementation of the Lean concept in manufacturing and service enterprises, as well as higher education institutions.

The chapter is closed with the author's original proposal of the Lean Culture Maturity Model in Higher Education (LCMMHE).

3.4   Lean Culture in Higher Education— The Results of the Author's Own Research

3.4.1 External Conditions for the Shaping of Lean Culture

The research conducted by the author allowed her to indicate the most important factors of the external context determining the effective implementation and maturity of Lean Culture in higher education. The factors listed below were selected the most often by the respondents and are supported by the decisive majority of interviews (the other factors are discussed in Chapter 2 and Part 3.2 of this chapter). They are the following (see Fig. 3.1):

- National culture.
- The dominant higher education model.
- Progress in the restructuring of the public sector and public organisations.
- The public perception of the concept of Lean Management.

These elements are discussed below.

National Culture

In the light of the conducted research, it is possible to notice that national culture, as well as organisational culture in higher education, influence the effectiveness of implementing the Lean concept. The respondents indicate that national culture can support or hinder the building of Lean Culture in higher education. For example, in the countries characterised by the evidence based approach to public policies, the implementation of changes in the higher education management system is believed to be more effective and efficient. However,

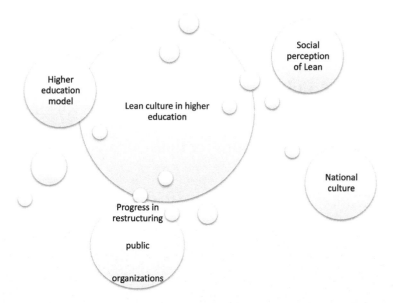

Fig. 3.1 The external context for the building of the maturity of Lean Culture in higher education—the results of the author's own research (the areas of the circles are proportional to the number of indications, and their distances from the central circle show the importance of the indicated factors) (*Source* The author's own work)

during the conducted interviews the decisive majority of the respondents were of the opinion that in view of the considerable and progressing internationalisation of universities and the standardisation of internal processes, national culture stops being of dominant importance. This proves that progressing globalisation is accompanied by institutional isomorphism, which was described in Chapter 2. What becomes more and more important is academic organisational culture through which the behaviour of organisation members can be influenced. This is supported by the following statements:

I think that the culture of the organization is the most important, and the leadership of the organization, they demand it. (A line manager, administration employee; participation in Lean projects; six years' experience in Lean, the first Lean experiences in HEI)

Maybe the culture of the workplace is more important than the culture of the nation. (A dedicated Lean position; an administration employee; participation in Lean projects; eight years' experience in Lean, the first Lean experiences in HEI)

An important role in the shaping of Lean Culture is played by culture manifested by individual employees (change leaders, Lean facilitators, organisational leaders). The conducted studies on the maturity of Lean Culture in higher education (the results are presented in Chapter 4) also appear to confirm the assumption that a university's organisational culture is more important. The criterion of a country of a university's origin did not diversify significantly the results of the assessment of Lean Culture maturity in the social dimension. A difference occurred in the process dimension of Lean Culture, which, in the author's opinion, may result from other factors such as a higher education model or progress in the process restructuring of public organisations in a given country.

The obtained results are partly concurrent with those achieved by other researchers. National culture manifests itself first of all at the level of fundamental premises for organisational culture (according to Schein's concept) (Parkes 2017, p. 640). There is no national culture (except for Japanese culture) which would fully support the implementation of the Lean Management concept (Pakdil and Leonard 2017; Erthal and Marques 2018; Parkes 2017). Therefore Lean Culture should be developed in such a way as to eliminate possible limitations resulting from national culture. What appears in this context is the notion of organisational culture management which is aimed at preventing an uncontrolled and spontaneous development of cultural processes (Sułkowski 2012, p. 253). In the process of adjusting to a national culture context, such key Lean Values as respect for people or the need for continuous improvement must not be sacrificed (Liker and Convis 2012, p. 48). Summarising her research results, the author concludes that national culture undoubtedly influences Lean Culture, but it is not a dominant factor determining the maturity of Lean Culture in higher education.

The Dominant Higher Education Model

A particular country's legal solutions consolidate a certain dominant model of higher education based on a collegial, bureaucratic, or enterprising culture (these issued were discussed in Chapter 1 and the first part of Chapter 2). However, attention should be drawn to the fact that higher education management models are usually specific hybrids comprising, to a smaller or larger extent, all three models referred to above. The following part describes these aspects of a higher education model that were mentioned the most often in the conducted research as those conditioning the process of building a Lean Culture. The content presented below was described on the basis of the following publications (Sowa 2009; Zeller 2011; Antonowicz 2015; Lacatus 2013; Davies 1995; Bonstingl 1995; Bugdol 2011; Magala 2006; Jóźwiak 1999; Kochalski 2011; Koj 1998; Kot 1996; Koźmiński 1999; Leja 2013; Kwiek 2010, 2015; McNay 1995; Rybkowski 2015; Woźnicki 2000).

In the collegial model, a university is governed by an academic oligarchy whose members are elected for a particular term of office from among members of the academic community according to the principle of *primus inter pares*. Decisions concerning university management are made individually on the basis of recommendations put forward by collegial bodies; in some cases, such recommendations are binding for the person holding a decision making position. Effectiveness and efficiency are measured in term of the achievement of the objectives of the academic oligarchy (the university is oriented first of all towards pursuing its own objectives). The university's functions, the necessity of cooperation among the collegial bodies with individuals holding managerial positions (e.g. between a faculty and a dean) as well as the considerable autonomy of organisational units (e.g. faculties) hinders the effective creation of organisational structures. The powers of the owner and the managing body are blurred and dispersed. The characteristic feature is a weak sense of organisational and financial responsibility for undertaken actions. From the perspective of building a Lean Culture, the elements of the collegial model of university management may constitute a serious barrier. The academic community may not be interested in changes in the status quo of the university management system and the lack of professionalisation in the area of management causes a situation in which proposals for changes may be misunderstood and rejected. The principle of rotation in office makes it difficult for people to perform the role of the leader and to maintain introduced changes (what appears is the syndrome of an electoral cycle, which is so significant in the world of politics). Because of collegiality, decision making processes are very long and require the approval of numerous bodies and teams whose changes made in proposed decisions can frequently distort their original character. This resembles critical comments targeted at participatory management. But in business organisations, they are perceived as beneficial for their development. Positions in collegial bodies are usually held by academics without professional preparation for managing a university. Stretching changes over long periods of time decreases employees' commitment and sense of initiative. The process of centralisation is hindered, there occur many overlapping actions and activities, it is difficult to reconcile different operational standards existing in different university organisational units. Furthermore, the course of processes may be very complicated. In complex organisational structures and processes there occur problems with assigning responsibility.

In the bureaucratic model, many areas of academic activities are under strict control of the state (e.g. tuitions, types of job positions, allocation of funds, salaries, teaching loads, forms of employment, minimum requirements applicable to teaching or research). Funds for activity are distributed mainly on the basis of algorithms which do not reflect the university's factual effectiveness and efficiency. Universities focus on ensuring their compliance with legal regulations and optimally adjusting to assessment and financing algorithms, even if it is not justified by their missions, objectives or the expectations of students, employees, etc. Legal regulations are often unadjusted to the specific character of academic activities (e.g. the public procurement law, the labour law, etc.). Additionally and for their own purposes, universities establish internal procedures whose objective is to ensure legal compliance. The algorithm-based distribution of funds frees decision makers from responsibility for where money is allocated, but simultaneously considerably limits their freedom to manage funds and follow their own financial management policies. The consequence is the appearance of a bureaucratic culture of audit and the lack of trust. The bureaucratic model generates many barriers to the building of a Lean Culture. The bureaucratisation of higher education is a huge source of wastage because considerable expenditures are incurred for activities which do not create any added value. The rigid operational framework of universities blocks or effectively hinders changes and, on the other hand, causes some kind of discouragement and apathy. It also constitutes an excuse and a line of defence against changes (this change cannot be implemented because it is prohibited by the law). There is no orientation towards the customer; students are treated like applicants in a public office and employees—like very small cogs in a huge machine.

The author is of the opinion that the principles of the Lean Management concept are the most compatible with the enterprising culture of a university. Its actions are oriented towards customers and meeting their expectations. This model, however, assumes the high flexibility and short-term nature of made decisions. This can be perceived as inconsistent with the unique character of higher education institutions and their didactic and research processes, as well as the social and culture-formative missions attributed to them. It should be noted that academic tradition, culture, and values constitute a part of a university's organisational identity and important elements ensuring the continuity of its functioning.

Therefore, implementing the Lean Management concept, decision makers should take into consideration the higher education model dominant in a given country because this is what determines the effectiveness of the implementation of required changes.

The research conducted by the author indicated also the universal features of higher education which can facilitate the building of a Lean Culture. They are as follows:

- Activities organised around didactic and research processes (a university is by nature a process organisation, which was discussed more broadly in Chapter 2).
- Common timeless and universal values and strong traditions which unite the academic community in pursuit of teaching and research excellence.

- Traditions of self-government, collegiality and team work.
- Traditional culture of cooperation and networking.
- Being a learning organisation oriented towards the creation and transmission of knowledge.
- Belief in science and scientific methods.
- Natural creation of matrix structures (assignment based on functions, processes or projects).
- Progressing centralisation of management forced by changes in legal regulations, implementation of computerised management systems or necessity to reduce operating costs.
- Progressing internationalisation which forces standardisation.
- Still dominating permanence of employment, low employee turnover, particularly in the university administration.
- Highly qualified employees.

The research results discussed above broaden the existing knowledge of the subject. So far researchers dealing with the issue of implementing Lean Management and other process management concepts have not studied the conditions for the implementation of this concept in a systematised way and from the perspective of higher education organisational models.

Progress in Restructuring Public Organisations

Progress in restructuring the public administration is an important factor which can influence success in the building of a Lean Culture. In many cases, the implementation of Lean Management in higher education institutions was inspired by changes introduced in other public organisations such as hospitals or public administration offices. This is also confirmed by the research conducted by Stoller (2015) (www1).

The Public Perception of the Concept of Lean Management

The conducted research shows that the implementation of Lean Management can trigger negative emotions. In many countries, Lean is associated with a radical organisational change whose visible consequence is the restructuring of employment and dismissals. This is supported by the following statement:

> *But it really worries me because there are a lot of people I work with, even here in the campus, who think that lean means that jobs will be lost. So we're trying now to use words which don't scare people, it's probably problematic.* (A Lean Leader, line manager, administration employee; sixteen years' experience in Lean projects; first experiences in the manufacturing sector)

Such a social perception of Lean Management results in a situation where the use of the name of the concept to refer to various initiatives, programmes or other undertakings causes negative reactions in university employees. The awareness of many people has developed a stereotypical and negative understanding of the concept. This constitutes a serious problem in the process of implementing the Lean concept in higher education, first of all in the psychological and social spheres (the dimensions of the Lean Language are described further in Chapter 3). Thus the conducted research indicates that many universities avoid using the word "Lean", replacing it with such phrases as "continuous improvement", "business improvement", etc. In the countries where such negative connections do not occur, Lean Management is perceived more favourably. The Lean concept is associated with the elimination of wastage. It should be noted that some university stakeholders, e.g. students or business partners, look forward to such changes, perceiving them very positively. For example, students of management sciences expect their universities to apply solutions that are studied in class.

As discussed above, the factors of the external context may influence the effectiveness of the building of a Lean Culture in higher education. They may exert a particularly strong impact on its invisible elements located, as it were, under the surface of an organisation. They play an important role in the shaping of attitudes, relations and functioning of a whole organisation (Schein 2004, p. 8).

3.4.2 Elements of a Lean Culture in Higher Education

On examining the external conditions for the maturity of a Lean Culture, the author carried out a qualitative analysis of the collected research materials. The objective was to identify the universal dimensions of a Lean Culture in higher education. The author used the elements of the methodology defined in the grounded theory. For this purpose, the author placed the transcripts of all interviews in one text file which was then entered in the Open Code programme used to conduct qualitative analyses of texts. According to the recommendations formulated by Charmaz (2009, p. 63), the first stage of the process was preliminary coding. The analysis covered more than 16,500 verses. The interviews were analysed verse by verse and subsequently assigned preliminary codes based on data (adhering to data) whose character is by definition temporary and comparative (Charmaz 2009, p. 64). The preliminary codes were used to divide the data according to categories and to identify processes occurring among them. The coding method has an emergent character. The application of the method detected 189 preliminary codes. In the next stage, the author went on to concentrated coding. For this purpose, the text was searched by means of the preliminary codes. The effect was a summary list showing the frequency of the appearance of the preliminary codes in the text. A fragment of the list is presented in Fig. 3.2.

An analysis of the frequency of the occurrence of the preliminary codes carried out by means of a word cloud confirmed that Lean Culture was deeply humanistic as its centre is occupied by man. It is also a process culture. The results of the analysis are presented in Fig. 3.3.

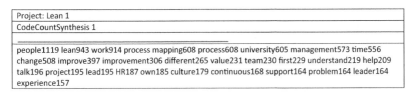

| Project: Lean 1 |
| CodeCountSynthesis 1 |

people1119 lean943 work914 process mapping608 process608 university605 management573 time556 change508 improve397 improvement306 different265 value231 team230 first229 understand219 help209 talk196 project195 lead195 HR187 own185 culture179 continuous168 support164 problem164 leader164 experience157

Fig. 3.2 A summary list of the preliminary codes (*Source* The author's own work)

Fig. 3.3 Lean Culture in higher education—a cloud of words associated with the Lean Management (*Source* The author's own work)

In the next step, using the focused coding of categories, the author divided the preliminary codes into more aggregated categories. Taking into consideration the accepted paradigm of the research on Lean Culture, the author adopted two code grouping criteria.

The purpose of the first criterion was to present Lean Culture on the basis of the relational definition of organisational culture referring to the interpretative-symbolic paradigm. The author followed the research recommendation formulated by Bogdan and Biklen (Creswell 2013, p. 203). The codes were divided into the following four groups: codes of actions, codes of emotions, attitudes and ways of thinking, codes of processes and phenomena, and codes of persons and social structures.

people, university, management, team, HR, leader, student, academic, customer, manager, admin, universities, role, structure, senior, higher education, director, leadership, facilitator, expert, professional, improvement unit, senior management, provost, head of, worker, chancellor, sponsor, workers, hierarchy, line manager, top management, hr department, supporter, member of staff, provider, human resources department, facilitator

work, process mapping, improve, understand, help, talk, lead, ask, job, learn, question, implement, looking, training, measure, involve, win, research, develop, challenge, answer, resist, plan, engage, aware, clear, asking, review, achieve, force, teaching, solve, sustain, control, afraid, empower, empower, collaboration, progress , coaching, assess, measuring, activity, empowering, questioning, mentoring,

value, first, own, support, problem, experience, effect, open, positive, resistance, effective, opportunities, opportunity, cannot, result, respect, questions, benefits, excited, language, efficiency, easier, trust, sense, obvious, freedom, trained, challenging, efficiently, inspired, exciting, quickly, inspiration, frustration, suspicious, limited, responsibility, common sense, directly, lack of, frustrating, experienced, good idea, clarity, new thing, day-to-day, new idea, small wins, typical day, awesome

Codes of actions

Codes of people and social structures

Codes of emotions, attitudes, ways of thinking

LEAN CULTURE

Codes of processes and phenomena

Lean, process, time, change, improvement, different, project, culture, continuous, tool, changes, success, waste, resource, meeting, map, environment, resources, across, barrier, workshop, principles, session, bottom, manufacturing, cost, excellence, differently, techniques, beginning, production, goals, risk, communication, task, outcome, flow, evidence, bureaucracy, enable, target, top-down, bottom-up, visible, interview, value added, system,

Fig. 3.4 Lean Culture from the perspective of the interpretative-symbolic paradigm (*Source* The author's own work)

Figure 3.4 includes codes divided into the proposed categories and within each category, codes are arranged according to the frequency of occurrence.

The analysis allowed the author to identify the codes through which it is possible to describe the fundamental and invisible premises of a Lean Culture. In the author's opinion, these codes include awareness, resistance, coercion, fears, sense of ownership, inability, trust, freedom, frustration, suspicion, common sense, wisdom, commitment, understanding, etc. The codes such as resistance, coercion, fear, sense of ownership, inability, frustration, and suspicion are not compatible with the premises of the Lean Management concept. Changing these codes is the most important because they constitute the most permanent element of organisational culture conditions by the external factors described above and a university's organisational culture. During the analysis of the interviews so-called in vivo codes were revealed. They are generally known terms hiding condensed but important meanings (Charmaz 2009, p. 76). Examples of such terms include "small wins", "make a difference", "true north". According to the research participants, "small wins" meant introducing changes in small steps, through small successes. "Make a difference" was understood as introducing a change which would have a real and permanent influence on work. "True north" meant a university's most important goals related to its pursuit of excellence.

The other criterion for the division of the codes was defined by the author from the perspective of the adopted functionalist paradigm, in which it was assumed that Lean Culture could be intentionally shaped by leaders in higher education institutions. The definition of the other grouping criterion was based on the conducted review of the literature on the subject, the results of the author's own research, as well as her experience. The codes were divided into the following seven categories: people (the code 'people'—1119 indications, the first place in the code list), the Lean Management principles—the process approach (the code "process, process mapping"—608 indications, the fourth place in the code list), leadership (the code "management"—573 indications, the seventh place in the code list), Lean Values (the code "lean values"—231 indications, the thirteenth place in the code list), team work and relations (the code "team"—230 indications, the fourteenth place in the code list) (the code occurrence frequencies are presented in Fig. 3.2), artefacts and relations with the environment. The particular code categories were used by the author to determine the dimensions of Lean Culture. A model of Lean Culture is presented in Fig. 3.5.

The dimensions of Lean Culture cannot be considered individually or separately because they are very strongly connected, thus creating a systemic, comprehensive and holistic approach towards the implementation of the Lean Management concept. In each of the dimensions, the research revealed descriptors specific for higher education which make it possible to understand their essence from the point of view of higher education.

In the subsequent part, the author presents the results of her research on the aforementioned dimensions.

Fig. 3.5 Lean Culture from the perspective of the functionalist paradigm (*Source* The author's own work)

3.4.3 Lean Values in Higher Education

The conducted research shows that Lean Culture in higher education is based on many strongly interrelated organisational values. Therefore, it is possible to talk about a certain system of Lean Values. The literature on the subject indicates respect for people and continuous improvement as the main values of Lean Culture (cf. Balzer 2010; Emiliani 2015). Using a word cloud as a tool, the author analysed the most frequently occurring words-codes in the category of value (Fig. 3.6).

The performed analysis allows a better understanding of the interpretation and perception of such values as respect for people and continuous improvement in the higher education environment. These values are expressed through other descriptors of Lean Culture such as change, understanding, openness to change, posing questions, identifying

Fig. 3.6 Lean Management values in higher education—a cloud of words associated with the value (*Source* The author's own work)

wastage, challenges, successes, common sense, trust, permanence, continuity, and wisdom. Below, the author presents how Lean Values are interrelated and understood within the context of higher education.

Respect for people is a fundamental Lean Culture value. It is discussed and interpreted in many dimensions in universities. This is supported by the following statements:

> (…) *respect for people is that we as a university, and especially the leaders, need to acknowledge that it's actually the employees who have the knowledge, the understanding and the power to change the things we are doing.* (A dedicated Lean position; an administration employee; participation in Lean projects; eight years' experience in Lean, the first Lean experiences in HEI)

The conducted research shows that it is defined and understood through such values as trust, a right to question, freedom of choice, safety, obligation, responsibility, cooperation, honesty, listening, understanding, and empathy. These values constitute a foundation for building relations among employees and superiors in an organisation.

Trust is of fundamental importance for the building of a Lean Culture. The research results indicate that trust is understood multidimensionally in universities, for example:

- trust built by top management on a top-down basis (management legitimises changes through received support),
- trust in employees with respect to changes under implementation (not every small change has to undergo a long acceptance procedure; trust manifests itself in delegation of authority and empowerment),
- trust and belief in people's good intentions,
- trust in line managers.

It is emphasised that Lean Management builds trust also through the transparency of processes and actions.

According to the interviewees, trust plays the key role in the building of relations between a leader and employees. If there is no trust, improvement is reduced to looking for a person to blame and shifting responsibility onto others. A method of building trust is joint work of employees and leaders (e.g. during workshops on improvements) and leaders' being familiar with their employees' problems due to regular contacts with employees in places where they perform work (from Japanese *gemba*). Trust is the essence of Lean Culture. It allows an organisation to adjust better to changes and to implement changes faster by minimising employees' resistance. According to the interviewees, trust is based on such values as transparency, responsibility, honesty, and safety.

The environment of Lean Management is characterised by a high level of transparency because the process approach allows an open disclosure of existing problems. A transparent presentation of a university's activities related to the expenditures-processes-effects system, identification, and allocation of scopes of responsibility and authority build trust in higher education management. It is an honest attitude towards employees and customers (students, employees, financing or sponsoring agencies, other entities). Transparency is connected with accountability understood as the ability to present the effects of undertaken restructuring actions by means of available quantitative and qualitative metrics.

Responsibility is another important dimension of trust. Lean Culture is based on the responsibility of leaders and employees. The pursuit of excellence is possible only where employees feel personally responsible for the functioning and improvement of processes. They can see clearly their objectives, made mistakes and their causes. The leader's responsibility is understood, on the one hand, as the necessity to be close to employees and to understand their problems (gemba). On the other hand, such responsibility entails the necessity to create space for making autonomous decisions (empowerment).

Another dimension of trust is honesty. It is understood as honesty towards external and internal customers, the ability to keep promises, to listen to and respond to customers' requirements and expectations. Emphasis is also put on another dimension of trust. Courage to provide information on existing problems is also an expression of honesty on the part of leaders and employees.

Trust was also interpreted by the interviewees as safety. Safety refers to both safety of the workplace and safety in expressing views and opinions or criticising generally accepted and ineffective ways of doing things (questioning). Employees should not be afraid to ask questions or express their opinions. For this purpose, it is important to create proper space based on trust and support.

Respect is also built in higher education on the basis of understanding. Understanding in an organisation takes place through the understanding of processes, people, systems, structures, culture, etc. Lean Management requires an in-depth reflection on a university's activities and the provision of answers to the following questions: What do we do? How do we do it? Why do we do it? When do we do it? Where do we do it? Who does it? etc. If this value is achieved, we move away from the unconscious management of higher education towards conscious actions based on a deep understanding of an organisation's functioning. Another dimension of this value is understanding through visualisation. Pictures, maps, tables, etc. allow people to overcome their psychological and perceptual limitations. On the one hand, they facilitate creativity and, on the other hand, they allow a thorough analysis and understanding of the essence of problems occurring in higher education.

Respect also manifests itself in the freedom of choice. A change in employees' attitudes is possible mainly through their voluntary participation in training courses, workshops and restructuring projects. The author's research conducted in universities shows that encouragement is a much better method of achieving employees' commitment; it is also true about promoting and emphasising the usefulness of the Lean Management concept in solving everyday problems related to process management. The research revealed also the principle of asking for help, which is an expression of understanding that Lean Management is a correct approach to problem solving. During meetings or project workshops everybody has the opportunity to demonstrate their knowledge and skills, and to be appreciated, which is an important factor in making people involved in the process of continuous change.

Respect and trust are conditions for building another Lean Culture value—Lean Value cooperation. It is understood multidimensionally, and first of all as sharing knowledge, helping other employees in solving their everyday work problems, providing assistance in the good and satisfactory performance of duties. Cooperation aimed at work processes improvement is consistent with human nature.

The other axis around which Lean Culture is built is improvement. In the light of the research results, it is visible that improvement is understood multidimensionally as continuous betterment and a permanent culture of everyday work. In the opinion of the interviewees, the value of improvement is based on openness to change, flexibility, being proactive, common sense, fact-based decision making, eliminating wastage and creating value, wisdom as well as permanence and continuity of change.

Lean Management provides for an evolutionary approach to changing a university's organisational culture. Such changes should have a rolling character. According to the Kaizen concept, they should be implemented through small projects, activities, and undertakings. The positive aspect of this approach is adjusting the pace of changes to the process of employees' learning and the easiness of performing improvement actions. The research participants stressed that it constituted

an additional element increasing employees' involvement. It stimulates employees' energy, enthusiasm and passion for changes and work
because effects become visible relatively quickly (sometimes during the
course of a one-day session).

Flexibility is understood as the ability to adapt. It becomes a value
in the changing environment in which universities function. Its success
does not depend on possessed tangible resources, but on the ability to
create and use knowledge. Flexibility requires that employees at every
level of an organisation have deep knowledge of processes, are able to
notice approaching changes, and react to them accordingly. Therefore,
they have to be continually trained, encouraged to think, and empow-
ered to implement changes. Being proactive is strongly connected with
flexibility. It is understood as the ability to foresee approaching changes
as well as to prevent problems and errors in the future.

Many respondents emphasised that Lean Management was a common sense concept. And this does not concern only the sphere of the
economisation of activities (considering them only through the prism
of the metrics of effectiveness and efficiency). The results of the conducted research indicate that common sense is understood first of all as
behaviour consistent with human nature. People tend to forget, therefore restoring order in an organisation is an opportunity to create a
well-organised workplace which inspires. Common sense is also making
decisions on the basis of facts and data analysis.

During the course of improvement processes, a university acquires
knowledge and learns. The effect of this is the creation of another value
to which the respondents referred to as wisdom. Wisdom is connected
with reflection, the necessity to check regularly whether work could
not be performed better. Lean Management shows that despite a mass
of things to take care of and the quick pace of life, it is necessary to
slow down and spend some time on reflection. Reflection is of essential
importance. It is used to recover time which has been previously wasted.

Hence, the elimination of wastage is an important dimension of
improvement. The key to defining wastage is the notion of value
(not always identical with economic values, which was discussed in
Chapter 2). The conducted interviews revealed a phenomenon which
the author referred to as "adding value through ineffectiveness". At the

level of a university, a conflict may occur between value understood through the prism of economic metrics and value understood through the prism of a university's mission. In some situations, the creation of value is associated with undertaking actions which, from the economic or technical-organisational point of view, are ineffective or are categorised as wastage. The author's research shows a few examples of such situations: a student expects consultations with a lecturer to last as long as it is necessary for them to understand a particular problem (in this case, time is not a measure of value; value is measured by the fulfilment of the student's expectations).

The respondents were also asked about their perception of the relations between the Lean Values and the value traditionally associated with higher education. These relations are fully presented in the following statement:

> *Yes it's kind of creating new values, like open communication, working together, more respect for people. And the whole idea of continuous improvement, we cannot keep the old processes for millions of years. I think that traditional academic values are striving for excellence, to be the world leader in research, to be the best in teaching, the best in everything. I think that it's important to have a benefit of working together, of communication, common language, culture, current state mapping, continuous improvement, end of wastage. When you're talking a common language, people understand the words and expressions in the same way.* (Lean Management Department Director, administration, twelve years' experience, first experiences in HEI)

The analysis conducted above allows the author to conclude that the catalogue of Lean Values in higher education should be extended. The values such as respect for people and continuous improvement should be accompanied by others, for example, understanding, questioning, proactivity, and trust. Using Krzyżanowski's definition of value, it is possible to regard the aforementioned categories as Lean Culture values because they are considered as positive and desirable; they are the product of feelings and convictions based on people's beliefs and observations (Krzyżanowski 1997, p. 143). They constitute an interpretation of reality and with time determine people's behaviour and way of being. Using Bugdol's work, it is possible to state that the Lean Values proposed above can be also described as organisational values because they are rooted in (Bugdol 2006): relations among people, organisational culture (ways of operating, styles of management, missions, etc.), as well as generally accepted value end ethical systems. The literature on the subject presents the current discussion on the role of values in organisational culture. Schein (2004), Cameron and Quinn (2015), and Hofstede et al. (2011) draw attention to their considerable importance. Cardona and Rey emphasise that it is impossible to build unity in an organisation without a common mission and common values going beyond purely economic effectiveness (Cardona and Rey 2009, p. 30).

Organisational values evolve and change with time. Therefore, a notion of key values appears in the literature (Cardona and Rey 2009, p. 85). In the context of the Toyota management philosophy, Liker regards the following as key values: a spirit of challenge, the Kaizen mind, *genchi genbutsu* (a philosophy of deep respect for an organisation's activities which creates added value), team work, and respect (Liker and Meier 2005). What is emphasised is a certain dualism or even an internal contradiction in understanding the basic Lean Values such as, for example, respect for people and continuous pursuit of excellence (Pakdil and Leonard 2017). Standardisation of work as a tool for improvement may simultaneously cause employees' resistance, demotivate them and restrict their creativity. The author may also use another example of contradiction, i.e. the relation between trust and continuous questioning. Asking questions the whole time may be perceived as an expression of a lack of trust. The conducted research allows also the author to ask the question about the relation between Lean Values and organisational values specified in a university's culture. The division proposed by Lencioni may be used to show such relations (Lencioni 2002; Jashapara 2006). The author divided organisational values into four categories: fundamental values, desirable values, required values, and accidental values. In higher education, fundamental values reflect tradition and academic principles. These are values such as the master–disciple relation, truth, knowledge, autonomy, independence, freedom, transnationality, and communitarianism. In the author's opinion, Lean Culture will certainly strengthen such values as the master-disciple relation, transferring it also to the sphere of administration (e.g. the use of the kata technique, learning through practice), pursuit of the truth by posing questions, knowledge as information acquired by learning in the process of continuous improvement, transnationality through building external relations (e.g. in communities of practitioners), communitarianism as a dimension of team work. The research shows that tensions appear between Lean Values and such values as autonomy and independence. In the author's opinion, it usually results from the improper understanding of these notions. Autonomy and independence are notions which constitute the research process, provide researchers with freedom to choose research subjects and methods as well as to decide about themselves within this process. These notions are not attributed to administration processes whose essence is characterised by standardisation and repeatability. Desirable values are values which a university will need to build and develop Lean Culture. None of the Lean Values defined above such as respect for people, continuous improvement, understanding, questioning, proactivity or trust are foreign to higher education organisational culture. They will be strengthened. Required values are defined as minimum standards with respect to attitudes and behaviour applicable to employees and determined by the Lean Management principles. As it has already been emphasised many times, the Lean Management concept is consistent with human nature and common sense. From the point of view of employees, changes in organisational values will certainly not cause considerable tension. Tension may, however, occur between Lean Values and principles on the one side and a collegial, bureaucratic and to some extent enterprising culture of higher education (which has already been described above). The last category comprises accidental values. Such values may appear spontaneously with the passing time. They constitute a reflection of a commonality of interests or similarities among employees' personalities. Their character may be positive, for example, better cooperation among university employees or higher work culture, or negative, for example, a lack of trust in management. The author knows that there are many classifications of organisational values and is fully aware that the above description does not exhaust all those referred to in the literature and theories.

Summing up, the author would like to emphasise that if the higher education organisational culture is to change towards Lean Culture, this will require changes in the values on which universities' functioning is based. The knowledge of contradictions and tensions among values is important for the conscious building of a mature Lean Culture. Lean Values should eventually become integral elements of a university employee's individual culture.

3.4.4 The Principles of Lean Management—The Process Approach Oriented Towards Creating Value

The Lean Principles and process approach were discussed extensively in Chapter 2. Although their character is organisational and technical, they play an important role in the building of a mature Lean Culture. They exert influence on attitudes, behaviour, and culture of everyday work connected with managing organisations focused on creating value by eliminating wastage. The analysis of codes based on the use of a word cloud showed through which notions and meanings these principles were understood in higher education. The results of the analysis are presented in Fig. 3.7.

The most important notions associated with the principles of Lean Management include the following: work, process mapping, process, time, continuous improvement, value, project, ownership, problem, student, business as usual, implementation, effect, and tools. A code meaning analysis shows that the implementation of the Lean Management principles is associated with the essence of the process approach. The central items are value determined by a customer-student and time. This is connected with obtaining a thorough knowledge of higher education processes by means of various tools, and particularly process mapping.

Work on processes has the character of a project. The principles of Lean Management constitute an integral part of the operational excellence of higher education and employees' everyday work targeted at solving problems. What appears in the analysis is a code concerning ownership. In most cases, it means independence, one's own area of

Fig. 3.7 The principles of Lean Management in higher education—a cloud of words associated with the Lean Principles (*Source* The author's own work)

activities, way of working, motivation, language, initiative, and creativeness. Thus it can be concluded that employees independently and for their own needs interpret the concept of Lean Management and its principles. They create *"their own lean journey"*. It can be interpreted as a manifestation/expression of autonomy and independence in the area of their own activities.

Below, the author analyses the results of her own research. The Lean Principles and the process approach in Lean Culture are presented in light of the respondents' statements. Attention is focused on the manner of defining, understanding and interpreting these principles as the descriptors of Lean Culture.

According to the first principle of Lean Management, it is necessary to establish precisely the value of a particular product. Such value should be defined from the point of view of all (internal and external) customers of a higher education institution. This principle means that an employee should know the expectations and requirements of the recipient (internal and external customers) of the effects of their work. The respondents' statements indicate a certain practice in the functioning of universities. According to them, university employees often know what they do, but they do not know why they do it or what value is delivered to their customers. Knowledge of processes cannot be restricted, exclusive or available to the chosen few. Work performed by an employee within a process should be sensible and valuable for end users/customers (employees, students, etc.). Continually asking the question about value and what it means for the process customer allows a reduction in the number of actions performed within a given process.

Another Lean Management principle is identifying a value stream for every product. This principle is defined as identifying a flow of value within a process from the perspective of a customer or, more broadly, an internal or external stakeholder. For university employees, it means first of all understanding in what way a particular conducted process contributes to the achievement of the university's objectives and how it is connected with the other key processes of the institution. This principle refers also to the adequacy of resources necessary for process execution (information, material, equipment, software, etc.). The employee is familiar with the correct manner of process execution and knows its particular stages and actions. An important element of implementing this principle is the possession of necessary documentation (instructions, procedures, regulations, guidelines, etc.). It should be useful, relevant, simple, understandable, and easily available. The respondents draw attention to the fact that the number of documents in a process should be reduced to the necessary minimum. They also emphasise the need to define risks in processes.

Ensuring an undisturbed flow and eliminating sources of wastage constitute another Lean Management principle. A condition for its implementation is process reorganisation based on employees' bottom-up creativity and commitment as well as management's competences and involvement. The respondents' statements and conducted observations indicate the dimensions of this principle. First of all, it is reducing the volume of data, information, documents, etc. which are useless and redundant. Another dimension is the right to interrupt process execution if problems appear which could result in errors (andon). A very important aspect is good communication during process execution among employees in a given organisational unit and among departments. The respondents also drew attention to the need for the ongoing identification of the sources of wastage and undertaking corrective actions aimed at their elimination. At the same time it was emphasised that even if an employee is aware of problems, they may refrain from taking any action. The reasons for such situations include a lack of authority or the existence of various social, communication or psychological barriers. The interviewees also raised issues related to risks and the proper handling of risks. Employees should know what actions they can take when a particular risk occurs. The author would like to note that pursuant to the ISO 9001 standard, employees may adopt one of the following three strategies: to accept a risk, to avoid it or to minimise it.

Another important principle of Lean Management is that of creating value when it is expected by the customer. It means the necessity of making processes free from any disturbances or downtime and performing only actions required by the customer (a pull system). The interviewees drew attention to issues related to ensuring a uniform workload, refraining from performing certain actions in advance, and performing actions without unnecessary delays.

The last principle is continuous improvement. It is understood as unending betterment through the commitment of a university's employees and management. In the respondents' statements, it is understood as monitoring errors on a regular basis, analysing data on processes in order to make relevant decisions concerning improvement. They also draw attention to the necessity to connect actions oriented towards improvement with the factual requirements and expectations of customers—process users.

In the conducted analysis, the respondents frequently emphasised the role of higher education management and leader in the process of creating a Lean Culture. The author presents the results of the research in this area in the next part.

3.4.5 Lean Leadership in Higher Education Institutions

Issues related to Lean leadership featured prominently in the interviews conducted in the selected higher education institutions. The respondents interpreted the role of Lean leadership and Lean leaders in the light of their own experiences. This allowed an analysis of Lean Culture at the levels of its visible elements, deeply hidden assumptions, and resultant contradictions. The author again analysed the content of the interviews, using a word cloud as a research tool. In the analysis, she distinguished codes which were assigned to the dimension of leadership. The results of the analysis are presented in Fig. 3.8.

Fig. 3.8 Lean leadership in higher education—a cloud of words associated with Lean leadership (*Source* The author's own work)

The analysis of the frequency with which the codes appeared indicate the way of interpreting and understanding the functions of leaders in the implementation of Lean Management in higher education institutions. The most frequently occurring words are the following: help, lead, culture, leader, support, manager, understanding, meeting, structure, respect, engage, HR (human resources). First of all, leaders were assigned roles with respect to broadly defined support. This is proved by such words as help, leadership, support, understanding, commitment. Their role also has a culture-formative character. Their attitude should be characterised by respect for people. Also the code of meeting appears quite frequently. The author noticed a certain dichotomy in the respondents' approach to meetings; on the one hand, they are associated with the necessity to hold regular meetings, but on the other hand, meetings are perceived as a source of wastage (*It's a waste of time, I tend to avoid them, committee meetings sometimes don't even reach the decision making point*). Another important code revealed in the analysis is that of structure. On the one hand, it has positive connotations with supporting structures, but on the other hand, it reflects the specific character of higher education institutions and is perceived as a barrier in the context of a social hierarchy and extended organisational structures. Associations with HR are connected with the fact that HR departments frequently participate in the implementation of the concept of Lean Management.

Below the author analyses in detail the research results in the dimension of Lean leadership divided into the issues related to top management and those related to immediate superiors. Such a division appeared clearly in the research. The final part of this section is a discussion aimed at placing the obtained results in the context of the previous researches conducted in this area.

3.4.5.1 Top Management in a Higher Education Institution

The analysis of the content of the interviews revealed the most important descriptors of Lean Culture determining the tasks of top management in the process of building a mature Lean Culture. They are as follows:

- Understanding the need to change a university's organisational culture.
- Initiating and implementing a Lean strategy.
- Ensuring support for the Lean programme and people running it.
- Ensuring support for employees in the cultural and social dimensions.
- Ensuring support for employees in the technical and organisational dimensions.

Understanding the Need to Change a University's Organisaional Culture

The research showed that one of the major barriers to the implementation of the concept of Lean Management in higher education was not so much a lack of understanding of the need for changes as rather its incompetent implementation. Some universities continue to make attempts to solve new problems by means of old and traditional methods which turn out to be inadequate and ineffective. The interviewees confirmed that the implementation of Lean Management meant, first of all, a change in leadership. This is supported by the following statements:

> So that's really a 180 degree change, from thinking that this is about the employees and the money, to thinking that it's mainly about leadership. This is the biggest change. (A dedicated Lean position; an administration employee; participation in Lean projects; eight years' experience in Lean, the first Lean experiences in HEI)

Visiting the higher education institutions which had selected the Lean Management concept as a method of introducing changes, the author was able to sense in the interviews a deep understanding of the need for change and the adequacy of this concept for change in higher education institutions. This is supported by the following statements:

I think it's a natural tool for change, and if we get the senior leaders on board, absolutely, because we're showing cost-saving, efficiency effects, we're showing cost avoidance, we can prove that the work which is done is a result of these tools. (A Lean Leader, line manager, administration employee; sixteen years' experience in Lean projects; first experiences in the manufacturing sector)

The understanding of the need of change manifested itself first of all through permanent and open support for a Lean programme. It legitimised changes and built trust in them among employees. Such support was usually expressed in an official and formal opening of a programme (an internal order of top management, an academic conference, a newsletter, etc.). This is supported by the following statement:

Probably there was a kick-off in 2012, in August, when the University Director stood up in front of all the leaders at the University and said that we were going to work with this. (An administration employee, dedicated Lean position; participation in Lean projects; eight years' experience in Lean, the first Lean experiences in HEI)

An important activity was also building formal and permanent organisational structures making up a Lean Management system (dedicated positions, teams, departments). Top management supported also change programmes through participation in seminars and conferences. Informal support was expressed through public or private words of recognition and open communication. The respondents emphasised the importance of such behaviour. Through open, active and public support, top management builds employees' trust in the concept of continuous improvement of a higher education institution. The importance of this attitude is confirmed by the following statement:

You need a leadership senior's willingness to support this to allow this process to unfold. (A senior manager; participation in Lean projects; fifteen years' experience; the first experiences connected with writing a master's thesis)

Another issue in this area raised in the research was top management's understanding of the nature of implemented changes. The respondents noted that top management should be patient and understand that changes in people's attitudes and behaviour as well as in organisational culture were rather slow. It is a long-term task as opposed to organisational and technical changes which can be carried out in a relatively short period of time. In the interviews, the magical number of 10 years often appeared; based on previous experience, it is the expected duration necessary for changes in organisational culture to become effective and permanent. The need to be patient is confirmed by the following statement:

> *And this is also about culture, so it takes time, even though you give a leader a course in Lean Management, it would take time for them to change their own behaviour. I think it does have a potential, but it takes some time.* (An administration employee, dedicated Lean position; participation in Lean projects; eight years' experience in Lean, the first Lean experiences in HEI)

The respondents frequently referred to the necessity of following the principle of "zero exceptions" by top management. Experiences showed that this made it possible to reduce resistance among other representatives of top management who were not involved in a Lean programme, middle-level managers, academics, and administration employees. Tensions which occur in this respect in higher education institutions are confirmed by the following statement:

> *I think that the university culture is hard because of that… academic freedom. That's why I've talked about courage leadership they need to really define what academic freedom is. What are your rights as a faculty member, what are your obligation as an employee, two different things. Because faculty don't like to be called employees.* (A line manager; participation in Lean projects; six years' experience in Lean, the first Lean experiences in HEI)

Initiating and Implementing a Lean Strategy

In this area, the conducted research revealed two important issues: the need to connect a Lean strategy with a university's vision and mission and the importance of a holistic approach to implemented changes.

The respondents indicated that the important task of top management was coordination of activities conducted within the scope of a Lean strategy by skilfully combining top-down and bottom-up approaches. They also frequently referred to the problem of overlapping restructuring activities, e.g. establishing various teams to deal with the same or similar problems in the same functional areas of the university. Top management is expected to ensure that improvements in processes will be purposeful and sensible, related to the university's mission and vision, as well as coherent and mutually supplementary.

Ensuring Support for the Lean Programme and People Running It

Another problem indicated by the respondents responsible for change implementation was too little attention paid to them by top management. They perceived this as a lack of support. Such a situation constituted a huge challenge for them; in some circumstances, it was also a barrier to implementing the Lean Management concept and building a proper work culture. The occurrence of such situations is confirmed by the following statement:

> *We have to have top leaders with us and they have to do it. It doesn't help if the top leader, let's say the Director of Art Faculties, says: "Okay, you can do the Lean", but they themselves don't do it. I think we had bad experiences, but we had the experience that the top leaders told you: "Just do it, but if you are doing it, I just don't have to care".* (An administration employee; participation in Lean projects; six years' experience in Lean, the first Lean experiences in HEI)

It is important to treat employees seriously, to empower and motivate them, as well as to get them involved. It is expected that top management will actively support and promote managers and change leaders. This is supported by the following statement:

> *I think university leaders need to become more immersed in this. You've got people who are passionate about this and see the value, but that's not really*

enough. It's about the fragility of it, that we need to be a bit careful about.
(An academic, a CI/LM department manager, eighteen years' experience
in Lean, the first experiences in the manufacturing sector)

According to the respondents, the appointment of a representative of
top management responsible for the implementation of a Lean strategy
is an important factor determining success in the building of a Lean
Culture. In the described experiences, such persons had a deep understanding of the Lean Management concept and the idea of continuous
improvement. They also had specialist knowledge in Lean Management
(e.g. a Black Belt certificate) as well as experience in project execution.
Thanks to this, they could fulfil the function of both a mentor and an
intermediary between change leaders and the organisation's top management. They also acted as advocates and promoters of change. Each
of the surveyed universities had such an officer holding a top management position, e.g. deputy chancellor, member of the university board
or council. The need for such leaders is confirmed by the following
statement:

*We have a significant leadership gap in the way we manage. People who
are exceptional in their fields of expertise aren't necessarily good coaches,
good leaders, or good facilitators. And in the Lean environment we need
coaching, leading, and facilitating; we don't need expertise in particular
fields.* (A senior manager, participation in Lean projects, fifteen years'
experience, the first experiences connected with writing a master's
thesis)

Support in the Technical and Organisational Dimensions

Another important aspect of the activities of top management in the
process of building a mature Lean Culture is support for a programme
of change in the technical and organisational dimensions. Analysing the
research materials, the author identified the most important two dimensions of this type of support: communication and the decision making
process.

The respondents indicated that inappropriate communication was one of the barriers to the effective implementation of the Lean Management concept. They drew attention to the qualitative and quantitative dimensions of communication. In the quantitative sense, the problem was an excessive number of actions within the communication process, e.g. too many meetings, documents, or procedures. The communication process should be simplified and contain only indispensable actions and documents. In the quantitative sense, the respondents stressed problems with language (this will be discussed in the further part of the book), communication channels (especially along processes), and their openness. One of the raised problems was difficulties with reporting problems occurring within processes and with recommending preventive and corrective measures (particular universities did not have any, or had rather ineffective, reporting systems or systems handling employees' suggestions, etc.).

The research results show that one of the main sources of wastage is the process of making decisions in higher education institutions. Functioning (to a smaller or greater degree) in many universities, the collegial decision making process manifests itself in establishing numerous teams or committees, usually deprived of decision making powers. The decision making process is also often complicated by an extensive, multilevel organisational structure and a lack of an unambiguously established scope of a university's centralisation or decentralisation (a decision has to move through many management levels of the central and departmental administration units). This results in unwillingness to assume responsibility for made decisions and to put binding signatures on documents. In the respondents' opinion, it has a particularly negative impact on the attitude of lower level managers and regular employees towards changes. They expect quick effects of changes identified as necessary by teams and within projects. The long decision making process causes a decline in motivation, slows down the pace of implementing changes, and, in extreme cases, stops the introduction of changes. Therefore, it is expected that the process of making decisions concerning the implementation of changes will be quick, simple, and free from unnecessary steps.

3.4.5.2 Immediate Superiors

The research results indicate the important role of immediate superiors in the implementation of the Lean concept. What is important is their support, involvement, and belief in the concept. The respondents emphasised that they exerted direct influence on maintaining employees' enthusiasm and commitment. The support of immediate superiors was of particular importance at the beginning stage of Lean implementation. For the vast majority of employees, it was a new approach to work which generated a wide range of reactions from enthusiasm to deep fears. This is confirmed by the following statements:

> *So typically when I brought it there was a fear associated with this, what are you doing?, why are you doing this?, what are you changing? don't touch me, my staff.* (An administration employee, Lean leader, line manager; sixteen years' experience in Lean projects; first experiences in the manufacturing sector)

The research results allowed the author to define the most important descriptors of Lean Culture which determine the functions of immediate superiors. They were divided into technical-organisational functions and social functions, with the latter regarded as more important. It was emphasised that training and encouraging employees to accept changes made no sense if immediate superiors were not involved in the process. This is confirmed by the following statement of one of the leaders:

> *Because when you are a leader you know that collaborating is the best thing you can do. I collaborate a lot with other institutions, other departments. I ask people what works, what doesn't work, so it really increases my knowledge of relationships and collaboration. So it definitely causes change; my relationships are stronger.* (An administration employee, Lean leader, line manager; sixteen years' experience in Lean projects; first experiences in the manufacturing sector)

The interviewees draw attention that immediate superiors should not regard appearing problems as a basis for assessing and punishing employees. With respect to the social dimension, the respondents very broadly defined the role of immediate superiors in everyday work. They emphasised the following:

- The immediate superior should be a mentor and coach who motivates employees to change and gets them involved in the process of change; employees can always count on their superior's support in improvement activities.
- The immediate superior's relations with employees are open, deformalised, based on partnership, trust, and authority.
- The immediate superior discusses and formulates the objectives of changes to be implemented together with employees and does not exert pressure on employees in the course of such formulation (objectives and tasks result from an analysis of a situation, and not from the superior's personal priorities or ambitions).
- The immediate superior takes into consideration all proposals submitted by employees and regards them as important and valuable.
- The immediate superior treats mistakes made during the change implementation process as important experience which can be used in the future to prevent similar mistakes and learn from them. They focus on solving problems, and not on looking for somebody to blame.
- The immediate superior ensures that the effects of implemented improvement will be maintained.

The following statement confirms the necessity to build Lean leadership that serves others: *Well, I think that in Lean Management, the Lean leaders, they have to understand that they are not the ones that should decide how you should do your work. They should coach their employees on how to do their work best, encourage them to do work with changes and the improvements in the team* (an administration employee; participation in Lean projects; six years' experience in Lean, the first Lean experiences in HEI).

Another fragment of the interview is important for the description of managers' behaviour:

People started to enjoy coming together. It was energizing. The only problem was with managers, because it was difficult to find a place. Sometimes it was a room, but the sessions didn't go quite well, because they wanted to be in control. They put their priorities on top. People don't want to have managers in the same room. People want to do what they want and give feedback to managers. But, you know, managers worried all the time about what was going to happen. So initially, it was quite hard to get everybody to accept the whole process. (An administration employee, senior management; participation in Lean projects; twelve years' experience in Lean, the first Lean experiences in HEI)

In the technical-organisational dimension, superiors should support employees through the following:

- Understanding the specific character of processes and actions performed by employees (the superior is a direct observer of such processes and communicates with employees in their work environment—gemba).
- Being individually involved in diagnosing and solving problems in the places where they occur (decisions are not made "from behind a desk").
- Planning and organising work in such a way so as to ensure that employees have time for improvement activities (meetings, projects, training courses, etc.).

In the conducted research, the respondents stressed the necessity of strong involvement of middle-level, line, and operating managers in change programmes and the building of a Lean Culture. They should be responsible for improvement projects carried out in their organisational units. Individually or supported by a Lean expert, they should identify and solve problems in cooperation with employee teams. The necessity of understanding processes is proved by the following statement:

Sometimes people go to the line manager and say I have got a problem with that, but they don't understand the whole inconsistency of this process, the line manager, I think they feel that they don't listen, because the line manager doesn't truly understand the whole process. (An administration employee; participation in Lean projects; six years' experience in Lean, the first Lean experiences in HEI)

Superiors should also provide employees with opportunities to work in peace and combine participation in improvement projects with the fulfilment of their ongoing duties. The importance of such actions is confirmed by the following statement:

> *That the leaders need to create the space and the room for that. This is difficult. Where do we find the time for this?* (An administration employee, dedicated Lean position; participation in Lean projects; eight years' experience in Lean, the first Lean experiences in HEI)

The interviewees emphasised that a lack of support from immediate superiors who are not enthusiastic about the Lean concept as a method of change constituted a serious problem and barrier to Lean implementation in higher education. This can be noticed in the following statement:

> *I attended an improvement workshop and came back to work. I was really fired up, really motivated and excited about new things which could be done. And when your line manager isn't interested, that's not good.* (An administration employee; participation in Lean projects; three years' experience in Lean, the first Lean experiences in HEI)

The interviewees were able to explain such situations. Firstly, a particular process may have been a source of prestige in the organisation (the superior had specialist knowledge and competences which gave them power; the standardisation and disclosure of the process were perceived as a threat). Secondly, the process had been created by that superior, therefore they had a strong sense of attachment to the project and were not able to distance themselves from the changes which were being implemented. Thirdly, the superior was afraid of losing control of the process, the necessity of sharing their knowledge of the process and powers with other managers or employees (delegating authority, empowerment). The same as employees, line managers may have felt unprepared for changes and afraid of them. Hence the great importance of support provided by top management. This is supported by the following statements:

> *I would say that a leader should be supported, and very top leaders need to say this is important to the university and we need to look at this and put it into the values and strategies.* (A Lean Leader, line manager, administration employee; sixteen years' experience in Lean projects; first experiences in the manufacturing sector)

The conducted research shows that managers at all higher education management levels are expected to evolve away from their typical and traditional roles in administration management towards Lean leadership.

Issues related to the role of leaders in the building of a Lean Culture are discussed thoroughly in the literature on the subject (Liker and Convis 2012; Stoller 2015; Mann 2014; Liker 2005, Balzer 2010; Emiliani 2005, 2015; Yorkstone 2016; Antony 2014; Balzer et al. 2016; Lu et al. 2017). The research conducted by the author constitutes a contribution to this discussion.

The research results confirm that Lean leadership is different from conventional leadership and centralised administration management characteristic of higher education institutions (Emiliani 2015, p. 43) as well as visionary leadership based on the strong will of an individual and charismatic leader (Liker and Convis 2012, p. 176). In order to describe Lean leadership, the researchers use such notions as servant leadership, a new type of institutional leadership (Liker and Convis 2012, p. 166; Stoller 2015, p. 256; Lu et al. 2017), or value-added leadership (Emiliani 2015, p. 63). In the author's opinion, Lean leadership in higher education institutions is the closest to the ethos of service—Lean leaders create value only by serving their teams (the concept of servant leadership). Similar conclusions were reached by Emiliani (2015, p. 46). There are two aspects of the Lean leadership concept which manifest themselves strongly in the conducted research. On the one hand, it is a personal task consisting in the development and improvement of one's own skills; on the other hand, it involves leading others focused on building consent developing other people's skills based on the Lean concept. Through the development of others, the Lean leader pursues the development of the whole organisation (Liker and Convis 2012, p. 119). In order to ensure the occurrence of such a process, researchers attempt to indicate the qualities and behaviours of a perfect Lean leader (Stoller 2015, p. 338; Liker and Convis 2012, p. 36; Emiliani 2015, p. 44; Antony 2014, p. 260; Antony 2014; Waterbury 2011, p. 114; Balzer 2010, p. 99; Mann 2014, p. 46). They are as follows:

- Self-improvement.
- Stimulating development, self-improvement, and independence in employees (e.g. through delegating authority, empowerment, encouraging employees to look for answers individually using the KATA learning method).
- Participating actively in the work environment (teaching leaders and managers to observe what happens in the workplace, managing through gemba, participating in Kaizen, orientation towards processes and results).
- Subordinating one's actions to transformation efforts undertaken by the whole organisation (emphasis put on the strengthening of the culture of continuous improvement).
- Creating a culture of trust and empowerment (respect for people, sensitivity to other people's problems, listening to others, openness and acceptance of criticism, cooperation, proving that others in the organisation are treated seriously by participating personally in improvement activities).
- Pursuing objectives in a disciplined manner and solving problems on a step-by-step basis (subordinating actions to improvement goals and ensuring the whole organisation's involvement in a comprehensive programme of changes, standard work).
- Maintaining the continuity of organisational improvement through committed leadership and the culture of continuous improvement and learning.
- Ensuring a continuous and multidirectional flow of information.

Using the concept formulated by Bugdol (2018) and the results of the author's research, it is possible to indicate the following dimensions of Lean leadership in an organisation:

- The ethical dimension (it manifests itself in the application of the Lean Principles and values based on respect for people).
- The social dimension (it manifests itself through servant leadership and the building of a mature Lean Culture).
- The strategic dimension (it manifests itself through Lean strategy implementation).
- The tool dimension (understood as knowledge and skills related to process management and Lean Management, work in accordance with adopted standards).
- The operational dimension (improving operational activities, delegating authority and empowering employees, participating actively in projects, and becoming familiar with the work environment).

Lean leadership is developed at the levels of both a whole institution and individuals. Researchers draw attention that institutional Lean leadership may occur only with the support of strong individuals who share the same philosophy and values at every rung of a hierarchy. Considerable emphasis is put on leadership at lower levels of management (working groups, teams) because this is where everyday problems occur and sources of wastage can be identified (Liker and Convis 2012, p. 176). The results of the author's research show that this requires the delegation of authority and empowerment of employees. Without this, the involvement of employees, team leaders, and immediate superiors in the process of building a Lean Culture cannot be achieved.

The author would like to stress that the problem of Lean leadership in higher education institutions has a unique character because of their strong organisational cultures. The conducted research shows that particularly in strong collegial management models, initiatives aimed at changes appear among lower level employees or managers. The problem is how to persuade top management to accept that changes are necessary. Thus a dilemma arises to what extent Lean managers can change Lean Culture and to what extent Lean Culture can change Lean managers in higher education institutions. The research shows that Lean leaders adopt specific approaches/strategies in this respect, taking into consideration the level of involvement of managers at various higher education management levels. The author categorised and named such strategies. They are as follows:

• the total strategy,
• the side-door Lean Management introduction strategy,
• the virus infection strategy,
• the dripping water strategy.

The total strategy provides for the introduction of the Lean Management concept with the strong commitment and support of a university's top management, in accordance with the "no exceptions" principle. Conventional leadership evolves strongly towards Lean leadership.

The strategy of introducing Lean Management through a side door usually assumes the following form: In a university there is at least one representative of top management, the Lean Leader, who promotes, advocates, and supports the concept, ensuring the availability of resources necessary for its implementation. Subsequently, through a formal and informal network of internal Lean leaders, their training events, projects, and various forms of promotion, Lean Culture extends its range in the university.

The virus strategy is followed mainly when there is a lack of support on the part of top management, but at lower levels, there is a group of managers who strongly support changes and believe that Lean Management is a good method of their implementation. It focuses mainly on training employees, stimulating their creativity, and using informal communication channels. This is the shaping process of Lean leaders. It is expected that with time, bottom-up forces will force university top management to change their attitudes. The strategy of "dripping water" may be used successfully as an auxiliary element in all aforementioned strategies. Water wears the rock and with time changes become irreversible. The author's experience in project execution shows that in principle, after the completion of the first Lean project every person starts to look differently at the university's processes, wastage, and possibilities of changes. Such a person's way of thinking and attitude change irrevocably.

Lean leaders in higher education have to face numerous challenges and requirements. They are the source of many dilemmas they have to cope with in change implementation processes. The literature on the subject refers the most often to the following dilemmas:

- The dilemma about maintaining balance between questioning everything continuously and building the image of a self-assured leader (Stoller 2015, p. 270). Ensuring some kind of balance between these two attitudes becomes a starting point for true cooperation.
- The dilemma of a new leader from outside higher education (people who are not familiar with the specific character of higher education should be given time to get to know the rules and principles of their new organisation, time for learning and reflection) (Liker and Convis 2012, p. 127).
- The dilemma of transparency (it is connected with disclosing secrets, processes, and procedures to managers, employees, customers, and other stakeholders. So far such information has usually been protected as know-how, a sphere of personal interests, or for other reasons. Aversion to transparency may result in attempts to hide or distort data or facts) (Emiliani 2015, p. 48).
- The dilemma of turning a university into a "production plant" (it is believed that Lean is a business concept which will turn a university into a corporation oriented towards pursuing exorbitant economic indexes, which will lead to, for example, employee dismissals) (Emiliani 2005, p. 46; Yorkstone 2016).
- The dilemma of the non-academic character of Lean (academics believe in the scientific methods of change implementation, therefore they usually reject proposals for changes put forward by the administration without a full understanding of their essence; they prefer changes proposed by academics or are more open to changes offered by others if they have gained experience in the business or industrial sectors) (Emiliani 2005, p. 47; Emiliani 2015, p. 48).
- The dilemma of a lack of interest (a part of the academic community is not interested in any changes, maintaining the status quo is their main objective) (Emiliani 2005, p. 46).

- The dilemma of continuous improvement (leaders in higher education have to abandon ad hoc thinking, quenching fires, and focusing on crucial changes only; instead, they have to start thinking in the categories of continuous work aimed at improving everyday operating activities, and this change is a never-ending process) (Emiliani 2005, p. 48).
- The dilemma of a blame culture (similar to many other organisations, universities are characterised by a strong blame culture; leaders have to change this attitude, stop looking for people to put blame on, and opt for looking for systemic solutions to existing problems) (Emiliani 2005, p. 46; 2015, p. 48).

The author's research shows that higher education institutions have to deal with specific dilemma such as:

- The dilemma of the electoral cycle (this applies to universities where governing bodies are elected for a term of office; people in authority avoid making unpopular decisions or implement changes quickly at the beginning of their term of office; it is mainly changes legitimised by the law that is introduced).
- The dilemma of freedom and creativity (academic freedom and institutional autonomy are used as a shield against changes; furthermore, many processes are knowledge or creative processes which, because of their character, are difficult to standardise; the Lean leader has to understand the specific character of their university perfectly well).
- The dilemma of a culture of professionals (higher education employees are very well educated, are specialists in their fields, therefore, they have to be persuaded to accept changes; changes cannot be imposed on them from the outside or from the top as this could hurt their pride of specialists and professionals; also, they will not want to embrace changes which they do not understand). The research shows that in the process of building a Lean Culture, separate roles are assigned to top management and immediate superiors.
- The dilemma of *'primus inter pares'* (the strong structure and hierarchy based on academic degrees and titles constitute barriers to open

criticism, discussions and communication; frequently, there occurs a problem of a lack of managerial skills; managerial positions are held by people who have some administrative preparation, but are poorly familiar with modern management methods).

- The dilemma of subcultures (the statistical analyses conducted by the author confirmed again the existence of two distinct subcultures in higher education institutions: a subculture of superiors and a subculture of subordinates) (Maciąg 2016b; www2). Superiors have a higher opinion of various aspects related to the maturity of Lean Culture than their subordinates; thus employees belonging to the respective subcultures perceive the reality of higher education institutions differently (the results of the statistical research are presented in Chapter 4).
- The dilemma of a false start (the implementation of the Lean concept may be influenced by earlier negative experience related to the concept or other difficult changes).
- The dilemma of frustration (frustration, disappointment, and discouragement may appear in employees when, after the first successes, the Lean programme is not continued at a proper pace or is abandoned).
- The dilemma of "decisions made from behind a desk" (despite the fact that many universities are managed in a collegial manner and the mechanisms of power should ensure the participation of the whole academic community in decision making processes, it can be observed that certain groups such as administration employees, employees at the lower levels of the organisational structure, students, and other stakeholders do not participate in such processes. This causes a situation in which their voice is not heard and their problems are disregarded; therefore it is very important that Lean leaders be strongly present in their work environment, close to other employees and their problems).
- The dilemma of a holistic approach (It manifests itself in difficulties with combining the economic, human, and cultural dimensions of an organisation's activities. It becomes particularly visible when a Lean programme is being carried out only for the purpose of implementing further IT management systems and is focused only on the organisational-technical sphere).

- The dilemma of priorities (a lack of understanding that Lean is a holistic university management concept leading towards the effective achievement of all other objectives; the building of a Lean Culture cannot be one of many priorities, it has to become the most important priority; opponents often use the argument that it is not a good time for such changes because important modifications in the law are to be introduced, the university is involved in a big construction or IT project).
- The dilemma of a lack of distance (many leaders feel personally responsible for processes taking place in the university; every case of criticism is perceived personally; there is a lack of distance necessary for initiating the process of changes).
- The dilemma of standard work (a change in top management in higher education institutions usually entails a change in the management style, the manner of work organisation, priorities, etc.; the leader determines the shape of the management system. It is a strong and partly accepted element of a management culture in higher education, which may constitute a serious problem with maintaining management standards and the continuity of followed management practices).

The dilemmas and challenges described above require well-prepared leaders. The training of Lean leaders is a long-term task. But, as the literature on the subject emphasises, leadership can be learned (Lu et al. 2017). Researchers indicate the possibility of following a few approaches in training future leaders (Liker and Convis 2012, p. 140). One of them is based on KATA (which will be described in Chapter 4), while the other uses a more structured approach based on training conducted outside an organisation's structures (e.g. during the periods of academic placements in other universities, within the framework of practitioners' communities, by external training firms). The author is of the opinion that in collegial university management models, problems may appear in this respect (this concerns particularly positions other than typical university administration jobs). In view of the principles of rotation in office and election of authorities, it is difficult to plan in advance a career path of a Lean leader. In the author's opinion, in such circumstances, a comprehensive execution of employee training programmes becomes even more important. Stoller emphasises that in the Lean concept, leaders and managers are the same employees as all others; therefore, they also need clear guidelines, adequate tools, processes, and support (Stoller 2015, p. 169). Emiliani emphasises that Lean leaders grow through becoming aware of the importance of time and the flow of information, the necessity to ensure employees' commitment and to provide them with help and support, the importance of their own personal participation in improvement projects, as well as the maintenance of permanent contact with employees in their work environment (Emiliani 2015, p. 95). Ending the analysis of the results of her research, the author would like to summarise the benefits resulting from the building of a Lean Culture by paraphrasing Stoller: The building of a Lean Culture in higher education results in the following two most important benefits: managers and leaders acquire an in-depth understanding of the external and internal contexts in which their organisations function and people are given the opportunity to give their best (Stoller 2015, p. 341). The author is fully aware of the fact that the issues related to leadership, in particular, leadership in the Lean concept, have not been exhausted in this section. The author has focused on the presentation and discussion of the results of her research. They will be explored further in subsequent publications.

3.4.6 People

People constitute another dimension of Lean Culture distinguished in the model. The author again started her analysis with the use of a word cloud. The results are presented in Fig. 3.9.

An analysis of the preliminary codes allows a deeper understanding of how people in an organisation interpret and understand Lean Culture. The words/codes which appeared in the interviews the most often were the following: team, job, training, involve, positive, engage, excited, force, fear, and empower. Employees understand the building of a Lean Culture as an element of everyday work. Work has the character of a team effort. This process is accompanied by training. The interpretation

Fig. 3.9 People in higher education—a cloud of words associated with the people/employees (*Source* The author's own work)

indicates the advantage of the employees' positive attitude manifesting itself in involvement, excitement, and empowerment. It is also possible to notice certain negative aspects connected with the implementation of the Lean concept in higher education. These are employees' fears (which are discussed in detail below). Another code is force, which is interpreted as being forced to change (by an external factor), the necessity of forcing oneself to change (in the sense of a positive change) or the absence of any factor forcing one to change, i.e. freedom of choice in undertaking any activities. The results of the research in this respect are discussed in detail below. Their analysis allowed the author to indicate the most important descriptors of Lean Culture in the dimension of People. They are as follows:

• First reaction.
• Reaction to change.
• Reaction to wastage.
• Preparing employees for changes.

- Empowering employees to deal with changes.
- Professional support.
- Appreciation of commitment.
- Employee assessment.
- Fears.

First Reaction

The conducted interviews indicate clearly that at its preliminary stage the Lean Management implementation process brought various reactions in employees. The most frequent reactions were enthusiasm coupled with fears of the unknown, a certain dose of naivety, and awkwardness. The respondents emphasised that an understanding of the Lean concept might be hindered by the specific character of processes and organisational culture of higher education institutions (which were described in Chapter 2), previous negative experiences related to changes, as well as numerous myths propagated about the Lean concept (which were discussed earlier, together with the social perception of Lean).

Employees' Attitude Towards Change

The author divided the issues raised by the respondents into two groups: positive attitudes and negative attitudes. The positive reactions were discussed first. The respondents drew attention to opportunities for personal and organisational development connected with implementation of Lean Management; they had a sense of influence on conducted processes and the building of a community. They associated Lean with mutual support, joint efforts and cooperation for the good of the university. They emphasised that Lean gave them a chance to go beyond everyday routine and boredom at work as well as the mechanical performance of job duties. This is supported by the following statement:

> *But the positive effect is the elimination of frustration; people have more satisfaction, knowing what they are doing and what they should focus on today.* (An administration employee, line manager; participation in Lean projects; three years' experience in Lean, the first Lean experiences in the manufacturing sector)

This manifested itself for example through changes in the scope of duties related to a particular position or even a change of a position within an organisation (some employees were transferred to departments dealing with Lean, process management, and continuous improvement or became Lean experts, facilitators, or leaders). The implementation of Lean allowed employees to develop their careers within organisational structures and to take advantage of the potential of these employees who continually look for challenges and opportunities for development. An important element of building a Lean Culture was the strong unification of employees around the common mission, the building of the conviction that they were working together for the success of their university. The phrase 'to make a difference' appeared frequently in the respondents' statements. They emphasised that Lean gave them a sense of having an influence on the processes carried out in their universities.

This, in turn, gave them a sense of sensible work and simultaneously motivated them to undertake further improvement activities. An important issue was a sense of community built through cooperation and team work. Employees were not left alone with their new duties. Under the pressure of effectiveness metrics this could have caused stress and frustration.

The interviewees emphasised that previously changes in universities had been introduced improperly, which also had an effect on their reaction to another change in the form of implementing the Lean concept. They indicated the following emotions and attitudes in consequence of implementing the Lean concept: a sense of chaos connected with the change implementation process, aversion to changes, a sense of ownership expressed through an emotional attachment to one's own ideas and solutions, a fear of having one's solutions criticised and of expressing one's own opinions, as well as a fear of superiors.

Another important aspect was the learning of the philosophy of a rolling change (Kaizen). This is supported by the following statements:

Many people want to try to experiment with Lean; they watch videos on the Internet, they want to do something, and this is great. But what we have to do is to emphasize the importance of small wins. (A senior manager; participation in Lean projects; fifteen years' experience; the first experiences connected with writing a master's thesis)

At the beginning of the Lean implementation process, the problem was to find time for the performance of everyday duties, work in projects, and participation in training courses. This lasted until the Lean Values, principles, methods, and tool had become an integral part of a university's work culture and way of working. Employees' resistance was also caused by forcing them to participate in training courses and restructuring projects. The respondents indicated that it was important to follow the principle of free choice and encourage employees to participate in such events. During the conducted research the author also paid attention to another principle. It was the principle of asking for help. The point was for employees and superiors to ask people dealing with Lean (leaders, facilitators, experts) for help and support in problem solving. This proved that in their opinion, Lean was the proper method of dealing with problems. Besides, it guaranteed a serious approach, responsibility, and commitment of the superior and team members; it also had a strong impact on the building of a mature Lean Culture. The conducted research showed that employees represented very different approaches to change, not always regarding it as a positive phenomenon. First of all, change forced employees to exit their comfort zones. Suggestions concerning improvement were perceived as criticism and attack, which, in turn, leads to defensive reactions. This is why openness and honesty are very important elements of Lean Culture. It was possible to treat suggestions for change as opportunities for improvement. Obviously, this required employees to distance themselves from conducted processes and to stop identifying with them because a decisive majority of problems with processes in organisations have a systemic character and result from bad management practices for which managers are responsible.

It is expected that employees' participation in improvement projects will change their attitudes and strengthen their commitment to continuous improvement processes. Their work will become interesting and inspiring; they will not suffer from boredom and routine thanks to their ability to change things. Changes implemented in everyday work will be maintained and employees will not return to the old and ineffective methods of work. They will regard suggestions as challenges and opportunities for change. They will be also ready to extend their knowledge necessary for the improvement of their higher education institution.

Reaction to Wastage

The essence of Lean is pursuing the elimination of wastage sources in higher education institutions. During the conducted research the author encountered a situation in which university employees drew attention to the dissonance between what was understood as positive actions from the Lean point of view and what was rewarded. For example, frugality is perceived generally as a positive quality which should be rewarded because an employee is concerned about the good of their workplace. Unfortunately, in many cases, this is not so. The law and universities' internal by-laws force employees to perform actions which are uneconomical, sometimes even unethical, but consistent with applicable regulations. The author notes that it is a serious problem in higher education institutions which should be dealt with at the levels of both particular universities and educational authorities.

Empowering Employees to Deal with Changes

The issue of employee empowerment featured prominently in the conducted research. The analysis of the obtained results allowed the author to indicate three dominant aspects of the understanding of this notion in the surveyed universities. These were the possibility of initiating changes, the possibility of making decisions and performing corrective actions, and the possibility of signalling problems occurring in processes. An important issue raised in the research was determining the extent to which employees could make decisions related to the scope of changes and the methods of their implementation. Employee empowerment in this respect was of particular importance. The interviewees stressed many times that approving even the smallest changes through a complex administrative approval procedure killed employees' initiative and commitment and frequently distorted the idea of change. Lean Culture follows the logic of small steps, i.e. small, quick and simple changes which bring about positive effects in a short period of time. Furthermore, employees should be persuaded to accept changes by getting them involved in change processes and providing them with responsibility. Changes cannot be imposed in a top-down manner. Firstly, this hurts employees' pride as specialists and professionals and secondly, it makes them unwilling to accept such changes and get involved in them. Another issue was the possibility of employees' signalling problems occurring in processes. In this respect, the author noticed three major limitations. The first one is a lack of clearly defined solutions in this area, e.g. a system through which employees could submit their suggestions or proposals for improvement (Kaizen, a dedicated website, etc.). The second limitation comprises fears of other employees' or superiors' reactions, a fear of exclusion or perceiving oneself or being perceived by others as a person who cannot cope with problems (who is less intelligent, less educated, etc.). The third limitation is unwillingness to undertake any actions or a lack of interest, which may result from a sense of routine and hopelessness as far as work improvement is concerned ("I won't be able to change anything, anyway") or an employee's personal attitude (work is not an important source of satisfaction and success; it is just a means of earning money).

Preparing Employees for Changes

The conducted research shows that the process of preparing employees for changes related to Lean comprises cultural, social, technical, and organisational issues. The research participants emphasised the necessity of maintaining continuity between a vision of a university's development and improvement and changes under implementation. The awareness of how even the slightest change contributes to the development of a university builds a sense of purpose and has a positive influence on employee motivation. It should be remembered that universities are organisations employing highly qualified employees, specialists in their fields. Therefore, communicating the objectives of changes and their connections with a university development vision is of considerable importance. Employees expected that they would be informed how their actions contributed to the implementation of their university's development and improvement vision. They also expected that the university would prepare them for the implementation of changes with respect to knowledge and applicable techniques and would also inform them of progress in the change implementation process.

An important issue raised in the interviews is that employees unprepared for changes oppose them, build an atmosphere of fear, and stimulate one another negatively. The respondents indicated that the source of such behaviours could be previous experiences as well as human nature. Therefore, such important roles were played by the key Lean Values, the attitudes of top management and immediate superiors as well as the quality of interpersonal relations in higher education institutions.

Professional Support

An important success factor in implementing the Lean concept in higher education was ensuring professional support for employees in their everyday work. Employees expected that they would be able to contact specialist units or people obliged to provide professional assistance in problem solving.

The surveyed universities usually established expert teams consisting of trained employees; in some cases, they hired external experts or consulting firms (more on this topic in Chapter 4).

Appreciation of Commitment

According to the respondents, appreciation of employees' commitment to change processes was very important. They emphasised strongly that various forms of recognition were welcome, verbal or non-verbal ones, expressed by members of the university top management, superiors or colleagues. Appreciation should have a continuous character and be expressed in the case of even small proposals for change or improvement. It is important to promote and reward employees' active attitudes towards submitting proposals for the improvement of processes and activities. This strengthens their openness, allows the elimination of fears of dismissal or having an opinion different from that of a superior. Employees expect that their initiatives will be appreciated and they will be given the opportunity to present in public the results of their improvement activities or projects.

Employee Assessment

Another important issue which appeared in the research is connected with approaches to employee assessment in higher education. Employees expect that they will be assessed comprehensively for the results of their actions and for their involvement in improvement processes (they will not be assessed for incidental events). According to the respondents, employees should be involved in the process of their assessment.

The conducted research revealed clearly a thread connected with the possibility of supplementing periodic employees assessments with an evaluation of undertaken improvement actions. There were different opinions about this. The respondents emphasised that on the one hand, such an element of employee assessment could stimulate employees' commitment to work, initiative, and creativity. On the other hand, however, the dominant opinion was that this could result in such negative phenomena as creating systems of interests and conflicts or strengthening internal competition among employees and teams, which would translate negatively into the quality of cooperation. In view of the strong culture of assessment and audit in higher education institutions, the aforementioned negative scenario is quite probable. It should be also taken into consideration that every employee is different, has different personal goals, and does not have to be passionate about their work. Thus the author is of the opinion that employees should be assessed first of all for properly performed work, while initiative for continuous improvement should be an additional element taken into consideration in connection with bonuses, promotions or additional organisational benefits.

Fears

The research results indicate a few sources of fears which appear during Lean implementation processes in higher education. The first source is the possibility of losing a job triggered by myths about Lean. Another source is a possibility of disclosing a lack of competence. Employees worry that they do not have sufficient knowledge and skills necessary to perform new duties and tasks. Another source of fears is a loss of monopoly on knowledge, power, and prestige connected with the previous exclusivity for the execution of a particular process. On the one hand, the necessity to share knowledge and, on the other hand, disclosure of process execution mechanisms may be sources of fears. Other employees and superiors are able to identify and recognise process mechanisms, as well as to assess or change them. This can be perceived as a manifestation of criticism and undermining one's competences. If a process is made transparent, it ends a certain monopoly determining a sphere of influence. During the course of the research the author also heard the opinion that employees' fears, but also top management's fears, and resistance to change could result from the existence of 'grey zones' in higher education institutions. This is the consequence of, among other things, a high level of the autonomy of organisational units within a traditional functional structure. Grey zones have become the sources of unjustified privileges and informal power.

The above results of the author's research continue and broaden the threads followed by other researchers in discussions on the role of employees in the process of building a mature Lean Culture in higher education institutions. This subject has been studied, among others, by the following researchers (Liker and Convis 2012; Stoller 2015; Mann 2014; Liker 2005, Balzer 2010; Emiliani 2005, 2015; Antony 2014; Balzer et al. 2016; Lu et al. 2017; Allan and Sinha 2013). Research and publications pose the question about the methods of persuading employees to accept changes, to get them involved in change processes, to maintain the effects of implemented changes, and to continuously improve a university's functioning.

The conducted analysis of the codes included in Fig. 3.3 confirms that the Lean concept is focused on people. Its basis is a conviction that employees are the most valuable organisational resource (Liker and Convis 2012, p. 49; Emiliani 2005, p. 47). It is necessary to develop personnel management policies and systems ensuring equity as well as to foster mutual trust in employees because it is only in such an environment that every employee notices problems, reports them, and gets involved in solving them (Liker and Convis 2012, p. 47; Emiliani 2005, p. 47;

Emiliani 2005, p. 61; Lu et al. 2017). The author's research confirms that the key role in this respect is played by the concept of empowerment developed originally within the trend of human relations, i.e. delegating duties and decision making powers to regular employees (Mann 2014, p. 224; Cardona and Rey 2009, p. 38). The foundation for employees' development is their self-improvement, including voluntary learning (from Japanese jishuken) (Liker and Convis 2012, p. 125). In light of the acknowledged theories of motivation, Lean constitutes a perfect environment for motivating employees (Stoller 2015, p. 154). Appreciation, diversification, autonomy, and opportunities for learning are the inherent qualities of the role of an employee in the culture of continuous improvement. A condition for effective motivation is the full commitment of top management (Stoller 2015, p. 155).

The author's research highlighted the discussion on whether employees should be rewarded additionally for participation in restructuring projects. Liker and Convis are of the opinion that employees should not be paid for something they wanted to do anyway because this could kill their internal motivation (Liker and Convis 2012, p. 44). The research results indicate that what employees value more is non-monetary expressions of appreciation, words of praise from a superior or team members.

Another conclusion is that the implementation of Lean as an organisational change may trigger a sense of threat or uncertainty. This problem is addressed, among others, by Schein. He distinguishes fears of the necessity to learn and existential fears (Schein 2004, p. 330). The conducted research shows that a fear of learning has its source mainly in concern about temporary incompetence, punishment for incompetence, a loss of personal identity or group affiliation. An existential fear is anxiety about losing one's job. The research results confirm, for example, the conclusions reached by Emiliani (2015, p. 63). Lean programmes must not be associated in any way with a reduction in employment because this would have a devastating impact on employees' commitment.

The key to understanding Lean is team work. The Lean concept moves away from assessing and building a reward system based on individual work results because of the risk of focusing on individual performance instead of group work (Liker and Convis 2012, p. 44).

3.4.7 Team Work and Relations

The author's research revealed that team work as well as building relations inside and outside an organisation constituted important dimensions of Lean Culture in higher education. Therefore, these two elements, i.e. team work and internal relations or relations with the environment, are included in the model as separate dimensions of Lean Culture.

The conducted research allowed the author to indicate the roles played by team work in the creation of Lean Culture in a higher education institution. These roles are providing mutual inspiration, sharing knowledge and experiences, supradepartmental cooperation, as well as celebrating common successes. Sharing knowledge, experiences and ideas was a particularly important aspect of cooperation in a university aimed at continuous improvement. This is supported by the following statements:

> *Team work integrates the staff, allows everybody to take a part in solving a problem and implementing a new idea. So they are able to get a lot of respect for the work which one of them did.* (A Lean Leader, line manager, administration employee; sixteen years' experience in Lean projects; first experiences in the manufacturing sector)

The respondents frequently drew attention that knowledge of processes must not be private knowledge used for private purposes.

The research shows that relations are also built through the promotion of concepts and initiatives related to Lean in higher education. The process of building relations is usually carried out on many planes, using people, processes, structures and various promotion tools. So-called word-of-mouth marketing turned out to be an effective promotion tool. Employees encouraged one another to participate in training events and to apply various Lean techniques and tools in their everyday work. This was helped by visual materials (Kanban tables, dashboards, process map diagrams, cartoons, photographs, etc.).

The other popular tools for promoting and building relations were meetings, conferences, seminars, workshops, and newsletters about projects under implementation. Internal networks of Lean experts, angels, and advocates were a good carrier and stimulus for building relations in higher education institutions. All these activities, processes, and structures allowed the building of a culture of cooperation and interaction at the level of departments and among departments. The results of the conducted research confirm the theses included in the literature on the subject and broaden the perspective of research on Lean in higher education. The research confirms that Lean can serve initially to persuade teams to communicate with one another (Stoller 2015, p. 181). It is particularly important in such complex structures as higher education institutions, where strong divisions in organisational structures (departments, faculties, schools, institutes, administration, academic sections) are usually clearly visible (Emiliani 2015, p. 83). A university is a special organisation because, unlike in a manufacturing enterprise, its employees have to cooperate in multidimensional relations comprising a whole organisational structure, creating formal and informal networks (e.g. while preparing and carrying out research projects, working in various teams, committees, etc.). The author's research shows that common projects, training events, conferences, and other forms allow employees to get to know each other, to become familiar with each others' expectations, requirements, and process-related problems. This reduces the level of conflicts or mutual accusations and builds trust, thus minimising the generation of waste. An important function in organising the work of teams is performed by Lean team leaders and facilitators (Waterbury 2011, p. 122; Balzer 2010, p. 117). A facilitator is a Lean expert who performs the role of a mentor and supports a team leader. A team leader is responsible for project execution.

The issues related to people, relations among them, and team work are very numerous and complex. The author is fully aware of the fact that they have not been exhausted in this section of the book. They will be explored further in subsequent publications.

3.4.8 Artefacts in Lean Culture

The notion of artefacts and their role in organisational culture was discussed in the first part of the chapter. The research conducted by the author indicates the existence of many artefacts which are manifestations of Lean Culture in higher education. According to the typology proposed at the beginning of the chapter, they can be divided into linguistic artefacts (language, concepts), behavioural artefacts (dress codes, ways of addressing others in an organisation), and physical artefacts (technology, products, tangible works, databases, knowledge bases). The author examined Lean Culture artefacts from the perspective of their tangibility, looking for their manifestations and trying to describe their authenticity and reality from the point of view of members of an organisation. It should be noted that tangibility and intangibility, visibility and invisibility have a conventional character as it is difficult to determine their limits unambiguously. The task is made even harder by the fact that every university is a different organisation with an original organisational culture. Therefore the above description contains a certain synthesis and generalisation of the results of the conducted research.

3.4.8.1 Lean Language

The language used by change creators and employees is an important aspect of building a Lean Culture in a higher education institution. The problem of the Lean Language, particularly in the context of implementing Lean in higher education, is not a very popular research topic. This subject was studied, among others, by Emiliani (2014), Stoller (2015, p. 324), and Waterbury (2011).

At the beginning of the author's research language was a subject matter of secondary importance, but after some time it surfaced as another important research problem generating such questions as: What language should be used in the implementation of organisational changes in a higher education institution so that the language itself does not become a source of resistance to and rejection of the concept? Is it necessary to use the language characteristic of the Lean concept in higher education or is possible to replace its typical expressions with others? Will it not cause far-reaching distortions which will eventually distort the essence of the concept? Does the Lean Language have to be understandable to all university employees?

In order to present the problem more thoroughly, the author followed an analytical approach different from that applied in the case of the Lean Culture dimensions discussed above. The author combined the analysis of her research results with the analysis of the notions and approaches to the role of language in organisational culture as defined in the literature on the subject.

Language is referred to as an integral and complex element of organisational culture (Ott 1989, p. 26). It is assigned the following roles: ensuring communication in an organisation, identifying organisation (subculture) members, providing a means of shaping and controlling thoughts and ideas, providing a means of excluding members from organisational culture/subculture, providing a means of shaping content (certain expressions can be added to or eliminated from the language, e.g. "maximise" or "optimize" is replaced by "continuously improve", "data-driven" is replaced by "fact based") (Emiliani 2014; Ott 1989, p. 27; Schein 2004, p. 121). Language can adopt the form of spoken words, written words or signs. Language is a product of culture, its transmitter, and a means of its maintenance (Ott 1989, p. 28). As Schein emphasises, language comprises not only words and expressions but also categories whose meanings have to be agreed within an organisation (Schein 2004, p. 113). In the author's opinion, examples of such categories include a high quality of education, a quick process, and academic excellence. People in higher education institutions use many such categories and frequently understand them differently. This may become a source of misunderstandings and conflicts. Stoller emphasises that language is the key to motivation by adjusting a message to the way in which people think and feel, by avoiding unnecessary jargon and technical information (Stoller 2015, p. 324).

Analysing the role of language in Lean Culture, it is necessary first of all to define the notion of the Lean Language.

Referring to the definition in the Encyclopaedia Britannica, the author defined the Lean Language as a system consisting of spoken and written symbols as well as body language which is used by people dealing with the concept of Lean Management and organisations using this concept in defining, communicating, expressing and stimulating emotions as well as determining their own identity.[1] Broadening this definition, it can be said the Lean Language is a means of communication used by people dealing with the Lean concept and working in this area to record and convey information on Lean Management.[2]

In the individual dimension, the Lean Language differentiates specialists and organisation members from other people in groups or social networks. In the organisational dimension, it is an element of building an organisational culture and being different from other organisations. The Lean Language is a specific language, which is determined by the history of the development of the concept. It contains many words and phrases from the English and Japanese languages which usually are not translated into national languages. One of the reasons for such a situation is often a lack of a good equivalent of a particular term in a national language (e.g. the word Lean does not have a good counterpart in Polish, Dutch, or Norwegian; the same is true of such Japanese words as Kaizen, Poka Yoke, Kanban, etc.). Another element which may hinder the understanding of the Lean Language is the fact that it is based on scientific management, and thus it uses specialist terms from the field of management, particularly process management, additionally incorporating words and phrases from other disciplines such as information science, statistics (e.g. Six Sigma, psychology, sociology, etc.), as a matter of fact, the Lean Language becomes a new separate language used by specialists.

The author's research indicates that the Lean Language is strongly associated with business and a culture based on indexes, accountability, and efficiency, the result of which is budget and employment cuts. Thus, the very use of the word Lean can in itself be a source of resistance without a person's becoming familiar with the essence of the concept and its variety used in higher education. Also Wilson emphasises this aspect. He indicates that the Lean Language, particularly in public organisations, can be a powerful source of misunderstandings and resistance on the part of employees, despite the fact that they perceive

---

[1]The author used the definition included in Encyclopaedia Britannica (www3).

[2]The authors used the definition included in The Dictionary of the Polish Lnaguage (www4).

the same problems and try to solve them (Wilson 2015). The Lean Language is closer to people connected with management, but can be completely incomprehensible for employees who do not perform any managerial functions. The research conducted by the author shows that it can be perceived as a hermetic, corporate-bureaucratic newspeak, and because of its form, it can be completely incomprehensible and enigmatic, which will constitute a source of resistance. The respondents emphasised that if they were not understood, new words and expressions made people suspicious, biased and hostile towards those who spoke the new language. People feel isolated and such an attitude may evolve into distrust, fear or divisions among employees.

In the light of the research results, it is possible to indicate the functions fulfilled by the Lean Language in the creation of a Lean Culture in higher education. First of all, it creates new organisational reality by introducing new words and expressions (e.g. customer, waste, process). As Emiliani emphasises, sometimes old words and expressions well known in higher education institutions are eliminated, and sometimes they are stressed, strengthened or provided with new contexts (Emiliani 2014). For example, the scope of using expressions previously associated mainly with the areas of research and teaching, but having little in common with university management, is being broadened. A case in point is the notion of excellence, previously dominant in the contexts of academic or teaching excellence. At present, the word is used to refer to organisational or operational excellence.

The research conducted by the author shows that language is used as a measure of the maturity of a Lean Culture: the deeper the changes, the greater the role of the Lean Language in everyday communication in higher education institutions. This is supported by the following statements:

I think that in a highly successful organisation, you will not use the word Lean, because people behave in the lean way as a part of everyday conversations with line managers. (An administration employee, dedicated Lean officer, Lean leader; twelve years' experience in Lean, experience gained in HEI)

As Buczkowska emphasises, there occurs a natural and very important feedback loop facilitating communication and interpretation of cognitive content. Such a feedback loop leads to the strengthening and development of the conceptual system which, through language, becomes an externalised social system (Buczkowska 2015, p. 86). It is a quick and universal method of communication. Such conclusions are confirmed by the presented research results. The respondents emphasised that using well defined notions allows specialists and other people involved in change implementation in higher education institutions to spend less time necessary for communication.

The research shows that the Lean Language can be a source of prestige for people involved in change implementation. Using the Lean Language makes it possible to build an individual identity and to emphasise the possession of a particular status or specialist knowledge, or membership in a group of people dealing with the Lean concept. The Lean Language can become a means of eliminating old and routine approaches. The Lean Language is a synonym of an attractive novelty and a source of prestige for universities and people involved in the Lean implementation process. On the other hand, however, it should be kept in mind that the Lean Language can sometimes stigmatise people or universities. In certain circles, they can be perceived as advocates of a hostile business culture which destroys the time-honoured identity. Misunderstanding the Lean Language can become a reason for dividing a university into those who know the language, and those who do not. With time such divisions can become stronger.

The analysis of the research results shows that the issues related to the Lean Language and its role in the creation of an organisational culture is important and multidimensional. Hence the question arises about what should be done to make the Lean Language an effective tool for the building of a Lean Culture, about the qualities and functions it should have to support and strengthen changes in an organisation's culture towards continuous improvement. The conducted research allows the indication of a few desirable qualities of the Lean Language. The Lean Language should be:

- Comprehensible for users—every language expression as a defined sign has an interpretation assigned to it in a given language; such an interpretation carries certain information and determines how a given word or expression is understood. Therefore, properly and unambiguously defining particular notions as well as adjusting them to the context of a given organisation and the functions performed in it by employees (a superior, a subordinate, a specialist, etc.) are important aspects of Lean Culture implementation. At the beginning of the change implementation process, the new language should not be introduced at any cost because this may meet with resistance. It is recommended to try to describe phenomena and problems by means of known notions that are generally used and typical of a given organisation. The typical Lean Language should be converted into the language of a given organisation and the language of everyday work. Also, Wilson draws attention to this. It is necessary to adjust the Lean Language to the language used in the organisation by its employees (Wilson 2015). The author would like to emphasise that if so far the notion of Lean has not been used and its equivalents have been, for example, continuous improvement or process improvement, this should not be changed. The author's research shows that many words and expressions typical of Lean are completely incomprehensible for an average university employee. For example, the notion of "customer" raises the question about who it really is because there are no customers in universities (e.g. in Norway or Poland, students do not have to pay tuition, it is taxpayers that pay all related costs). Therefore, another approach should be followed in order to interpret this notion in the academic context. Questions should be asked about people benefiting from university employees' work. The word customer can be replaced by other words with which employees are very well familiar, for example student, dean, employee in another department, researcher, lecturer, etc. In other words, the pull principle can be also used in creating a language—words and expressions are defined if it is necessary or expected.

- Consistent—in order to build a conceptual apparatus and to strengthen the Lean Language in organisational culture, it is necessary to use the defined notions in a consistent manner. Emiliani draws attention to the fact that despite the implementation of changes based on the Lean concept, top management continues to use the traditional and conventional language of management, which causes confusion and misunderstandings (Emiliani 2014).

- Used universally—the principle of collegiality means that the whole academic community, including students and external entities, participates in university management processes. This forces all participants to use a common language if they are to understand each other on the way towards consensus. Following Buczkowska, the author (Buczkowska 2015, p. 86) distinguishes the following maturity levels of the Lean Language: the first level—defining and understanding concepts (words and expressions); the second level—assigning some cognitive content to such concepts; the third level—communication in which such concepts are used; the fourth level—creating a conceptual system comprehensible for everybody inside and outside the organisation. The author's observations indicate that growth in the maturity of the Lean Language is not linear; it depends on the employee's function in the organisation, held position and the time of implementing the concept in the university.
- Useful in facilitating communication in all functional areas of the university and with external entities—many entities with which universities cooperate also implement process management concepts, including Lean Management. Therefore, a common language will definitely facilitate mutual understanding and communication. The Lean Language is an international language of specialists. Therefore, its knowledge allows undertaking activities and participation in communities of practitioners, networks, conferences, seminars, etc.

Summarising the presented analysis, it should be emphasised that the Lean Language plays a very important role in the building of organisational culture. Language is the vanguard of changes planned for implementation and hence it has to be adjusted to the context in which a given university functions. If the language is not adjusted to the specific character of a university, this may cause a rejection of planned changes; even if both the reformers and the reformed have the best intentions, they will fail to find a common ground for agreement. A university should create its own, unique and simple Lean Language. A lack of a common language may constitute a serious barrier to reaching success and maintaining the consequences of changes. It is even often suggested that the word Lean be not used and be replaced by continuous improvement (because of business connotations and bad experiences); consequently, Lean should be defined as a useful way of working. The respondents noted that Lean Management could be regarded as yet another management fashion. Nevertheless, the essence of this concept is timeless and universal. Thus it will continue to exist under different names and so will the language created on its basis as a permanent element of organisational culture.

Language is also associated with such notions as jargon, metaphor, myth, history, anecdote, heroes, organisational script, saga, and legend. During the course of the research, the author listened to many stories about how Lean was being introduced in a university and how people faced changes, about successes and failures. Many stories were also told about functioning Lean systems. The respondents described how their universities had weathered various crises, what corrective actions had been taken and what preventive actions should have been taken, and how employees should deal with particular problems in the future. In each of the surveyed university, a Lean hero appeared. In the interviews, a Lean hero was frequently referred to, their role in and contribution to the development of the Lean concept in a university was emphasised. A lean hero was a representative of top management or a person operationally responsible for Lean implementation. They usually performed the functions of a Lean leader, facilitator, initiator, promoter, advocate, executor, or coach. In the light of the interviews, they were a certain axis connecting employees in the organisation. Almost everybody knew such a person, which was confirmed by numerous greetings, short talks and jokes observed by the author while passing between university buildings or rooms, at meetings or seminars.

The research conducted by the author certainly broadened the knowledge of this dimension of Lean Culture in higher education as it is not presented exhaustively in the literature on the subject. The author is of the opinion that issues related to the Lean Language should become a subject matter of in-depth interdisciplinary research to be conducted by specialists in linguistics, Lean and continuous improvement. The author wishes to emphasise that there are certain limits to the use of language in research on organisational culture. On the basis of conducted analyses, Ott indicates the following three situations in which a language may be incomprehensible for the researcher: when members of an organisation use a specialist language incomprehensible for the researcher, when employees speak the same language, but define particular categories differently, and when employees use correctly defined categories in an improper way (Ott 1989, p. 112). Such a situation can become an additional source of knowledge for the researcher of organisational culture. Therefore, the most effective ways to study a language are interviews as well as analyses of documents, texts, and video or audio recordings. The author draws attention to the basic barrier which occurred in the research conducted by her. It was the national language. The research was carried out in the English and Polish languages. English was used in both Anglo speaking countries and non-Anglo speaking countries such as Norway, the Netherlands, and Poland. There may have appeared inaccuracies in understanding and at the stage of translating. Relying on her experience related to process concepts and Lean Management and the assistance of a professional translator (a native speaker), the author made all possible efforts to perform all activities correctly.

3.4.8.2 Behavioural Artefacts

Although behavioural artefacts present a less visible element of organisational culture, their existence is perceived especially by people from outside an organisation. Hence, as an outsider, the author was very well positioned to carry out such observations during the course of her research. An analysis of behavioural artefacts was based on open observations during meetings, visits, conferences, seminars and when moving between offices or building on university premises. An important source of knowledge of behavioural artefacts was an analysis of the language, myths, histories, sagas, etc. Behavioural artefacts were analysed in the individual dimension and the group dimension. With respect to the individual dimension, the author paid special attention to the ways in which organisation members addressed each other, their attitudes, expression of emotions or indicating their position in the organisation. Such behaviours were included in certain organisational standards and leadership styles. A particularly important experience was taking part in meetings during which participants used their national language only (e.g. in the Netherlands). During such meetings, the author was able to focus on observing participants' behaviours and emotions. The author is perfectly aware that behaviours can be analysed through the prism of national culture, but this thread is omitted deliberately. The descriptions below constitute a certain generalisation and arrangement of collected observations. During the course of the research the author observed the following individual behaviours characterising Lean Culture, including leadership:

- the boss's informal behaviour: the boss knows the employees' forenames, smiles, greets everybody; during the meeting the boss sits together with the employees in a circle, listens to everybody carefully, discusses problems with all employees, does not treat his position in the organisation too formally, does not manifest his status, does not create communication barriers, stimulates openness and freedom of expressing opinions and views,
- the boss's behaviour as a mentor: the boss explains things if the employees do not understand sufficiently certain events or are wrong about something (e.g. they lack some information or use unverified information), ensures the proper course of the discussion, uses information and facts, is open, keeps the proper pace of the discussion and sticks to the agenda,
- the boss's behaviour as a member of the team: the boss sits together with the employees in a circle, some people stand, some people move freely about, the atmosphere is casual, the boss nods his head and produces utterances expressing his understanding or confirmation, is focused on the people and the discussion,
- the employees' behaviour: they ask questions, discuss, admit openly that they could be wrong; the atmosphere is relaxed, there is no tension or distance; small technical problems are turned into jokes; they are enthusiastic, open, and not afraid of expressing their own opinions.

The author's research revealed certain patterns and standards of routine groups' behaviours such as meetings, celebrations, ceremonies or rituals. Group behavioural artefacts typical of Lean Culture include the following:

- Meetings are very short, some participants stand, some sit in a circle, participants hold mugs with beverages in their hands (mostly coffee), respect for time.
- Meetings are often supported with visualisations (tables, drawings), short meetings at dashboards, typical duration—15 minutes, frequency— once or twice per week, according to a predetermined schedule.
- Celebration of small victories (formal and informal meetings to celebrate successes in executing restructuring projects).
- Cyclical, e.g. annual, internal seminars to summarise the work of teams, to present the results of projects; Kaizen events.
- Conferences in which representatives of other schools or public organisations can participate.
- Workshops, e.g. rapid improvement events (small projects oriented towards quick changes in processes conducted by a university).

One of the respondents referred to the necessity of celebrating small victories.

Celebrating every small win, I think the organization, particularly in the University we do a great job about celebrating the champions and the leaders, the winners. To make Lean Management successful in the long term you need to go right to the person who had the idea, who identified waste, who highlighted the problem, and celebrate every one of the contributors if you want to sustain Lean Management. (A senior manager; participation in Lean projects; fifteen years' experience; the first experiences connected with writing a master's thesis)

Adopting the position of an independent observer allowed the author to notice behaviours which are invisible or partly visible for organisation members. In some situations, people's behaviours indicated their fears (e.g. in consequence of resignation of a person strongly involved in the building of a Lean Culture), boredom, tiredness, or impatience. It can be concluded that Lean is based strongly on people rather than on systemic solutions implemented in an organisation. Additionally, some employees still do not perceive the Lean concept as a culture of work but treat it as an additional duty. This may be characteristic of the early stages of Lean Culture development processes.

3.4.8.3 Tangible Artefacts

During the course of the research the author focused on the following tangible artefacts which can be regarded as manifestations of Lean Culture: documents, maps, diagrams, tables, photographs, office design, drawings, signs, thought maps, word clouds, etc. The unique character of Lean Culture consists in emphasis put on the visual aspect. Hence a person from the outside visiting an organisation implementing the Lean concept realises immediately that such actions are undertaken.

The author is of the opinion that analysis of documentation is very important in research on Lean Culture. The implementation of Lean Culture in higher education strongly influences the methods of documentation management, the visual side of documents, their substantive content (e.g. names and language used in descriptions), a particular layout—often resulting from adopted international standards (e.g. organisational process maps, standard organisational procedures). With respect to their duration, documents can be of a short-term character, can be created on an ad hoc basis (e.g. dashboards, thought maps, process stream maps, notes, records), and can become a basis for subsequent documents (e.g. a process map is a basis for developing a standard operational procedure). The research shows that documents can fulfil the following functions in Lean Culture: the prescriptive function (documents unambiguously determine the correct methods of executing processes or tasks, e.g. procedures, regulations, instructions, guidelines, organisation charts, process maps); the evidence function (records confirming the performance of actions, e.g. registers, confirmation, reports); the control function (documents constitute a basis for control actions and include the results of such actions, e.g. inspection reports, project execution reports); the promotional function (documents promote Lean Management and encourage people to participate in various activities; they promote the university); the informative function (documents inform about the university's activities and undertakings, e.g. newsletters, notes, university periodicals, leaflets, invitations, and the didactic function). Documents may appear in various formats, e.g. as hard copies, electronic files, or Internet materials. Activities are also documented by means of films, video clips, or multimedia presentations. Documents can be addressed to the inside of the organisation or to external addresses.

During the course of the research, the author noticed less official artefacts proving the existence of Lean Culture. Such artefacts include conference publications, case studies presented during meetings, seminars or conferences, as well as articles in specialist journals or interview transcripts. Another source of information is entries on Internet forums or results of research conducted in a university (e.g. during a seminar presenting the results of conducted Lean programmes the participants were asked to fill in an online questionnaire whose results were shown immediately on a screen. The objective was to collect employees' opinions on a particular Lean programme, their involvement and major fears related to the programme).

Summarising the analysis of the conducted research, the author would like to emphasise that an analysis of artefacts should have a multidimensional character. Such an analysis should cover both official documents created by the university and documents coming from other sources. In the author's opinion, in the case of studies on Lean Culture, the very fact of the existence of some documents confirms that the university relies on the process approach methodology and Lean Management in the process of creating a Lean Culture (e.g. during the course of the research the author was able to notice various dashboards, block diagrams, slogans, competence matrixes, etc. in the offices and corridors of the visited institutions). The respondents drew attention that tangible artefacts had changed their way of perceiving the organisational reality. This is supported by the following statement:

My brain is changed. I prefer pictures, colours, dashboards, and others. I have a lean brain. Maybe we should do a deeper study in this area, how lean changes a brain. (Lean Management Department Director, administration, twelve years' experience, the first Lean experiences in HEI)

The life cycle of artefacts is determined by their usefulness for creating and maintaining organisational culture.

Issues related to artefacts in Lean Culture are rather complex. The author focused on discussing the most important threads that had been revealed during the course of the research. Studies on these issues need to be broadened, particularly with respect to the Lean Language. It will be the subject matter of subsequent publications.

3.4.9 Relations with the Environment

Visiting the surveyed institutions, the author drew attention to another important dimension of Lean Culture. It is the building of relations and cooperation with external entities. Such an attitude is an integral element of the external context of the functioning of the modern university described in Chapter 2. The essence of the university includes a certain servant function towards society. Lean makes it possible to perform this function at a deeper level, which can be confirmed by the following statement:

> *I think overall it can be a win-win not just to be the first at the gate but, you know, improving these processes, saving dollars, doing something more efficiently and effectively with respect to waste. We have a huge opportunity to make a difference also outside the university.* (An academic, administration employee, Lean leader, six years' experience in Lean, the first Lean experiences in HEI)

As is indicated by the conducted research, knowledge shared among organisations has a measurable value, but only in a given organisation's external and internal contexts. Therefore within Lean Culture, cooperation, the sharing of experience and openness to partners are not perceived as threats because solutions implemented in one institution usually cannot be copies implemented in another. Every institution builds its own individual culture based on the PDCA (Plan, Do Check, Act) cycle of continuous improvement. More or less formal cooperation networks come into being through communities of practitioners, conferences, seminars and study visits. The LeanHE Hub (www5) is a global platform connecting people who deal with Lean

Management in higher education. An example of a national initiative is the Improvement Community of Practice[3] in the United Kingdom (a cross-sectoral community of practitioners) or the author's project to establish a network of Polish universities under the auspices of the international Lean HE network[4] (it is to be a community of higher education practitioners implementing the process approach, including Lean Management).

The research conducted by the authors shows that cooperation networks bring many advantages. First of all, it is the sharing of knowledge and the creation of new knowledge through the transpositions of experiences from other universities or sectors (Sułkowski 2017b; Prawelska-Skrzypek et al. 2019). The author's research also confirms the conclusions resulting from Stoller's research according to which the sharing of knowledge increases the satisfaction of employees and leaders resulting from the participation in improvement projects (Stoller 2015, p. 348). It is also a form of assistance provided to partners (although in this context there may occur ethical problems resulting from the simultaneous cooperation and competition among higher education institutions).

3.5   A Model of Lean Culture in Higher Education

The conducted research allowed the author to create a model of Lean Culture in higher education. The presented model of a Lean Culture is based on the following three pillars: theoretical research (analysis of literature), practical research (conducted in higher education institutions), and the author's experience gained during the execution of various Lean

---

[3]During the research conducted at the University of Winchester in the United Kingdom, thanks to the kindness of Dr. Tammi Sinha, the author participated in a meeting of the Improvement Community of Practice. The objective of the meeting was to develop a plan of work and meetings for 2018. The activities of the community are described in more detail in *A community of practice as a form of voluntary academic cooperation*.

[4]The aforementioned Polish network organizes biannual seminars dedicated to *Lean Higher Education* (www6). The author is the initiator and organizer of these events.

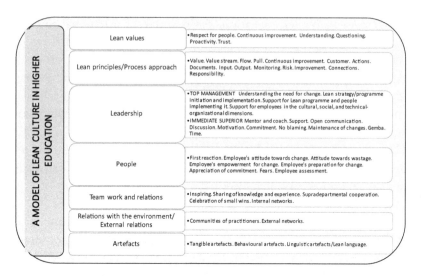

Fig. 3.10   A model of Lean Culture in higher education—a theoretical framework (*Source* The author's own work)

projects. It consists of 7 dimensions (see Fig. 3.10). Each of the dimensions presents the most important descriptors of Lean Culture which were identified during the course of the research. The proposed Lean Culture model has a holistic and universal character. It is meant to constitute a useful theoretical framework for the arrangement of knowledge on Lean Culture in higher education. It can be used by university management teams in research on organisational culture, its identification and the determination of the required direction of changes. The model makes it possible to examine gaps between a university's current organisational culture and Lean Culture. Such gaps explain why implemented changes may not bring about the full range of expected benefits or indicate the areas which require actions on the part of leaders before any decisions are made about the implementation of the Lean Management concept.

The presented model became a basis for developing a research tool for diagnosing the maturity of Lean Culture in higher education. It is presented in detail in Chapter 4. It can be used in research on the evaluation of a higher education institution's preparedness for change (Balzer 2010, p. 105; Antony 2014; Balzer et al. 2016).

3.6   Chapter Summary

The literature on the subject is consistent about Lean Culture being an important factor conditioning the effectiveness of implementing the Lean concept in higher education. It is not only a part of a university's organisational culture but also becomes a new quality based on the values and principles of Lean Management. The process of building a Lean Culture is accompanied by various tensions resulting from the internal and external contexts in which higher education institutions function. The understanding of Lean Culture, its essence and importance, as well as the way in which it is created and the factors which influence it was the subject matter of the deliberations undertaken in this chapter.

The objective of this chapter was to present the author's proposal of a model of Lean Culture maturity in higher education as well as conditions necessary for the building of such maturity. On the basis of the study of the literature, the conducted research, and the experience gained in various projects, the author identified the external and internal contexts for the building of a Lean Culture in higher education, defined Lean Culture with respect to various research perspectives and approaches to studies on organisational culture, and proposed a theoretical framework in the form of the Lean Culture Maturity Model in HE describing the dimensions and descriptors of Lean Culture. The author reflected on not only how higher education organisational culture changes in the process of implementing the Lean concept but also the degree to which the Lean Management concept changes in the process of its implementation in higher education. The adopted research perspective broadened by tools typical for the interpretative-symbolic paradigm allowed the author to gain a deeper insight into Lean Culture in higher education, a better understanding of its essence, dimensions, and descriptors. In her research, the author treated Lean Culture as a social construct and a metaphor of organisational culture in higher education. The analysis conducted in the chapter made it possible to find arguments in support of the correctness of the theses formulated at the beginning of the chapter:

- Lean Culture is strongly influenced by factors resulting from traditions, the models of organisational culture in higher education, and the national culture of a particular country.
- The use of the interpretative-symbolic perspective in research on Lean Culture allows the identification of its new dimensions and descriptors which have not been previously defined, as well as their prioritisation.
- The interpretative-symbolic perspective makes it possible to capture the fundamental premises of organisational culture in higher education and to identify interdependences, contradictions, and gaps in Lean Culture.
- The external and internal contexts of higher education institutions, including their organisational culture, cause changes in the understanding of the essence of Lean Management as compared to business organisations.

The conducted research indicates that the list of the external context factors which exert influence on the shaping of Lean Culture in higher education includes factors connected with progress in the restructuring of public organisations in a given country as well as the social perception of Lean Management. The broadening of the research perspective allowed the author to expand the catalogue of Lean Values, to determine which of them are the most compatible with traditional academic culture, to identify the Lean Culture dimensions which are of particular importance for higher education, to determine the interpretations of Lean Culture dimensions from the point of view of individual university employees, as well as relations occurring among them. The conducted research inspired the author to an in-depth reflection on Lean Culture in higher education. In its primary essence, Lean Culture is based on foundations other than those of higher education organisational culture. It is based on the optics of business and manufacturing. Hence the recurring question about the usefulness and justifiability of applying this concept in higher education in the light of its specific qualities resulting from tradition and the nature of the knowledge creation process. The conducted research shows that certain solutions which constitute the foundation of Lean Culture, e.g. those related to leadership or the

Lean Principles, may appear to be very difficult or impossible to implement in their original versions in higher education institutions or may require a wide range of changes or adjustments. There is a serious risk that the concept will become very much distorted and its original sense will be lost. In the author's opinion, the panaceum for such situation is a consistent compliance with the Lean Values and the notions of value and wastage, which constitute the core of Lean thinking. Value should be the axis for all discussions and the method of obtaining value should be pursuing an agreement on what value is for the internal and external stakeholders of a higher education institution. Such an approach to defining values opens new areas of creative thinking about higher education management going beyond the standard, currently applied solutions. Contrary to the critical opinions of the opponents of applying Lean in higher education, in the author's opinion, the Lean concept allows universities to return to their identity, the essence and core of the processes on which it is based and defined in terms of the master–disciple and new–known (ignorance-knowledge) relations (Lenartowicz 2016, p. 65). Lean makes it possible to eliminate bureaucratic, corporate or NPM-related degeneration and to fight against the two curses of contemporary higher education, i.e. bureaucratisation and economisation. In the author's opinion, it is a considerable challenge because it requires an unconditional undertaking to create value and assume responsibility for this process. In light of the conducted research, the Lean concept appears to be compatible with the specific character of higher education. On the one hand, it is well received by employees as a common sense idea consistent with human nature. On the other hand, it is based on some kind of consensus built on a bottom-up basis by participants of processes. Thus Lean Culture becomes their own individual culture of work. Lean Culture is created in the individual and organisational dimensions. It is a rolling change. Hence the question is raised about how to ensure the maturity of Lean Culture in higher education, how to measure it, and which strategy to adopt. This is the subject matter of the deliberations undertaken in the next chapter.

Issues related to Lean Culture should obviously become the subject matter of in-depth interdisciplinary research combining the disciplines of management, psychology, sociology, linguistics, and others.

References

Allan, R. R., & Sinha, T. (2013). Core training and staff motivation: An assessment of improvement initiatives in HE; and Lean. In J. Antony, N. M. Nor, S. A. H. Lim, & S. Albliwi (Eds.), FICL6 [sigma]-2013: *First International Conference on Lean Six Sigma for Higher Education*, 24–25 June 2013. Glasgow, Scotland: University of Strathclyde.

Al-Najem, M., Dhakal, H., & Bennett, N. (2012). The role of culture and leadership in Lean transformation: A review and assessment model. *International Journal of Lean Thinking, 3*(1), 119–138.

Alvesson, M. (2009). At home ethnography: Struggling with closeness and closure. In S. Ybema, D. Yanow, H. Wels, & F. H. Kamsteeg (Eds.), *Organizational ethnography: Studying the complexity of everyday life* (pp. 156–217). London: Sage.

Alvesson, M., & Willmott, H. (1992). On the idea of emancipation in management and organization studies. *Academy of Management Review, 17*(3), 432–464.

Angelis, J., Conti, R., Cooper, C., & Gill, C. (2011). Building a high-commitment Lean culture. *Journal of Manufacturing Technology Management, 22*(5), 569–586.

Antonowicz, D. (2015). *Między siłą globalnych procesów a lokalną tradycją. Polskie szkolnictwo wyższe w dobie przemian* [Between the strength of global processes and local traditions. Poland's higher education in the age of transformation]. Toruń: Wydawnictwo Naukowe Uniwersytetu Mikołaja Kopernika.

Antony, J. (2014). Readiness factors for the Lean Six Sigma journey in the higher education sector. *International Journal of Productivity and Performance Management, 63*(2), 257–264.

Antony, J. (2017). Lean Six Sigma for higher education. *International Journal of Productivity and Performance Management, 66*(5), 574–576.

Atkinson, P., & Nicholls, L. (2013). Demystifying Lean culture change and continuous improvement. *Management Services, 57*(3), 10–15.

Babbie, E. R., (2013). *Podstawy badań społecznych* [The basics of social research]. Warszawa: Wydawnictwo Naukowe PWN.

Balzer, K. (2010). *Lean higher education*. New York: CRP Press, Taylor & Francis.

Balzer, W. K., Francis, D. E., Krehbiel, T. C., & Shea, N. (2016). A review and perspective on Lean in higher education. *Quality Assurance in Education, 24*(4), 442–462.

Bergquist, W. H. (1992). *The four cultures of the academy: Insights and strategies for improving leadership in collegiate organizations.* San Francisco: Jossey-Bass.

Bergquist, W. H., & Pawlak, K. (2008). *Engaging the six cultures of the academy: Revised and expanded edition of the four cultures of the academy.* San Francisco: Wiley.

Beytekđn, O. F., Yalçinkaya, M., Doğan, M., & Karakoç, N. (2010). The organizational culture at the university [Öğretmenlerin Profesyonel Öğrenmesini Etkileyen Faktörlerin Đncelenmesi]. *The International Journal of Educational Researchers, 2*(1):1–13.

Bicheno, J., & Holweg, M. (2000). *The Lean toolbox* (Vol. 4). Buckingham: PICSIE books.

Billings, L., Llamas, N. A., Snyder, B. E., & Sung, Y. (2017). Many languages, many workflows: Mapping and analyzing technical services processes for East Asian and international studies materials. *Cataloging & Classification Quarterly, 55*(7–8), 606–629.

Bonstingl, J. J. (1995). *Szkoły Jakości. Wprowadzenie do TQM w edukacji* [Schools of quality. An introduction to TQM in education]. Warszawa: Wydawnictwa CODN.

Buczkowska, J. (2015). Poznawcza geneza języka a informacyjna struktura znaczenia [The cognitive origins of language and the information structure of meaning]. *Studia Philosophiae Christianae, 51*(4), 75–96.

Bugdol, M. (2006). *Wartości organizacyjne. Szkice z teorii organizacji i zarządzania* [Organizational values. Essays on the theory of organization and management]. Kraków: Wydawnictwo Uniwersytetu Jagiellońskiego.

Bugdol, M. (2011), Zarządzanie zasobami ludzkimi w szkolnictwie wyższym według modeli doskonałości [Human resources management in higher education based on excellence models]. In T. Wawak (Ed.), *Wyzwania zarządzania jakością w szkołach wyższych.* Kraków: Wyd. UJ w Krakowie.

Bugdol, M. (2018). *System zarządzania jakością według normy ISO 9001:2015* [A quality management system based on the ISO 9001:2015 standard]. Gliwice: One Press.

Burrell, G., & Morgan, G. (2005). *Sociological paradigms and organisational analysis: Elements of the sociology of corporate life.* Ardershot: Ashgate.

Caffyn, S. (1999). Development of a continuous improvement self-assessment tool. *International Journal of Operations & Production Management, 19*(11), 1138–1153.

Cameron, K. S., & Quinn, R. E. (2015). *Kultura organizacyjna – diagnoza i zmiana. Model wartości konkurujących* [Diagnosing and changing

organizational culture: Based on the competing values framework].
Warszawa: Wolters Kluwer.

Cano, M., Moyes, D., & Kobi, A. (2016). A framework for implementing Lean operations management in the higher education sector. In *Toulon-Verona Conference "Excellence in Services"*.

Cardona, P., & Rey, C. (2009). Zarządzanie poprzez misje [Management by missions]. Warszawa: Oficyna a Wolters Kluwer business.

Charles Bruno, T. (2013). Assess, enhance, repeat: Fostering a culture of continuous improvement in document delivery. *Interlending & Document Supply, 41*(3), 75–80.

Charmaz, K. (2009). *Teoria ugruntowana. Praktyczny przewodnik po analizie jakościowej* [Constructing grounded theory: A practical guide through qualitative analysis]. Warszawa: Wydawnictwo Naukowe PWN.

Clark, B. R. (1972). The organizational saga in higher education. *Administrative Science Quarterly, 17*(2), 178–184.

Creswell, J. W. (2013). *Projektowanie badań naukowych: Metody jakościowe, ilościowe i mieszane* [Research design: Qualitative, quantitative, and mixed methods approaches]. Kraków: Wydawnictwo Uniwersytetu Jagiellońskiego.

Czarniawska, B. (2010). *Trochę inna teoria organizacji. Organizowanie jako konstrukcja sieci działań* [A little bit different theory of organization. Organizing as constructing a network of activities]. Warszawa: Poltext.

Czerska, M. (2003). *Zmiana kulturowa w organizacji. Wyzwanie dla współczesnego menedżera* [Cultural change in the organization. A challenge for the contemporary manager]. Warszawa: Difin.

Davies, J. (1995). Cultural change in universities in the context of strategic and quality initiatives. In P. Tabatoni, J. Davies J., & A. Barblan, *Strategic management and university's institutional development*. www.eau.

Deem, R. (1998). New managerialism and higher education: The management of performances and cultures in universities in the United Kingdom. *International Studies in Sociology of Education, 8*(1), 47–70.

Deming, W. E. (2012). *Wyjście z kryzysu* [Out of the crisis]. OpExBooks.pl.

Doolen, T. L., & Hacker, M. E. (2005). A review of Lean assessment in organizations: An exploratory study of Lean practices by electronics manufacturers. *Journal of Manufacturing systems, 24*(1), 55–67.

Douglas, J., Antony, J., & Douglas, A. (2015). Waste identification and elimination in HEIs: The role of Lean thinking. *International Journal of Quality & Reliability Management, 32*(9), 970–981.

Dragomir, C., & Surugiu, F. (2013). Implementing Lean in a higher education university. *Constanta Maritime University: Constanta, Romania, XIII, 18,* 279–282.

Emiliani, B. (2014). *The language of Lean*. Downloaded from https://bobemiliani.com/the-language-of-lean/. Accessed 9 July 2018.

Emiliani, B. (2015). *Lean university: A guide to renewal and prosperity*. Wethersfield: CLBM, LCC.

Emiliani, M. L. (1998). Lean behaviours. *Management Decision, 36*(9), 615–631.

Emiliani, M. L. (2005). Using kaizen to improve graduate business school degree programs. *Quality Assurance in Education, 13*(1), 37–52.

Erthal, A., & Marques, L. (2018). National culture and organisational culture in Lean organisations: A systematic review. *Production Planning & Control, 29*(8), 1–20.

Francis, D. (2014). Lean and the learning organization in higher education. *Canadian Journal of Educational Administration and Policy* (157), 1–23.

Francis, D. E., Krehbiel, T. C., & Balzer, W. K. (2017). *Lean applications in higher education*. Downloaded from https://the-lmj.com/2017/03/.

Gioia, D. A., Schultz, M., & Corley, K. G. (2000). Organizational identity, image, and adaptive instability. *Academy of Management Review, 25*(1), 63–81.

Goffee, R., & Jones, G. (1998). *The character of a corporation: How your company's culture can make or break your business*. London: HarperCollins Business.

Hamrol, (2015). *Strategie i praktyki sprawnego działania: Lean, Six Sigma i inne* [Strategies and practices of efficient operation. Lean, Six Sigma, and others]. Warszawa: Wydawnictwo Naukowe PWN.

Hatch, M. J. (2002). *Teoria organizacji* [Organization theory]. Warszawa: Wydawnictwo Naukowe PWN.

Hines, P., Holweg, M. Rich, N. (2004). Learning to evolve. *International Journal of Operations & Production Management, 24*(10), 994–1011. http://www.emeraldinsight/. Accessed 15 February 2008.

Hines, P., & Lethbridge, S. (2008). New development: Creating a Lean university. *Public Money and Management, 28*(1), 53–56.

Hofstede, G., Hofstede, G. J., & Minkov, M. (2011). *Kultury i organizacje: Zaprogramowanie umysłu* [Cultures and organizations: Software of the mind]. Warszawa: Polskie Wydawnictwo Ekonomiczne.

Holloway, J. B. (2012). Leadership behavior and organizational climate: An empirical study in a non-profit organization. *Emerging Leadership Journeys, 5*(1), 9–35.

Hoseus, M., & Liker, J. K. (2008). *Toyota culture: The heart and soul of the Toyota way*. New York: Print Matters.

Jabłecka, J. (2000). Misja organizacji a misja uniwersytetu [Mission of an organisation versus mission of a university]. *Nauka i Szkolnictwo Wyższe, 2*(16), 7–25.

Jakubik, M., Kagan, R., Hanusyk, K., & Koch, T. (2012). Motywowanie pracowników w środowisku Lean [Motivating employees in a Lean environment]. In *Ciągłe doskonalenie w oparciu o zasady Lean Manufacturing.* Wrocław: Wyd. Lean Enterprise Institute Polska.

Jashapara, A. (2006). *Zarządzanie wiedzą* [Knowledge management]. Warszawa: Polskie Wydawnictwo Ekonomiczne.

Jo Hatch, M., & Schultz, M. (1997). Relations between organizational culture, identity and image. *European Journal of Marketing, 31*(5/6), 356–365.

Jones, A. P., & James, L. R. (1979). Psychological climate: Dimensions and relationships of individual and aggregated work environment perceptions. *Organizational Behavior and Human Performance, 23*(2), 201–250.

Jørgensen, F., Matthiesen, R., Nielsen, J., & Johansen, J. (2007). Lean maturity, lean sustainability. In J. Olhager, & F. Persson (Eds.), *Advances in production management systems* (pp. 371–378). Boston: Springer.

Jóźwiak, J. (1999). Tradycyjne koncepcje instytucji akademickiej [Traditional concepts of academic institutions]. In J. Woźnicki (Ed.), *Model zarządzania publiczną instytucją akademicką.* Warszawa: JSP.

Kamp, P. M. (2017). *The Lean journey for Dutch higher education institutions: A way to go?* (Master's thesis). University of Twente.

Kawalec, P. (2017). Ewaluacja – teoria i metodologia [Evaluation—Theory and methodology]. In G. Prawelska-Skrzypek (Ed.), *Ewaluacja w procesie tworzenia polityki naukowej i innowacyjnej.* Warszawa: Dom Wydawniczy Elipsa.

Kezar, A., & Eckel, P. D. (2002). The effect of institutional culture on change strategies in higher education: Universal principles or culturally responsive concepts? *The Journal of Higher Education, 73*(4), 435–460.

Kochalski, C. (Ed.). (2011). *Model projektowania i wdrażania strategii rozwoju w publicznych szkołach wyższych w Polsce* [A model of designing and implementing development strategies in public higher education institutions in Poland]. Poznań: Wyd. UE w Poznaniu.

Koj, A. (1998). Rola uniwersytetu w systemie edukacji [The role of a university in an educational system]. In K. Pacławska (Ed.), *Tradycja i wyzwania. Edukacja. Niepodległość. Rozwój.* Kraków: UNIVERSITAS.

Kostera, M. (2005). *Antropologia organizacji: Metodologia badań terenowych* [Anthropology of organizations: Field research methodology]. Warszawa: PWN.

Kot, W. (1996). *Historia wychowania. t. II* [History of education. Vol. II]. Warszawa: Żak.

Kotter, J. P., & Heskett, J. L. (1992). *Corporate culture and performance*. New York: The Free Press.

Koźmiński, A. K. (1999). Misje i strategie szkół wyższych [Missions and strategies of higher education institutions]. In J. Woźnicki (Ed.), *Model zarządzania publiczną instytucją akademicką*. Warszawa: ISP.

Krzyżanowski, L. (1997). *Podstawy nauk o organizacji i zarządzaniu* [Rudiments of management science]. Warszawa: PWN.

Kusy, M., Diamond, M., & Vrchota, S. (2015). Why culture change is critical to Lean initiatives. Lean training and coaching alone are not enough to improve customer satisfaction. *Healthcare Executive, 30*(6), 48.

Kvale, S. (2010). *Prowadzenie wywiadów* [Doing interviews]. Warszawa: Wydawnictwo Naukowe PWN.

Kwiek, M. (2010). *Transformacje uniwersytetu. Zmiany instytucjonalne i ewolucje polityki edukacyjnej w Europie* [Transformations of the university. Institutional changes and educational policy evolution in Europe]. Poznań: Wydawnictwo Naukowe UAM.

Kwiek, M. (2015). *Uniwersytet w dobie przemian* [The university in the period of changes]. Warszawa: PWN.

Lacatus, M. L. (2013). Organizational culture in contemporary university. *Procedia-Social and Behavioral Sciences, 76*, 421–425.

Langer, T. (2011). *Lean university. The application of Lean thinking for Improving processes in higher education institutions: Evidence from three UK case studies*. Belfast: Queen's University Belfast.

Leja, K. (2013). *Zarządzanie uczelnią. Koncepcje i współczesne wyzwania* [University management. Concepts and contemporary challenges]. Warszawa: Oficyna Wolters Kluwer business.

Lenartowicz, M. (2016). *Natura oporu Uniwersytet jako samowytwarzający się system społeczny* [The nature of resistance. The university as a self-creating social system]. Poznań: CSPP UAM.

Lencioni, P. M. (2002). Make your values mean something. *Harvard Business Review, 80*(7), 113–117.

Liker, J. K. (2005). *The Toyota Way*. Warsaw: Esensi.

Liker, J. K., & Convis, G. L. (2012). *Droga Toyoty do lean leadership* [The Toyota way to Lean leadership]. Warszawa: MT Biznes.

Liker, J. K., & Meier, D. P. (2005). *Droga Toyoty* [The Toyota way]. Warszawa: Wydawnictwo MT BIZNES sp. z oo.

Liker, J. K., & Morgan, J. M. (2006). The Toyota way in services: The case of Lean product development. *Academy of Management Perspectives, 20*(2), 5–20.

Lindahl, F. W., & Fanelli, R. (2002). Applying continuous improvement to teaching in another culture. *Journal of Accounting Education, 20*(4), 285–295.

Losonci, D., Kása, R., Demeter, K., Heidrich, B., & Jenei, I. (2017). The impact of shop floor culture and subculture on Lean production practices. *International Journal of Operations & Production Management, 37*(2), 205–225.

Lu, J., Laux, C., & Antony, J. (2017). Lean Six Sigma leadership in higher education institutions. *International Journal of Productivity and Performance Management, 66*(5), 638–650.

Maciąg, J. (2016a). Uwarunkowania wdrożenia koncepcji Lean Service w polskich szkołach wyższych [The conditions of implementing the Lean Service concept in Polish higher education institutions]. *Zarządzanie Publiczne, 1*(33), 51–64.

Maciąg, J. (2016b, November 1–3). *The determining role of organizational culture in the implementation of the Lean management concept as examplified by Polish universities*. Lean Conference 2016 "People, Culture and Lean in Higher Education", University of Stirling, Scotland. Downloaded from http://www.leanhehub.ac.uk/conference/former-hosts.

Magala, S. (2006). Trzy światy uniwersyteckiej społeczności (badacze, nauczyciele, obywatele) [The three worlds of the academic community (researchers, lecturers, citizens)]. In J. Chłopecki (Ed.), *Uniwersytet, społeczeństwo, gospodarka* [University, society, economy]. Rzeszów: Wyd. WSIZ.

Mann, D. (2009). The missing link: Lean leadership. *Frontiers of Health Services Management, 26*(1), 15–26.

Mann, D. (2014). *Creating a Lean culture: Tools to sustain Lean conversions.* New York: Productivity Press.

Martin, J. (1992). *Cultures organizations: Three perspectives.* London: Oxford University Press.

Martin, J. (2001). *Organizational culture: Mapping the terrain.* Thousand Oaks: Sage.

Masland, A. T. (1985). Organizational culture in the study of higher education. *The Review of Higher Education, 8*(2), 157–168.

McNay, I. (1995). Universities going international: Choices, cautions and conditions. In P. Blok (Ed.), *Policy and policy implementation in internationalisation of higher education.* Amsterdam: EAIE.

McNay, I. (2006). *Values, principles and integrity: Academic and professional standards in higher education.* Downloaded from https://www.oecd.org/site/imhe2006bis/37245044.pdf.

Miller, L. M. (2011). *Lean culture. The leader's guide.* Annapolis, MD: LM Miller Consulting.

Morest, V. S. (2009). Accountability, accreditation, and continuous improvement: Building a culture of evidence. *New Directions for Institutional Research, 143,* 17–27.

Morgan, G., & Wiankowska-Ładyka, Z. (2013). *Obrazy organizacji* [Images of organizations]. Warszawa: Wydawnictwo Naukowe PWN.

Ostroff, C., Kinicki, A. J., & Tamkins, M. M. (2003). Organizational culture and climate. *Handbook of Psychology, 12,* 565–593.

Ott, J. S. (1989). *The organizational culture perspective.* Chicago, IL: The Dorsey Press.

Pakdil, F., & Leonard, K. M. (2015). The effect of organizational culture on implementing and sustaining Lean processes. *Journal of Manufacturing Technology Management, 26*(5), 725–743.

Pakdil, F., & Leonard, K. M. (2017). Implementing and sustaining Lean processes: The dilemma of societal culture effects. *International Journal of Production Research, 55*(3), 700–717.

Parkes, A. (2015). Lean management genesis. *Management, 19*(2), 106–121.

Parkes, A. (2017). *Kulturowe uwarunkowania Lean Management* [The cultural conditions of Lean Management]. Warszawa: Difin.

Paro, P. E. P., & Gerolamo, M. C. (2017). Organizational culture for Lean programs. *Journal of Organizational Change Management, 30*(4), 584–598.

Prawelska-Skrzypek G., Sinha T., Welch Ch., Ward N., & Maciąg, J., (Eds.). (2019). *Community of practice as a form of voluntary academic cooperation.* Chapter in the peer reviewed monograph. Warszawa: Publishing House PWN (accepted for a print).

Radnor, Z., & Bucci, G. (2011). *Analysis of Lean implementation in UK business schools and universities.* London: Association of Business Schools.

Radnor, Z., Walley, P., Stephens, A., & Bucci, G. (2006). Evaluation of the Lean approach to business management and its use in the public sector. *Scottish Executive Social Research, 20.*

Robinson, M., & Yorkstone, S. (2014). Becoming a Lean University: The case of the University of St Andrews. *Leadership and Governance in Higher Education, 1,* 42–72.

Rybkowski, R. (2015). Autonomia a rozliczalność–polskie wyzwania [Autonomy versus accountability—Polish challenges]. *Nauka i Szkolnictwo Wyższe, 1*(45), 95–115.

Schein, E. H. (2004). *Organizational culture and leadership (Jossey-Bass business & management series).* San Francisco: Jossey-Bass.

Shah, R., & Ward, P. T. (2007). Defining and developing measures of Lean production. *Journal of Operations Management, 25*(4), 785–805.

Siehl, C., & Martin, J. (1984). The role of symbolic management: How can managers effectively transmit organizational culture? In J. Hunt, D. Hosking, C. Schriesheim, & R. Stewart (Eds.), *Leaders and managers: International perspectives on managerial behavior and leadership*. Elmsford, NY: Pergamon [After:] Ott, J. S. (1989). *The organizational culture perspective*. Dorsey Press.

Sikorski, C. (2009). *Kształtowanie kultury organizacyjnej: filozofia, strategie, metody* [The shaping of organizational culture: Philosophy, strategies, methods]. Łódź: Wydawnictwo Uniwersytetu Łódzkiego.

Sinclair, J., & Arthur, A. (1994). Inhospitable cultures and continuous improvement. *International Journal of Contemporary Hospitality Management, 6*(1/2), 30–36.

Smart, J. C., & St. John, E. P. (1996). Organizational culture and effectiveness in higher education: A test of the "culture type" and "strong culture" hypotheses. *Educational Evaluation and Policy Analysis, 18*(3), 219–241.

Smircich, L. (1983). Concepts of culture and organizational analysis. *Administrative Science Quarterly, 28*(3), 339–358.

Sowa, K. Z. (2009). *Gdy myślę uniwersytet... ...*[When I think of a university...]. Kraków: Wydawnictwo Uniwersytetu Jagiellońskiego.

Starbird, D. (2017). The value of a Lean culture. *The Journal for Quality and Participation, 39*(4), 19.

Stoller, J. (2015). *Lean CEO: w drodze do doskonałości* [The Lean CEO: Leading the way to world-class excellence]. Warszawa: MT Biznes.

Sułkowski, Ł. (2008). Czy warto zajmować się kulturą organizacyjną [Whether organizational culture is worth studying]. *Zarządzanie Zasobami Ludzkimi, 6*, 9–25.

Sułkowski, Ł. (2012). *Kulturowe procesy zarządzania* [Cultural management processes]. Warszawa: Difin.

Sułkowski, Ł. (2014). Zmiana kultury organizacyjnej – paradygmaty, modele i metody zarządzania [Changes in organizational culture—Management paradigms, models, and methods]. In Ł. Sułkowski, & Cz. Sikorski (Ed.), *Metody zarządzania kulturą organizacyjną*. Warszawa: Difin.

Sułkowski, Ł. (2016). *Kultura akademicka: koniec utopii?* [The academic culture. The end of a utopia?]. Warszawa: Wydawnictwo Naukowe PWN.

Sułkowski, Ł. (2017a). Doskonalenie organizacyjne polskich uczelni [Organizational improvement of Polish higher education institutions].

In Ł. Sułkowski, & A. M. Migdał (Eds.), *Przedsiębiorczość i Zarządzanie, Tom XVIII, Zeszyt 2, Część II, „Zarządzanie humanistyczne i publiczne"* (pp. 9–21). Łódź-Warszawa: Wydawnictwo Społeczna Akademia Nauk.

Sułkowski, Ł. (2017b). *Fuzje uczelni. Czy w szaleństwie jest metoda?* [Mergers of universities. Is there a method in this madness?]. Warszawa: WN PWN.

Svensson C., Ba-Essa M., & Bakhsh, M. (2013). Establishing a Lean Six Sigma in higher education. In J. Antony, N. M. Nor, S. A. H. Lim, & S. Albliwi (Eds.), FICL6 [sigma]-2013: *First International Conference on Lean Six Sigma for Higher Education*, 24–25th June 2013. Glasgow, Scotland: University of Strathclyde.

Svensson, C., Antony, J., Ba-Essa, M., Bakhsh, M., & Albliwi, S. (2015). A Lean Six Sigma program in higher education. *International Journal of Quality & Reliability Management, 32*(9), 951–969.

Taherimashhadi, M., & Ribas, I. (2018). A model to align the organizational culture to Lean. *Journal of Industrial Engineering and Management, 11*(2), 207–221.

Thomas A., Francis M., Fisher R., & Chilton K. (2013). Can higher education Lean itself up? Can the further education sector show us the way? In J. Antony, N. M. Nor, S. A. H. Lim, & S. Albliwi (Eds.), FICL6 [sigma]-2013: *First International Conference on Lean Six Sigma for Higher Education*, 24–25th June 2013. Glasgow, Scotland: University of Strathclyde.

Thomas, A., Antony, J., Francis, M., & Fisher, R. (2015). A comparative study of Lean implementation in higher and further education institutions in the UK. *International Journal of Quality & Reliability Management, 32*(9), 982–996.

Tierney, W. G. (1988). Organizational culture in higher education: Defining the essentials. *The Journal of Higher Education, 59*(1), 2–21.

Toma, J. D., Dubrow, G., & Hartley, M. (2005). The uses of institutional culture: Strengthening identification and building brand equity in higher education. *ASHE Higher Education Report, 31*(2), 1–105.

Urban, W. (2015). The Lean management maturity self-assessment tool based on organizational culture diagnosis. *Procedia-Social and Behavioral Sciences, 213*, 728–733.

Van der Merwe, K. R., Pieterse, J. J., & Lourens, A. S. (2014). The development of a theoretical Lean culture causal framework to support the effective implementation of Lean in automotive component manufacturers. *South African Journal of Industrial Engineering, 25*(1), 131–144.

Van Maanen, J. (2011). *Tales of the field: On writing ethnography*. Chicago: University of Chicago Press.

Vyas, N., & Campbell, M. (2015). Industry in crisis. *Six Sigma Forum Magazine, 15*(1), 18–22.

Walentynowicz, P. (2013). *Uwarunkowania skuteczności wdrażania Lean Management w przedsiębiorstwach produkcyjnych w Polsce* [The conditions for the effective implementation of Lean management in production enterprises in Poland]. Gdańsk: Wydawnictwo Uniwersytetu Gdańskiego.

Wallace, J., Hunt, J., & Richards, C. (1999). The relationship between organisational culture, organisational climate and managerial values. *International Journal of Public Sector Management, 12*(7), 548–564.

Wallach, E. (1983). Individuals and organization: The cultural match. *Training and Development Journal, 12*, 28–36.

Waterbury, T. (2011). *Educational Lean for higher education: Theory and practice*. Lulu.com.

Weick, K. (2016). *Tworzenie sensu w organizacjach* [Sensemaking in organizations]. Kraków: Wydawnictwo Uniwersytetu Jagiellońskiego.

Willmott, H. (2003). Renewing strength: Corporate culture revisited. *Management, 6*(3), 73–87.

Wilson, N. (2015). Language of lean. *The Lean Management Journal*. Downloaded from https://the-lmj.com/.

Womack, J. P., Jones, D. T., & Roos, D. (1990). *The machine that changed the world: The story of Lean production* (p. 85). New York: Rawson Associates.

Woźnicki, J. (2000). Dylematy modelowe w kształtowaniu systemu szkolnictwa wyższego u progu XXI wieku [Model dilemmas in the shaping of a higher education system on the eve of the 21st century]. *Nauka, 4*, 55–6.

Yorkstone, S. (2016). Lean universities. In T. Netland & D. J. Powell (eds.). *The Routledge companion to Lean management*. Abingdon: Taylor & Francis (Routledge), 978-1138920590.

Zarbo, R. J. (2012). Creating and sustaining a Lean culture of continuous process improvement. *American Journal of Clinical Pathology, 138*(3), 321–326.

Zawadzki, M. (2014). *Nurt krytyczny w zarządzaniu: kultura, edukacja, teoria* [The critical trend in management: Culture, education, theory]. Warsaw: Wydawnictwo Akademickie SEDNO Spółka z oo.

Zeller, P. (2011). Specyfika zarządzania szkołami wyższymi w świetle literatury [The specific character of managing higher education institutions in the light of the literature on the subject]. In C. Kochalski (Ed.), *Model projektowania i wdrażania strategii rozwoju w publicznych szkołach wyższych w Polsce*. Poznań: Wyd. UE w Poznaniu.

Zohar, D., & Hofmann, D. A. (2012). Organizational culture and climate. *Oxford Handbook of Industrial and Organizational Psychology, 1,* 643–666.

(www1) http://www.newsweek.pl/inne/ranking-gmin/a-po-co-to-iso,55565, 1,1.html.

(www2) https://drive.google.com/drive/folders/0B0o0qNZiNb1uNkdNUD F5ZHNIME0.

(www3) https://www.britannica.com/topic/language. Accessed 9 July 2018.

(www4) https://sjp.pwn.pl/slowniki/j%C4%99zyk.html. Accessed 9 July 2018.

(www5) http://www.leanhehub.ac.uk/.

(www6) http://www.isp.uj.edu.pl/projekty-w-trakcie-realizacji/-/journal_ content/56_INSTANCE_n9v3lSFqAPGx/2103800/135045947.

4

Maturity of Lean Culture in Higher Education—Research, Assessment, and Improvement

4.1 Introduction

The objective of implementing Lean Management is to change higher education organisational culture in the dimensions of values, leadership, people, team work and relations, external relations, Lean Principles, and artefacts. These dimensions were described in detail in Chapter 3 of this book. The issue of Lean Culture maturity is discussed mainly in publications concerning manufacturing enterprises (Kaltenbrunner et al. 2017; Dos Santos Bento and Tontini 2018; Vinodh and Chintha 2011; Perera and Perera 2013; Vimal and Vinodh 2012; Chiarini and Vagnoni 2015; Perkins et al. 2010; Al-Najem Dhakal and Bennett 2012; Caffyn 1999; Jørgensen et al. 2007; Wu and Chen 2006; Doolen and Hacker 2005; Shah and Ward 2007). Researchers have developed a number of various models and tools for assessing the degree of the implementation of Lean Management and the maturity of Lean Culture in organisations, for example: CIRCA CI self-assessment tool, integrated CI structural model, Lean Capability Model, Questionnaire to measure the implementation of Lean practices, Lean Enterprise Self-Assessment Tool (LESAT), Multigrade fuzzy approach for assessing leanness, Lean

© The Author(s) 2019
J. Maciąg, *Lean Culture in Higher Education*,
https://doi.org/10.1007/978-3-030-05686-5_4

Culture Assessment Model (LCAM), Leanness Model Performance Measurement System (PMS) for Lean Manufacturing Organizations, Gap-based maturity assessment model, Lean in Healthcare Questionnaire (LiHcQ), Lean manufacturing maturity model, Lean Manufacturing Constructs. Nevertheless, from the perspective of higher education realities, they have numerous shortcomings. Research on this subject conducted in higher education institutions focused mostly on the assessment of their preparedness for implementing Lean Management and Lean Six Sigma (Radnor and Bucci 2011; Balzer et al. 2016; Anthony and Antony 2016). The growing popularity of the Lean Management concept as a method of changing management in higher education institutions results in the necessity of diagnosing an organisational culture in terms of its readiness for the implementation of the Lean Management concept. The models, methods, and tools proposed in the literature are insufficient or inappropriate, taking into consideration the external and internal management context and the specific character of higher education organisational culture. The conducted analysis of the literature on the subject allowed the author to indicate the following research gaps:

• A lack of basic definitions of such notions as Lean Culture maturity, Lean Culture maturity model, Lean Culture maturity assessment level.
• A lack of a concept of and tool for the assessment of Lean Culture maturity in higher education.
• Fragmentary research on Lean Culture maturity assessment in higher education as well as conditions for building such assessment. A lack of a typology of Lean Cultures in higher education institutions.
• A lack of research on factors diversifying Lean Culture assessment.
• Limited and fragmentary research on the implementation of Lean Management concept in higher education. A lack of a systematic approach to Lean Culture maturity improvement. Fragmentary descriptions of programmes aimed at building Lean Culture maturity in higher education.

The research gap identified by the author became the reason for undertaking research on developing a tool for the assessment of the maturity of Lean Culture in higher education. The main research problem can be expressed in the following questions: How should Lean Culture maturity be examined and assessed for the purpose of its further improvement? What are the conditions for such assessment? The general objective of this chapter is to present the author's original tool for the assessment of Lean Culture maturity in higher education, to determine the conditions for its application, and to present a concept of a programme for the building of Lean Culture maturity.

The particular goals of this chapter are the following:

- To define a conceptual framework for the examination, assessment, and testing of Lean Culture maturity.
- To create a tool for assessing Lean Culture maturity Lean Culture Maturity Questionnaire (LCMQ) and to determine the conditions for its application.
- To test the LCMQ and to determine the factors conditioning Lean Culture maturity assessment.
- To develop a plan of a programme for building Lean Culture maturity in higher education institutions.

In this chapter, the following research questions are posed:

- Does the LCMQ allow a reliable assessment of Lean Culture maturity in higher education?
- Is Lean Culture maturity assessment diversified with respect to a university management model?
- Do the results of Lean Culture maturity assessment indicate the existence of a separate subculture created by a university's top management?
- Do the results of Lean Culture maturity assessment indicate the existence of separate subcultures created by administration employees or academic employees?
- Do participation in restructuring projects and possession of experience in Lean Management influence Lean Culture maturity assessment?
- Taking into consideration the diversified external and internal contexts of functioning, including organisational culture, is it possible to develop a model programme of change in higher education organisational culture?

Answering the above research questions, the author formulated the following research hypotheses. The author assumes the following:

- The LCMQ allows a correct, accurate, and reliable assessment of Lean Culture maturity in higher education.
- Lean Culture maturity assessment is higher in private universities and universities implementing quality management models and other process management concepts.
- University management assesses Lean Culture maturity at a higher level (there is a separate subculture).
- With respect to maturity assessment levels, it is possible to distinguish two subcultures: the subculture of administration employees and the subculture of academics.
- University employees who have experience in implementing process management concepts are more critical in assessing Lean Culture maturity (an assessment level will be lower).
- It is possible to develop a model programme of change in organisational culture oriented towards the building of a Lean University which will be possible to apply in every higher education institution.

In order to verify the formulated hypotheses, the author used the following research methods: the analysis of the literature on the subject, the expert assessment method, the questionnaire research technique together with the Internet questionnaire technique, the statistical analysis method, the method of incomplete enumerative induction at the stage of generalising the results of observations and formulating statements in a research questionnaire, and the method of deduction at the stage of verification and formulating conclusions.

This chapter will discuss the problem of the assessment of Lean Culture maturity and present the author's original research tool for diagnosing Lean Culture maturity in higher education as well as the conditions for its application. The chapter ends with a proposal for a programme of building Lean Culture maturity in higher education institutions. The author discusses also at length the limitations of research on and assessment of Lean Culture maturity in higher education.

4.2   The Culture of a Process-Oriented Organisation

Undertaking a review and discussion of the most important Lean Culture maturity assessment models, it is necessary first of all to explain the notions of maturity, organisational culture maturity, and Lean Culture maturity. In language dictionaries, the notion of maturity is defined as "a very advanced or developed form or state" (www1), "the quality or state of being mature especially: full development" (www2). In view of the wide variety of used definitions, the author decided to refer to the international terminological standards proposed by the International Organization for Standardization. ISO (www3) defines maturity within the terminology concerning mainly information systems. The related standards include such terms as maturity, maturity level, and maturity model. Maturity is defined as *a state of a system, demonstrated by special characteristics and behaviour, that permits it to operate better in accordance with its business goals as a result of transformation and adoption (with respect to information systems)* (ISO/TR 13054:2012). Maturity level is defined as *a point on an ordinal scale of organizational process maturity that characterizes the maturity of the organizational unit assessed in the scope of the maturity model used* (ISO/IEC 33001:2015). The definition of maturity model is as follows: *a set of structured levels that describe how well the behaviours, practices, and processes of an organization can reliably and sustainably produce required outcomes* (ISO/TR 14639-2:2014), *means of and scale for evaluating and assessing the current state of maturity* (ISO/TR 13054:2012). In the light of the above definitions, it is possible to state that a maturity model is a set of levels, a scale, a means of assessing a degree of maturity with respect to assumed criteria.

In management, the notion of maturity is used the most often to determine a degree of maturity in comparison to assumed theoretical criteria (e.g. Jeston and Nelis 2008, p. 315, ISO 9004:2018, EFQM, CMMI). The subject matter of assessment is the maturity of various elements such as an organisation, system, process, resources, leadership, organisational culture, etc. or areas of activity in organisations, e.g. process management, quality management, project management, strategic management, information systems management, knowledge management, environmental management, risk management (Bugdol and Szczepańska 2016). Maturity is treated as a final assessment and a measure of progress (Jedynak 2007, p. 77).

In the case of organisational culture, an assessment of maturity is conducted with reference to adopted theoretical models. An approach to research on organisational culture is determined by a research perspective based on adopted paradigmatic premises, which was described in Chapter 3 (e.g. Sułkowski 2016). It can have the character of a qualitative assessment (organisational culture is examined by means of observations and interviews conducted in an organisation) (e.g. Schein 2004; Kostera 2003) or a quantitative assessment (survey questionnaires) (e.g. Cameron and Quinn 2003). A survey of the literature on the subject shows that in this respect there is some kind of epistemological pluralism, and researchers use the whole spectrum of social research methods.

As it has already been mentioned in the previous chapters of the book, Lean Culture is an organisational culture oriented towards processes. Consequently, Lean Culture maturity is also conditioned by an organisation's process maturity. Van Looy, Backer and Poels define process maturity as '*the extent to which an organisation has explicitly and consistently deployed processes*' (Van Looy et al. 2011). According to the terminology proposed by the ISO, *organizational process maturity* is defined as *an extent to which an organizational unit consistently implements processes within a defined scope that contributes to the achievement of its business needs (current or projected)* (ISO/IEC 33001:2015). Process maturity can be defined as follows (Van Looy et al. 2011; Rummler and Brache 2000):

- at the level of an individual process (maturity of a business process which comprises process development and modelling),
- at the level of processes and their mutual relations within an organisation (maturity of Business Process Management which comprises process management and optimisation), and
- at the level of an organisation (maturity of a business process approach which comprises a process structure and process culture).

It should be noted that this approach to classifying organisations' process maturity has a purely theoretical character. It shows the way towards acquiring the maturity of the process approach in an organisation. In practice, all these levels are regarded jointly, which is the consequence of the complexity of changes in the social, technical, organisational, economic spheres resulting from the implementation of process management concepts.

The most popular and universal process maturity assessment model is the model specified in the requirements of the ISO 9001 standard (ISO 9001:2015). These requirements concern process identification, definition, measurement, monitoring, assessment, and improvement. The literature on the subject mentions also assessment models dedicated to selected processes in an organisation (Rosemann and De Bruin 2005, p. 7), for example: the Process Condition Model developed by DeToro and McCabe, the maturity model for the fulfilment of the 48-h-service promise in the public sector developed by Zwicker, the collaboration maturity model developed by Magdaleno and the team or the Capability Maturity Model Integration (CMM, CMMI), Investors in People (www4). The CMM and CMMI models have been used in higher education institutions for more than twenty years. They are used, among other things, in the assessment of informatics and information systems, human resources management, quality management in e-learning processes, students' involvement in learning processes, the assurance of a learning system in business programmes (Garceau et al. 2015, p. 137).

The maturity of a process approach is frequently equated with the maturity of process management. It is defined in terms of organisational, technical, and social maturity. In the organisational and technical dimensions, the subject of assessment is the maturity of processes and process management as well as it institutionalisation (a process management system) (ISO 9001:2015). Maturity in the social dimension is conditioned by social processes in an organisation. Its meaning is close to that indicated in definitions of social capital. As Bugdol emphasises, definitions of social capital in organisations focus on its major dimensions such as knowledge, skills, talents, and cooperation abilities (competences of organisational actors), relations, social networks and their standards, as well as trust (Bugdol 2006, p. 120). Thus, in the social dimension, maturity can be defined as a measure of the maturity of an organisation's social capital. The creation of social capital is facilitated by both a well designed organisational structure and a work organisation system (Bugdol 2006, p. 120). In order to emphasise the unique character of process-based organisational culture, researchers use the notion of process culture (Bitkowska and Weiss 2015, p. 245; Grajewski 2012, p. 101). In such culture, the organisational-technical dimension and the social dimension are closely connected (Van Looy et al. 2011).

There are many models used to assess the maturity of a process approach. Such models comprise the organisational, technical, and social dimensions of process approach maturity. The author proposed a classification of these models, taking into consideration their structural premises and first of all the number of dimensions subject to assessment. In one-dimensional models, maturity is assessed on the basis of a predetermined set of criteria. In this context, the following models can be distinguished: Crosby's Maturity Grid Model 1979 (Crosby 1979), the model specified in the ISO 9004 standard (ISO 9004:2018) (www5), the model specified in the ISO 10014 standard (ISO 1001), Model Speyer (Bugdol 2011; Lisiecka 2009). In two-dimensional models, maturity is assessed with respect to expenditures and effects, with a separate set of assessment criteria for either of them. Criteria for expenditures include usually leadership, employees, strategy, partnership, resources, and processes; criteria applicable to effects comprise results for employees, customers, society, as well as results of key importance for an organisation. Examples of such models include Malcolm Baldrige's excellence model, Deming's model, the European Foundation for Quality Management (EFQM) model, and the Common Assessment Framework (CAF) model dedicated to public organisations. These models are used also to assess process maturity in higher education institutions (Mashhadi et al. 2008, p. 340; Calvo-Mora et al. 2005). There are also multidimensional models. In such models, maturity is assessed in terms of progress in managing an organisation's particular processes (e.g. Business Process Maturity Model (BPMM OMG) (Harmon 2010, p. 91; www6). It can also be assessed in the following three dimensions: the process management level (perspective), the assessment area (factor), and time/organisation (scope) (e.g. the model proposed by Rosemann and De Bruin) (Rosemann and De Bruin 2005). Researchers indicate the need for further research on process management maturity models taking into consideration the unique character of particular organisations.

Summing up, it should be stressed that maturity assessment models applicable to process management have different application objectives. They can be used to diagnose an organisation and its progress in implementing changes or achieving a particular maturity level, which is confirmed by the granting of a particular conformity certificate (e.g. CMMI, ISO 9001). Such models use different methods of assessing maturity. A particular organisational maturity level can be confirmed, for example, by the scope of processes covered by a process management system (every maturity level is assigned a different set of processes, e.g. CMMI, BPMM OMG) or a maturity level of selected organisational areas, functions or processes (a maturity level is established on the basis of a degree to which assessment criteria are met, e.g. ISO 9004, EFQM).

The implementation of the process approach influences the occurrence of so-called process culture, which is an important dimension of Lean Culture. Lean Management is one of the process management concepts. However, because of its specificity, attempts are made at developing separate models for assessing the levels of Lean Culture implementation and maturity.

4.3 Maturity of Lean Culture in the Light of an Analysis of the Literature on the Subject

Research on Lean Culture maturity was conducted first of all in manufacturing organisations. In order to determine the scope of such research and research gaps, the author carried out a systematic review of the literature on the subject. For this purpose, the EBSCO base was used. It was searched using the following key words: Lean Management, Lean Culture, assessment, evaluation, maturity. The results of the analysis are presented in Table 4.1.

The next part of the analysis covered articles in which the searched notions were defined as key words. The author rejected the articles

Table 4.1 The number of publications on maturity of Lean Management and Lean Culture in higher education institutions according to EBSCO as at 1 December 2018

Search criteria	EBSCO base— number of articles	First publication
Key words: Lean Management, assessment, evaluation (in abstracts)	86 (35[a])	1996
Key words: Lean Management, assessment, evaluation (key words)	62 (24)	2009
Key words: Lean Management, assessment, evaluation (in titles)	3	2013
Key words: Lean Management and maturity (in abstracts)	8	2009
Key words: Lean Management and maturity (key words)	2	2017
Key words: Lean Management and maturity (in titles)	1	2018

Source The author's own work
[a]Full-text publications

which did not concern directly the assessment of Lean Management implementation or Lean Culture maturity. The analysis of the literature on the subject was focused on the methodology of model development and testing. The results of the analysis are presented in Table 4.2.

Lean Management implementation maturity was also assessed by researchers in the context of comparisons among companies which had and those which had not implemented the concept. In the conducted statistical analysis, Meybodi (2010) showed that organisations which had implemented Lean: analysed better the external context, developed better their core competences on the basis of knowledge development and learning, were more consistent in translating challenges connected with competition into their own strategic and operational objectives, were more flexible and better oriented towards customers, developed new products faster, and were more consistent in using their competitive advantages to cope with market challenges.

The topic of Lean Culture maturity is also raised in the context of higher education institutions. Researchers use the notion of readiness for Lean Management implementation (Radnor and Bucci 2011; Balzer et al. 2016; Anthony and Antony 2016; Antony 2014). On the basis

Table 4.2 The models of assessing Lean Management and Lean Culture implementation maturity in organisations—the results of a systematic analysis of the literature on the subject

Name of model	Authors	Structure of model	Model development method	Lean Management/Lean Culture implementation maturity testing methods	Statistical methods of tool verification	Application, analysis results
CIRCA CI self-assessment tool (Caffyn 1999)	Sarah Caffyn (1999) and Bessant et al. (2001)	10 behavioural standards, maturity assessment at 5 levels	Case studies, literature analysis	Questionnaire based on self-assessment, surveys	None	Universal tools. The idea of continuous improvement is still wrongly understood in organisations
The integrated CI structural model (Wu and Chen 2006)	Wu and Chen (2006)	6 levels of organisational improvement	Analysis of literature, own research	Assessment with respect to a theoretical model	None	The concept of continuous improvement should have a holistic character and comprise a whole organisation
Lean capability model (Jørgensen et al. 2007)	Jørgensen et al. (2007)	2 dimensions—technical and organisational spheres (management, organisational and human capabilities, culture, and learning), 5 maturity levels	Interviews with employees conducted in workplaces	None	None	Production. Diagnosing a Lean implementation level is of primary importance for drawing up a roadmap for the process of implementing this concept
Questionnaire to measure the implementation of Lean practices	Shah and Ward (2007)	3 conceptual dimensions, 10 operational dimensions, 41 questions, scale of 1–5	Literature analysis, interviews with practitioners, expert opinions	The questionnaire measures a Lean Management implementation level in an organisation	Exploratory factor analysis (EFA), sample 63 Confirmatory factor analysis (CFA), sample 280	Oriented towards manufacturing organisations, the questionnaire measures the current status of Lean implementation

(continued)

Table 4.2 (continued)

Name of model	Authors	Structure of model	Model development method	Lean Management/Lean Culture implementation maturity testing methods	Statistical methods of tool verification	Application, analysis results
Lean Enterprise Self-Assessment Tool (LESAT)	Perkins et al. (2010)	The model comprises 3 dimensions, 15 criteria, 54 practices. A five-point scale, with each point describing a level of implementing a particular practice	Analysis of literature and case studies	Questionnaire based on self-assessment. It allows an assessment of the gap between the current state and the required state. Possibility of combining with a SWOT analysis	None	The tool may be used for internal comparisons, benchmarking with other organisations, tracking changes, learning
Multigrade fuzzy approach for assessing Leanness (Vinodh and Chintha 2011)	Vinodh and Chintha (2011)	The model contains 5 dimensions, 20 criteria, 61 attributes, and a 1–10 assessment scale; it is divided into 5 sections	Literature analysis, expert opinion	The Leanness index is calculated on the basis of an assessment of an attribute and the weight of a given attribute as established by experts	Assessment of the possibility of using the fuzzy approach by experts; measurement of consistency of opinions	Manufacturing, possibility of identifying areas requiring correction
Lean Culture Assessment Model (LCAM) (Al-Najem et al. (2012))	Al-Najem et al. (2012)	4 dimensions of Lean Culture, 8 critical factors	Literature analysis	12 hypotheses are formulated. Their verification will allow the testing of the model	None	Organisational culture is a critical success factor for Lean Management implementation
Leanness model	Vimal and Vinodh (2012)	The model comprises 5 dimensions, 30 Lean criteria, and 59 attributes	Literature analysis	Case study, assessment conducted by managers	Fuzzy logic methods for performance measurement	Manufacturing. Necessity of further research and assessment model verification
Performance Measurement System (PMS) for Lean manufacturing organisations	Perera and Perera (2013)	The model is based on the measurement of the same 8 indexes in 5 areas	Literature analysis, interviews	The model refers theoretically to the EFQM model and Balanced Scored Card (BSC)	The model is of a conceptual character; it has not been verified	Manufacturing. The model comprises expectations of shareholders and management, as well as qualitative and quantitative indexes

Name of model	Authors	Structure of model	Model development method	Lean Management/Lean Culture implementation maturity testing methods	Statistical methods of tool verification	Application, analysis results
A model of assessing maturity as a gap	Chiarini and Vagnoni (2015)	The model is based on comparing TPS premises with the Lean model in FIAT in 4 dimensions	Literature analysis, FIAT documentation analysis, interviews	Case study, open coding method	None	Manufacturing. The open coding method makes it possible to identify the true gap in the understanding of the Lean methods
Lean in Healthcare Questionnaire (LiHcQ) (Kaltenbrunner et al. 2017)	Kaltenbrunner et al. (2017)	The model is based on Liker's 14 principles (80 questions divided into 16 categories, a 1–5 scale describes the extent to which particular statements are used/applied in an organisation)	Interviews with 12 employees, survey of 386 employees, tool reliability testing	Survey of employees	Internal consistency, measured using Cronbach's alpha, was 0.60 for the factor people and partners, and over 0.70 for the three other factors	Health care. A reliable survey from the statistical point of view
Lean manufacturing maturity model (Dos Santos et al. 2018)	Dos Santos et al. (2018)	The model is based on Liker's 14 principles (8 dimensions, 38 Lean practices, 1–5 Likert scale, strongly disagree, totally agree)	Literature analysis, interviews with experts, survey of managers, statistical testing	Survey of managers in 90 manufacturing enterprises	Confirmatory factor analysis (CFA), composite reliability and Cronbach's alphas was 0.7, n R^2 was 0.499	Production. There is a relationship between maturity of Lean practices and operational excellence. Problems with acquiring data regarded as confidential
Lean manufacturing constructs (Nawanir et al. 2018)	Nawanir et al. (2018)	9 dimensions, 64 measures, scale from 1 (strongly disagree) to 6 (strongly agree)	Literature analysis, consultations with academics and practitioners	Survey of managers in 90 manufacturing enterprises	Structural equation modelling approach SEM, sample 236, confirmatory factor analysis (CFA)	The questionnaire allows a holistic assessment of a Lean Management implementation level

Source The author's own work based on Sarah Caffyn (1999), Bessant et al. (2001), Wu and Chen (2006), Jorgensen et al. (2007), Shah and Ward (2007), Perkins et al. (2010), Vinodh and Chintha (2011), Al-Najem et al. (2012), Vimal and Vinodh (2012), Perera and Perera (2013), Chiarini and Vagnoni (2015), Kaltenbrunner et al. (2017), Dos Santos Bento and Tontini (2018), and Nawanir et al. (2018)

of their research, Radnor and Bucci (2011) define readiness for Lean Management implementation in terms of combining a Lean programme with a university strategy, communicating activities related to Lean, understanding the process approach, understanding the customer concept, understanding the essence of balancing potential against demand. Antony (2014) identifies the following readiness factors: leadership and vision, commitment and resources, connections with a university strategy, orientation towards customers and choice, as well as training targeted at proper people (the analysis concerns LSS). In 2016 the author conducted pilot research on Lean Culture maturity in selected higher education institutions in Poland, using a modified survey questionnaire based on Liker's 14 principles. A statistical analysis confirmed the reliability and accuracy of the research tool (Maciąg 2016a).

The above analysis of the literature on the subject indicates that researchers do not define unambiguously such notions as maturity, maturity level or maturity assessment model. They do not differentiate between Lean Management implementation assessment and Lean Culture maturity. The core problems are often extended to include issues related to continuous improvement process assessment. Table 4.2 shows that the approaches to model development and testing are strongly diversified. They are usually based on analyses of the literature on the subject, supplemented with interviews, and sometimes tested by means of statistical analyses of research results. A wide spectrum of methods is used in the development and testing of models, from mathematical ones such as the fuzzy approach to deeply humanistic ones such as open coding (the grounded theory). Researchers refer also to problems with conducting surveys, especially in non-manufacturing organisations. Kaltenbrunner et al. (2017) point out that questionnaires that are too long, complex or incomprehensible for people who are not familiar with Lean cause respondents to omit difficult or unclear questions. This may influence the reliability of research results. Reviews of assessment maturity models were also conducted by Lameijer et al. (2017), Doolen and Hacker (2005), and Urban (2015). Urban draws attention to imprecise definitions of the basic notions (Urban 2015). Lameijer et al. (2017) emphasise that with respect to Lean and Lean Six Sigma, the models assessing the levels of implementation and maturity are unsatisfactory. Recommendations formulated by researchers are superficial, provide only a general outline of what should be achieved, do not contain any concrete solutions or implementation methods. Researchers stress that limitations in the application of particular models are frequently not specified. Their theoretical foundations are also insufficient as they do not take into consideration the theories of organisational development. There is a visible lack of a holistic approach (Wu and Chen 2006).

Presented in Table 4.2, the synthetic analysis results show that Lean Culture maturity assessment models definitely require in-depth research. The models used at present are oriented mainly towards the organisational-technical dimension of Lean Culture. Lean Culture maturity is examined mainly by way of assessing the scope of the application of Lean Principles, techniques, and tools in process management. The social dimension is not emphasised. Lean Culture is not studied from the perspective of employees' attitudes, behaviours, interpretations, and understanding of the essence of Lean Management. For the author, this became the reason for undertaking scholarly exploration in this area. In the next section, the author will present the assumptions concerning her original tool to examine Lean Culture maturity in higher education institutions.

4.4 The Assessment of Maturity of Lean Culture in Higher Education—The Research Methodology

4.4.1 The Method of Researching Maturity of Lean Culture in Higher Education—The Premises of the Research Procedure Adopted by the Author

The above analysis of the literature on the subject allowed the author to formulate the following definitions related to the assessment of Lean Culture maturity.

Lean Culture maturity is the state of organisational culture demonstrated in a desired, harmonised, consistent, and coherent model of behaviours which is the result of common learning in the process of organisational improvement based on the fundamental premises, system, and methods of Lean Management.

A Lean Culture maturity model is a structured set of dimensions and descriptors of organisational culture describing a desired model of employees' behaviours in the process of organisational improvement based on the fundamental premises, system, and methods of Lean Management.

A Lean Culture maturity level describes to what extent a model of behaviours existing in a particular higher education institution has achieved the desired level, is harmonised, consistent, and coherent, which makes it possible to acquire permanent effects in the process of organisational improvement based on the fundamental premises, system, and methods of Lean Management.

The process of creating the tool for the assessment of Lean Culture maturity in higher education was based on the Lean Culture Maturity Model in Higher Education (LCMMHE) as defined in Chapter 3. It comprises a set of descriptors divided into the following seven homogeneous dimensions: a process approach, values, management (with a distinction between top management and immediate superiors), employees in an organisation, relations and work in teams, artefacts (tangible artefacts, behavioural artefacts, and language), as well as relations with the environment. The specific character of the particular dimensions of Lean Culture makes it possible to use a wide spectrum of quantitative and qualitative social research methods in the examination and assessment of their maturity, which is presented in Table 4.3.

The necessity to use simultaneously many methods and tools makes research on Lean Culture a complex and complicated undertaking. Determining the level of its maturity is an additional difficulty. Therefore, the author's objective was to develop a tool to assess the level of Lean Culture maturity in higher education institutions.

The methodology of creating and testing the tool as well as research results are presented in the next section.

Table 4.3 The methods of assessing Lean Culture maturity in higher education

Subject matter of research	Research methods
Linguistic artefacts	Observation
	Analysis of texts/documents
	Analysis of statements (interviews)
Behavioural artefacts	Lean Culture Maturity Questionnaire (LCMQ)
	Observation
	Analysis of texts/documents
	Analysis of statements (interviews)
Tangible artefacts	Lean Culture Maturity Questionnaire (LCMQ)
	Observation
	Analysis of texts/documents
	Analysis of statements (interviews)
Process approach	Lean Culture Maturity Questionnaire (LCMQ)
Values	Analysis of texts/documents
Leadership	Analysis of statements (interviews)
People	
Team work and relations	
Relations with environment	Analysis of texts/documents
	Interview

Source The author's own work

4.4.2 The Lean Culture Maturity Questionnaire (LCMQ)— The Author's Proposal for a Research Tool

4.4.2.1 The Methodology of Developing the Lean Culture Maturity Questionnaire

Developing the tool for the assessment of Lean Culture maturity in higher education, the author consistently followed the adopted ontological and epistemological premises. In the interpretative-symbolic perspective, Lean Culture was studied with respect to the notions, values, symbols, meanings, and senses assigned to it by university employees. Such an ontological attitude allowed a fuller and deeper learning and understanding which attitudes were adopted by employees and how they personally assessed changes introduced in their universities. The essence of Lean Culture is change in employees' attitudes and behaviours. Consequently, it is only employees who participate in the process of change and are creators of change that are able to assess the level of Lean Culture maturity.

The basis for developing the LCMQ was the author's LCMMHE (presented and described in detail in Chapter 3). The model comprises the following 7 dimensions: artefacts, a process approach, values, leadership, people, relations and work in teams, as well as relations with the environment. The analysis conducted in Table 4.3 shows that not all dimensions of Lean Culture can be studied fully by means of the LCMQ. This problem concerns the dimensions related to artefacts (language, behaviours, tangible artefacts) and relations with the environment. Therefore, at the beginning the questionnaire was applied to the following 6 dimensions of Lean Culture: a process approach, leadership, values, people, team work, and tangible artefacts. The dimension of relations with the environment was excluded from the questionnaire (not all employees are involved in such relations or know anything about them). Within the Lean Culture Model, each dimension was assigned a set of descriptors which became a basis for the formulation of statements in the research questionnaire (the descriptors of Lean Culture are presented in Figs. 3.5 and 3.10). The first version of the questionnaire consisted of 91 statements divided into six dimensions of Lean Culture. Each statement corresponded to a given Lean Culture descriptor which had been established on the basis of the analysis of the conducted interviews. In the questionnaire, the author deliberately avoided specialist terminology used in Lean Management. The questionnaire was meant to have a diagnostic character. Hence the way in which the statements were formulated should allow an assessment of Lean Culture maturity also in those higher education institutions which did not officially declare following this change implementation method.

The survey questionnaire was drawn up in the Polish and English language versions. At the next stage the questionnaire was verified by means of the expert assessment method and statistical methods.

4.4.2.2 The Qualitative Assessment of the Research Questionnaire

For a preliminary qualitative assessment of the survey questionnaire, the author used the expert assessment method. The questionnaire was sent to seven experts specialising in the implementation of the Lean concept, as well as organisational culture, humanistic management, and process management. Selecting persons to perform the function of an expert, the author paid special attention to ensuring that they were people who had not had any influence on the shape of the questionnaire at the stage of the research conducted in higher education institutions. She also tried to ensure a balanced selection of experts assessing the questionnaire with respect to their theoretical and practical knowledge of Lean Management as well as their nationalities. Five professors, three from Poland and two from the USA, participated in the research. Additionally, assistance was requested from the person managing the international LeanHE network, as well as an expert in Lean Management holding a doctoral degree and running their own consulting business in Poland. Thus the group of experts consisted of: 3 women and 4 men; 4 persons from Poland, 1 person from the United Kingdom, 2 persons from the USA; 5 active Lean Management practitioners, including 4 active practitioners and researchers associated with higher education institutions. The experts were asked to review and comment on the survey questionnaire. The experts' opinions and comments on the particular statements included in the questionnaire were put together in an Excel spreadsheet. There were slight differences in the assessments. The experts were generally consistent in their opinions, which allowed the broadening of the survey questionnaire with issues related to the humanistic approach, from the point of view of organisational culture, process management, management psychology, as well as the practice of implementing Lean Management in organisations.

Additionally, the experts analysed the questionnaire with respect to the Lean Culture descriptors. The grouping of the questionnaire statements in various configurations allowed the author to reduce their number to 80 (first of all, the repeating statements were eliminated).

Eventually, the prototype of the questionnaire consisted of 80 statements divided according to the six dimensions of Lean Culture (the questionnaire omitted the dimension connected with relations with the environment because, taking into consideration their specific character, the more appropriate research methods are document analysis and interviews).

The assessment of the statements was based on a five-point Likert scale. The author's decision to use this scale was preceded by an in-depth analysis of its practical application in qualitative research (opinion and attitude surveys) and research on organisational culture. The analysis of the literature on the subject with respect to the reliability of the research results in relation to the ranges of scales (Babbie 2013a, p. 197) showed that there were no significant differences between the reliability of the research results obtained by means of a seven-point scale and an eleven-point scale. Obviously, from the statistical point of view, the wider the scale, the greater the reliability of the research; nevertheless, from the perspective of the adopted objective of the research, the identified differences were not significant. The analysis comprised also the scales used to examine organisational cultures in various models. For example, the five-point scale used by Cameron and Quinn detailed assessment and self-assessment forms concerning managerial skills, managerial effectiveness or managerial behaviours (Cameron and Quinn 2003). Deciding which scale to choose, the author took also into consideration the fact that in the case of such a long and detailed research questionnaire requiring a commitment of time and a considerable intellectual effort on the part of the respondent, the use of more extensive scales could cause the failure of the research and a low rate of returned questionnaires. Therefore eventually the author adopted a five-point scale, modifying it in such a way that it did not have the neutral middle value (I don't know). It was replaced by the assessment of "yes and no", which, in the interpretation of the research results, may indicate the respondent's indecisiveness or the fact that some elements of Lean Culture manifest themselves in their organisation, but they are not able to assess this unambiguously. The final version of the assessment scale was as follows: 5—"strongly agree", 4—"agree", 3—"neither agree nor disagree", 2—"disagree", and 1—"strongly disagree".

At the next stage, the LCMQ was prepared in the Internet version, in two language versions (Polish and English), and was sent to the selected higher education institutions which had given their consent to participate in the research. The research was conducted using Google forms. The author complied with all ethical principles in order to ensure the anonymity of the research. A detailed discussion of the method of selecting a research sample was presented in Chapter 1. Altogether twenty-three universities took part in the research, including institutions from the United Kingdom, Norway, the Netherlands, Canada, and Poland. The structure of the research participants was the following: 5 schools collected tuition fees, 2 schools were private institutions, 11 schools held various certificates confirming the implementation of various quality management models (e.g. ISO 9001, EFQM, other models based on excellence models).

The LCMQ was eventually filled in by 771 employees of higher education institutions.

The structure of the respondents was the following:

- The structure with respect to gender: women—60% of the respondents, men—40% of the respondents.
- The structure with respect to the length of employment with a higher education institution: up to 5 years—26% of the respondents, 5–10 years—26% of the respondents, more than 10 years—48% of the respondents.
- The structure with respect to the function fulfilled in a university: top management (the rector's office, the chancellor's office, the management of faculties, and other organisational units)—8% of the respondents, line managers/operational managers/department managers, etc.—18% of the respondents, managers of temporary teams—6% of the respondents, subordinates (without managerial functions)—68% of the respondents.
- The structure with respect to the type of performed work: administration employees—42% of the respondents, lecturers and researchers—58% of the respondents.
- The structure with respect to experience in Lean Management, continuous improvement or other process-based methods: 20% of the respondents had such experience, 80%—did not.
- The structure of the respondents who had such experience was as follows:

  - 51% of the respondents became familiar with process-based management concepts while working in higher education institutions, 37%—in business organisations, 12%—in public organisations.

- 70% of the respondents sporadically participated in training courses related to such concepts, 17% regularly participated in such training activities.
- 51% of the respondents were sporadically involved in improvement projects based on Lean Management, continuous improvement or other process-based methods; 38% were involved in such projects on a regular basis, and
- A half of the respondents belonged to formal teams dealing with Lean Management in their universities; a half of the respondents were members of a network of Lean leaders and facilitators.

The collected results of the questionnaire survey were used to assess the reliability and accuracy of the LCMQ as a tool for testing Lean Culture maturity.

4.4.2.3 Testing the Reliability of the LCMQ as a Research Tool

The LCMQ underwent statistical tests aimed at checking its reliability as a research tool to measure the maturity of Lean Culture in higher education. For this purpose, the following methods were applied:

- A confirmative analysis based on the principal components method (Spencer 2013; Tabachnick and Fidel 2014).
- Standardised Cronbach's alphas.

The factor loading matrix is presented in Table 4.4. Each of the dimensions of Lean Culture was marked as follows: V—number of dimensions, number of statements. Almost all factors (except for the questions concerning the third dimension) in which the absolute value of the loading was higher than 0.5 (positively and negatively) describe a separate dominant construct.

Using Kaiser's criterion, it is possible to state that there is one decidedly dominant factor accounting for more than 35% of the total observed variability; the subsequent two factors account for, respectively, just 6 and 4% of the variability. It means that the survey results

Table 4.4 The factor loading matrix

Number of statement in research questionnaire	Content of statement	Dimension and number of statement	Factor 1	Factor 2	Factor 3
1	I understand how the process I execute contributes to the achievement of the objectives of the university	V1_1	**-0.503**	0.058	0.281
2	I understand the relationships among the core processes in my university	V1_2	-0.467	0.148	0.234
3	The efforts which I need to execute the process of my work are sufficient and appropriate (i.e. information, materials, infrastructure, software etc.)	V1_3	-0.440	0.142	0.057
4	The documents (instructions, procedures, and other written rules) which I need and use in my process are useful, easy to understand and appropriate	V1_4	-0.482	0.312	0.021
5	I can easily find the documents I need for my work	V1_5	-0.493	0.280	0.099
6	The number of documents in the process is reduced to the necessary minimum	V1_6	-0.438	0.254	-0.023
7	I know the requirements of my customers (internal and external)	V1_7	-0.471	0.053	0.315
8	My work in the process is sensible and valuable for the final users/customers (staff, students etc.)	V1_8	**-0.526**	0.079	0.269
9	I know how to properly act in the process under which I work and I know the stages of its execution	V1_9	-0.489	0.105	0.259
10	My work is evenly distributed in the process execution (no downtime or excessive workload)	V1_10	**-0.395**	0.175	0.083
11	I execute activities in the process when they are needed by my customer/final user	V1_11	-0.426	0.043	0.209
12	Processes are executed without unnecessary delays (on time)	V1_12	-0.468	0.154	0.152
13	I don't create data and documents etc. in the process which are useless and unnecessary	V1_13	-0.459	0.211	0.196
14	Risks in my process are defined	V1_14	-0.493	0.167	0.266
15	I know how to treat a risk and I know what kind of activities I should take to accept, minimise, and/or avoid risks	V1_15	-0.460	0.150	0.411
16	I have the right to stop my work when I recognise the problems which can cause defects in the process	V1_16	-0.480	0.035	0.214
17	Communication among the staff members who operate in my unit assures the effective execution of the process	V1_17	**-0.556**	-0.118	0.120
18	Communication among the departments which operate under the process assures its effective execution	V1_18	-0.493	0.161	0.136
19	I identify the sources of waste on an ongoing basis	V1_19	**-0.153**	0.070	0.348

(continued)

Table 4.4 (continued)

Number of statement in research questionnaire	Content of statement	Dimension and number of statement	Factor 1	Factor 2	Factor 3
20	I can take corrective actions to minimise or reduce identified sources of waste	v1_20	−0.499	0.110	0.315
21	I monitor the level of defects in the process by using different indicators (i.e. time, cost, number of defects, etc.) on an ongoing basis	v1_21	−0.431	0.152	0.385
22	The collected information about defects and problems in the process of work is regularly analysed	v1_22	−0.551	0.076	0.277
23	The collected information about defects and problems in the process of work constitutes a basis for improvement	v1_23	−0.597	0.109	0.279
24	Implemented improvements make my work more compliant with my customers' requirements	v1_24	−0.586	0.105	0.348
25	Implemented improvements make my work better organised and effective	v1_25	−0.565	0.112	0.337
26	Via active, open and public support, the senior/top management have created an atmosphere of trust in continuous improvement	v2_1	−0.747	0.151	−0.178
27	The senior/top management are patient and understand that changes in behaviours and attitudes to work and organisational culture take time	v2_2	−0.673	0.064	−0.217
28	The senior/top management actively support and promote the managers and the leaders of change	v2_3	−0.750	0.115	−0.245
29	Changes in the university are complex and complement each other	v2_4	−0.747	0.262	−0.191
30	The improvements of the processes are purposeful and sensible, linked to the vision and mission of the university	v2_5	−0.739	0.261	−0.126
31	Changes in the university are complex and complement each other	v2_6	−0.711	0.272	−0.150
32	The process of communication in the university is simple and does not contain redundant steps/procedures/documents	v2_7	−0.698	0.330	−0.203
33	The process of making decisions about change implementation in the university is simple and does not contain redundant steps	v2_8	−0.721	0.294	−0.215
34	The process of approving change implementation in the university is simple and does not contain redundant steps	v2_9	−0.712	0.297	−0.207
35	My superior is my coach/mentor	v3_1	−0.602	−0.551	−0.157
36	My superior truly understands the character of the whole process of work that I do	v3_2	−0.629	−0.504	−0.034

Number of statement in research questionnaire	Content of statement	Dimension and number of statement	Factor 1	Factor 2	Factor 3
37	My superior supports me in the improvement of my daily work	v3_3	−0.652	−0.580	−0.025
38	Relationships with my superior are open, deformalised, and based on partnership, trust, and authority	v3_4	−0.599	−0.590	−0.049
39	The aims of changes are discussed before implementation and are not imposed by the managers	v3_5	−0.660	−0.490	−0.093
40	My superior takes my ideas into account and treats them as valuable and important	v3_6	−0.613	−0.595	−0.014
41	My superior treats mistakes as an important experience which can be used in the future to prevent other mistakes and to learn	v3_7	−0.656	−0.521	−0.056
42	The superior works to sustain the effects of implemented improvements	v3_8	−0.689	−0.498	−0.030
43	The superior motivates and engages me in the process of continuous improvement	v3_9	−0.665	−0.566	−0.068
44	The superior is personally involved in solving problems at their sources (these are not decisions made "from behind the desk")	v3_10	−0.618	−0.568	−0.097
45	The superior plans my work to allow time for developmental activities (i.e. meetings, training, workshops, etc.)	v3_11	−0.652	−0.453	−0.037
46	An important value in my university is respect for people	v4_1	−0.615	0.023	−0.227
47	An important value in my university is openness to change	v4_2	−0.683	0.173	−0.251
48	The university is proactive, faces changes, and prevents problems and defects	v4_3	−0.744	0.232	−0.260
49	The new methods of solving problems and improvement are continuously checked and tried	v4_4	−0.738	0.183	−0.186
50	A common sense approach is used in management	v4_5	−0.696	0.257	−0.287
51	An evidence-based approach is used in the decision making process at the university	v4_6	−0.716	0.216	−0.315
52	Continuous improvement is an inherent part of all activities and a way of performing everyday work in the university	v4_7	−0.752	0.236	−0.230
53	There is a culture of questioning any ineffective and routine ways and rules of working in the university	v4_8	−0.636	0.209	−0.175
54	There is a culture of trust in the university	v4_9	−0.701	0.082	−0.297
55	Waste identification and reduction is an important value in the university	v4_10	−0.703	0.203	−0.209
56	The main purpose of continuous improvement in the university is changing the behaviours and attitudes of the employees	v4_11	−0.706	0.186	−0.282

(continued)

Table 4.4 (continued)

Number of statement in research questionnaire	Content of statement	Dimension and number of statement	Factor 1	Factor 2	Factor 3
57	I can report problems in the processes carried out in the university and recommend preventive and corrective actions (there is a special reporting system, a system of work suggestions, etc.)	v5_1	-0.626	0.120	-0.120
58	I feel that I am prepared and competent to implement changes which improve the processes	v5_2	-0.705	0.132	0.024
59	I understand how my work contributes to the accomplishment, development, and vision of continuous improvement of the university	v5_3	-0.672	0.111	0.223
60	I am empowered to show initiative, be involved in projects, and implement changes in the processes	v5_4	-0.682	-0.033	0.126
61	All my initiatives and changes, even small ones, are appreciated	v5_5	-0.726	-0.129	-0.089
62	In my daily work, I use all knowledge and abilities acquired in past projects in the university	v5_6	-0.522	0.005	0.186
63	In my daily work, I use all knowledge and abilities acquired during training, workshops, and other events	v5_7	-0.442	0.010	0.252
64	Active participation in project improvement activities has changed my attitude to work and has engaged me more in the process of continuous improvement	v5_8	-0.620	0.089	0.161
65	My job is inspirational and interesting. I don't feel bored or stuck in a routine because I can make improvements	v5_9	-0.623	-0.083	0.180
66	I keep the positive effects of changes and don't come back to the old and ineffective ways of working	v5_10	-0.538	-0.038	0.270
67	I deepen my knowledge of the continuous improvement of myself	v5_11	-0.292	0.000	0.293
68	I am not afraid to lose my job due to process improvements	v5_12	-0.304	-0.102	0.137
69	I am informed on a regular basis about changes in my team/department/organization	v5_13	-0.640	-0.176	-0.126
70	When I have a problem in my work related to process improvement, I can expect help from a professional internal specialist, special departments, special teams, etc., which are obliged to provide assistance	v5_14	-0.680	0.088	-0.155
71	I treat every suggestion as an opportunity for change and as a challenge	v5_15	-0.504	0.022	0.208
72	I feel that we work together for the success of the university	v5_16	-0.743	0.045	-0.049

Number of statement in research questionnaire	Content of statement	Dimension and number of statement	Factor 1	Factor 2	Factor 3
73	I am evaluated holistically for the results of my actions, also for my engagement in improvement activities (and not for incidents)	v5_17	−0.687	−0.182	−0.058
74	I am involved in the evaluation of my work and actions	v5_18	−0.601	−0.175	0.023
75	The work and achievements of my colleagues are an inspiration for me to make improvements	v6_1	−0.542	−0.190	0.105
76	In my team, I share my knowledge and experience with my colleagues	v6_2	−0.470	−0.307	0.120
77	There are interdepartmental/interdisciplinary teams which help to solve different problems with communication	v6_3	−0.601	−0.057	−0.058
78	We celebrate small wins	v6_4	−0.482	−0.187	0.109
79	I can share the results of my own and my colleagues' work improvement initiatives (i.e. at conferences, seminars, meetings, in written, and online materials, etc.)	v6_5	−0.471	−0.110	0.083
80	I often use pictures, dashboards, tables and other forms of visualisation in my work	v7_1	−0.318	−0.063	0.221
		Output value	28.436	5.107	3.277
		Share	0.355	0.064	0.041

Source The results of the author's research conducted within the framework of the project: Title of project: The determinants of the maturity of Lean Management culture in higher education institutions. The project was executed under the research program 'Miniatura 1' financed by the National Science Centre, Poland (the dates of the project: 12 September 2017–12 September 2018) (No. DEC. 2017/01/X/HS/00619)

Legend Dimension V1—PROCESS APPROACH, dimension V2—LEADERSHIP—TOP/SENIOR MANAGERS, dimension V3—LEADERSHIP—LINE MANAGER/IMMEDIATE SUPERIOR, dimension V4—VALUES IN THE UNIVERSITY, dimension V5—EMPLOYEES, dimension V6—TEAM WORK AND RELATIONSHIPS, dimension V7—TANGIBLE ARTEFACTS are mainly affected by one dominant feature. In other words, the questionnaire measures one construct which can be identified with Lean Culture. The results of the confirmative analysis indicate also that the results of the assessment of the particular statements are consistent within the scope of one dimension of Lean Culture (a similar value of the factors with respect to the studied dimensions).

The results of the conducted confirmative analysis suggest another review of the statements included in the research questionnaire, particularly those whose factor loadings with respect to the first factor were below 0.3 (in Table 4.4, they are marked in grey). The analysis covered the five statements numbered 10, 19, 67, 68, and 80. In consequence of the analysis, the author decided to keep statements 10, 19, 67, and 68 in the questionnaire as important descriptors of Lean Culture, while statement 80 was moved to the dimension Process Approach (because of the similar value of the factor loadings). The final version of the research questionnaire is included in Appendix.

The modified questionnaire underwent subsequent assessments of reliability.

Assessing the reliability of the LCMQ, the author used standardised Cronbach's alphas which were calculated for all questions together and for the particular dimensions. Taking into consideration the analysis of the literature on the subject conducted at the beginning of this chapter, the author determined two major dimensions of Lean Culture, i.e. the process dimension (reflecting the descriptors of Lean Culture connected with organisational-technical issues) and the social dimension (comprising descriptors in the remaining dimensions of Lean Culture).

The acquired values of Cronbach's alphas are high ($\alpha > 0.8$) and very high ($\alpha > 0.9$), which proves the high consistence of the provided answers within the scope of the analysed Lean Culture dimensions. Simultaneously, the highest value of the coefficient in the case of the whole questionnaire (KL 0.974) shows a clear common variability formula observable for the whole questionnaire. This conclusion is confirmed by the high values of the correlation coefficients among the particular dimensions (Table 4.5). The obtained results of the analysis of the reliability of the research tool indicate that the developed questionnaire allows a one-dimensional identification of the type of

Table 4.5 The values of Cronbach's alphas

Variable	Description	Number of items on scale	Cronbach's alpha	Average correlation among items
KL	Lean Culture	80	0.974	0.341
KL_I (KL_1)	Process dimensions	26	0.912	0.286
KL_II	Social dimension	54	0.974	0.417
KL_II KL_2	Leadership—top/senior managers	9	0.940	0.647
KL_II KL_3	Leadership—line manager/immediate superior	11	0.963	0.708
KL_II KL_4	Values in university	11	0.942	0.605
KL_II KL_5	Employees	18	0.920	0.398
KL_II KL_6	Team work and relations	5	0.778	0.421

Source The results of the author's research conducted within the framework of the project: Title of project: The determinants of the maturity of Lean Management culture in higher education institutions. The project was executed under the research program 'Miniatura 1' financed by the National Science Centre, Poland (the dates of the project: 12 September 2017–12 September 2018) (No. DEC. 2017/01/X/HS/00619) organisational culture—Lean Culture. The results made it possible to carry out further analysis concerning the determination of Lean Culture maturity and types in higher education institutions as well as conditions for the maturity of Lean Culture.

4.4.2.4 A Typology of Approaches to the Assessment of Maturity of Lean Culture

At the next stage of the analysis of the results of the questionnaire research, the author conducted a statistical analysis, using descriptive statistics (Table 4.6).

The average assessment of Lean Culture is 3.00 (a 1–5 scale); the social dimension is assessed higher than the process dimension. In the social dimension, the highest assessments were received by the dimensions Leadership, Line Managers (the average assessment of 3.38), while the dimension Leadership, Top Management was given the lowest assessments (the average assessment of 2.64). The assessment of the particular dimensions of Lean Culture is characterised by a relatively high standard deviation (from 0.75 to 1.11), which indicates a certain diversification of individual assessments. Values of skewness above zero show that variable is skewed positively (to the right); variable is skewed negatively (to the right), if values of skewness are below zero. Positive skewness occurs in the assessment of Lean Culture and the following of its dimensions: Process dimension, Leadership—Top/senior managers, Values in the university, Employees. This means that the majority of the results are below the average assessment of a given dimension. Negative skewness indicates that in the following dimensions: Social dimension, Leadership—Line manager/immediate superior and Team work and relationships, the majority of the results are above the average assessment of a given dimension. The values of kurtosis are below zero, which means that flattened distribution occurs. In other words, there are quite a few results which are considerably distant from the average assessment.

The results of the conducted research and the statistical analysis of the questionnaire survey allowed the author to indicate three possible approaches to the assessment of Lean Culture maturity by means of the

4 Maturity of Lean Culture in Higher Education ... 277

Table 4.6 The descriptive statistics of the results of the questionnaire research on Lean Culture maturity in higher education

Variable	Description	Mean	Median	Minimum	Maximum	Standard deviation	Skewness	Kurtosis
KL	Lean Culture	3.00	2.99	1.09	4.86	0.75	0.10	−0.40
KL_I (KL_1)	Process dimensions	2.82	2.77	1.08	4.92	0.83	0.27	−0.58
KL_II	Social dimension	3.08	3.13	1.04	4.89	0.78	−0.01	−0.42
KL_II KL_2	Leadership—top/senior managers	2.64	2.67	1.00	5.00	0.94	0.15	−0.69
KL_II KL_3	Leadership—line manager/immediate superior	3.38	3.55	1.00	5.00	1.11	−0.46	−0.77
KL_II KL_4	Values in university	2.91	2.91	1.00	5.00	0.93	0.02	−0.66
KL_II KL_5	Employees	3.18	3.17	1.00	5.00	0.78	0.02	−0.32
KL_II KL_6	Team work and relations	3.26	3.20	1.00	5.00	0.89	−0.19	−0.35

Source The results of the author's research conducted within the framework of the project: Title of project: The determinants of the maturity of Lean Management culture in higher education institutions. The project was executed under the research program 'Miniatura 1' financed by the National Science Centre, Poland (the dates of the project: 12 September 2017–12 September 2018) (No. DEC. 2017/01/X/HS/00619)

LCMQ. It is possible to distinguish the following types of approaches to maturity:

- An assessment of maturity as an assessment of progress in the building of a Lean Culture.
- An assessment of maturity as an assessment of a cultural gap.
- An assessment of maturity as a result of a comparison of a given university with other universities in a benchmarking group.

In the first approach, Lean Culture is assessed from the point of view of progress in the building of a Lean Culture in a given university. On the basis of her own research, the author adopted the following three maturity levels:

- The low level of Lean Culture maturity—the average assessment in the range from 1 to 2.5.
- The average level of Lean Culture maturity—the average assessment in the range from 2.5 to 3.5.
- The high level of Lean Culture maturity—the average assessment in the range from 3.5 to 5.0.

Taking into consideration the results of her research and with a view to ensuring their thorough presentation, the author distinguished also two abstract notional categories describing Lean Culture maturity in higher education. These categories are maturity in the social dimension (social maturity) and maturity in the organisational-technical dimension (process maturity). Similar dimensions were included in the model proposed by Jørgensen et al. (2007). Social maturity comprises such Lean Culture dimensions and descriptors as leadership, people, team work and relations, and values. Process maturity includes the organisational-technical dimension determined by the application of the process approach. Its descriptors concern the process approach. Taking into consideration the paradigm of the system approach, it is assumed that there is a relationship between these dimensions of Lean Culture maturity. Using this relationship, Fig. 4.1 presents the levels of Lean Culture maturity with respect to the two dimensions presented above.

Social dimension of Lean Culture (social maturity)				
	3,51–5,00	The average level of Lean culture maturity (Social driven Lean Culture)	The high level of Lean culture maturity (Social driven Lean Culture)	The high level of Lean culture maturity (Sustainable Lean culture)
	2,51–3,50	The low level of Lean culture maturity (Social driven Lean Culture)	The average level of Lean culture maturity (Sustainable Lean culture)	The high level of Lean culture maturity (Process driven Lean culture)
	1,00–2,50	The low level of Lean culture maturity	The low level of Lean culture maturity (Process driven Lean culture)	The average level of Lean culture maturity (Process driven Lean culture)
		1,00–2,50	2,51–3,50	3,51–5,00

Organizational—technical dimension of Lean Culture (process maturity)

Fig. 4.1   The Lean Culture maturity assessment matrix (*Source* The author's own work)

The results of the research conducted in the universities confirm the thesis about the strong relationship between the social dimension and the organisational-technical dimension of Lean Culture. Figure 4.2 presents this relationship.

The analysis of the research results presented in Fig. 4.2 confirms that in accordance with the paradigm of the system approach, the implementation of changes generates effects in all subsystems of an organisation. There is a strong correlation between the social dimension and the organisational-technical dimension of Lean Culture in higher education. The majority of the institutions participating in the research are located in the quarter indicating the average level of Lean Culture maturity. The results of this analysis will be discussed more broadly in the next section.

In the other approach distinguished by the author, Lean Culture maturity can be assessed by examining the cultural gap. For this purpose, it is possible to use a radar graph which shows the particular Lean Culture dimensions, their expected and perceived levels, as well as the Lean Culture gap (Fig. 4.3).

J. Maciąg

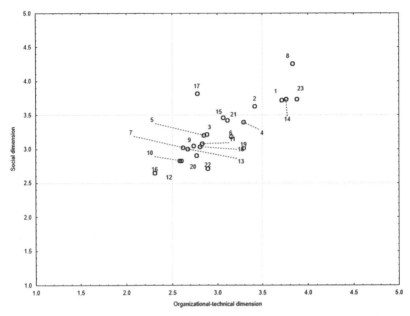

Fig. 4.2 Lean Culture maturity assessment based on the adopted assessment scale (*Source* The results of the author's research conducted within the framework of the project: Title of project: The determinants of the maturity of Lean Management culture in higher education institutions. The project was executed under the research program 'Miniatura 1' financed by the National Science Centre, Poland [the dates of the project: 12 September 2017–12 September 2018] [No. DEC. 2017/01/X/HS/00619] *Legend* The numbers from 1 to 23 are identification numbers for the particular universities participating in the research)

In the third proposed approach, a Lean Culture maturity level can be assessed indirectly by comparing a given institution to other institutions within a benchmarking group created by communities of practitioners. An example of such a comparison is presented in Fig. 4.4.

The universities were divided according to quartiles. 25% of the institutions with the lowest assessments of Lean Culture maturity are below the first quartile. The median (Me) divides the studied group into two equal parts; 50% of the schools with the assessments lower than those of the other half are below the median. 25% of the institutions with the highest assessments of Lean Culture maturity are located above the third

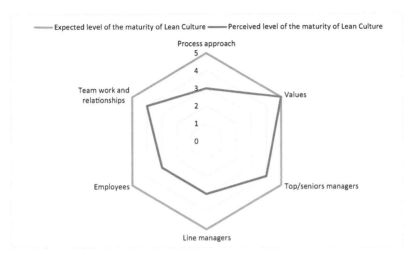

Fig. 4.3 Maturity assessment in the particular Lean Culture dimensions by means of a cultural gap (*Source* The author's own work)

quartile. The division of the universities according to quartiles allows a real assessment of a particular school's position in comparison to the results of other schools and not with respect to any assessment value criteria adopted in advance.

Nevertheless, the author wants to emphasise that she is against direct comparisons and the use of the results of the research based on the LCMQ, for example, in rankings of higher education institutions. Such direct comparisons are impossible in view of the fact that every institution has its own separate external and internal contexts, as well as its own specific organisational culture. However, the author is of the opinion that such comparisons can become a stimulus for a benchmarking group to initiate inspiring discussions on the use of Lean methods and tools, the conditions for their implementation, the role of the internal and external contexts, as well as the assessment of the effectiveness and efficiency of adopted solutions.

The results of the research conducted with the use of the LMCQ questionnaire also allowed the author to propose two typologies of Lean Culture.

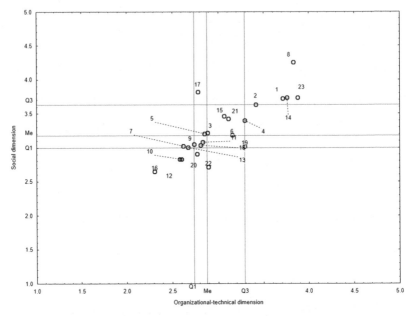

Fig. 4.4 Lean Culture maturity assessment based on the assessment scale discovered during the benchmarking process (*Source* The results of the author's research conducted within the framework of the project: Title of project: The determinants of the maturity of Lean Management culture in higher education institutions. The project was executed under the research program 'Miniatura 1' financed by the National Science Centre, Poland [the dates of the project: 12 September 2017–12 September 2018] [No. DEC. 2017/01/X/HS/00619])

4.4.2.5 The Types of Lean Culture

As Schein observes, creating a typology of organisational cultures is a useful procedure as it allows researchers to give sense to and arrange studied phenomena, to define their structure and basic premises, to build a theory explaining such phenomena, and to foresee, to some extent, how a particular phenomenon will develop in the future (Schein 2004, p. 190). Developing typologies, researchers usually use abstract dimensions or categories, and assume that there are hypothetical relations among them. The author is aware that such simplification of reality by way of categorising and modelling may involve some risks, but it is a useful research procedure. On the basis of the results of her research, the author distinguished two typologies of Lean Culture: a typology based on the criterion of Lean Culture maturity and a typology based on the criterion of an approach to building Lean Culture maturity.

An assessment of Lean Culture maturity makes it possible to assign each of the studied universities to a concrete group. On the basis of the adopted premises concerning the maturity assessment scale (Fig. 4.2), the author preliminarily distinguished three types of Lean Culture. This division is supported by the results of not only the statistical analysis but also the qualitative research conducted in higher education institutions. These types are the following: Lean Culture with a low level of maturity, Lean Culture with a medium level of maturity, and Lean Culture with a high level of maturity. As is shown by the research conducted by the author, Lean Culture with a medium level of maturity is a characteristic feature of the majority of the examined universities (Fig. 4.2). This group is the most diversified. In order to present a detailed characterisation of Lean Culture with a medium level of maturity, it is necessary to conduct further in-depth research in the particular higher education institutions. The research carried out within the scope of the project was aimed at verifying the reliability of the LCMQ tool. Therefore, the collected results do not allow a detailed characterisation of Lean Culture with a medium level of maturity. This requires further in-depth research in the particular higher education institutions. The author assumes that it will be possible to develop Lean Culture with a medium level of maturity by indicating its subtypes. Taking into consideration the specified limitations resulting from the research objectives and the range of the collected data, the author is able to describe only Lean Culture with the lowest or highest level of maturity (Table 4.7).

The research conducted by the author shows that in the Lean Culture building process, it is possible to use various approaches which differ with respect to emphasis put on the particular elements of the organisational-technical (process) dimension and the social dimension. Thus the author proposes to distinguish the following three types of Lean Culture in higher education:

Table 4.7 Lean Culture maturity levels—a preliminary characterisation

The levels of Lean Culture maturity in higher education	Low maturity Lean Culture (average assessments from 1 to 2.5—low maturity level)	Medium maturity Lean Culture (average assessments from 2.5 to 3.5—medium maturity level)	Mature Lean Culture (average assessments from 3.5 to 5.0—high maturity level)
The leading motto	*We have new problems, but we try to solve them, using the old methods*	*We are beginning to realize that the old methods do not work. We use process approach methods, including Lean Management, but our approach is not comprehensive and holistic*	*We know that Lean Management is an effective method of implementing changes. We know that improvement is a never ending process, therefore, we cannot stop on the way towards excellence*
Values	Customer-applicant. A lack of openness to changes, a reactive attitude. Pretending that the needs of customers and other stakeholders are taken into consideration	change in the approach towards	The objective is to create value for customers. Business Process Management s are fully accepted and determine the character of everyday actions
Lean strategy, system, structures, procedures	No reference to the concept of continuous improvement in the university strategy. A lack of a system, structures, and procedures	change in the approach towards	Lean strategy or continuous improvement, measuring the strategy implementation degree; Lean Management system

The levels of Lean Culture maturity in higher education	Low maturity Lean Culture (average assessments from 1 to 2.5—low maturity level)	Medium maturity Lean Culture (average assessments from 2.5 to 3.5—medium maturity level)	Mature Lean Culture (average assessments from 3.5 to 5.0—high maturity level)
Lean Principles—the process approach	A hierarchical, functional structure. Strong departmentalisation and fragmentation of processes. A lack of the process and system approaches. Sporadic attempts to apply the process approach, mainly in consequence of implementing information student affairs handling and management systems	change in the approach towards …….	A process is a basic criterion for the creation of structures. The process and system approaches as well as the Lean Principles are implemented in full. Balance between the top-down and bottom-up approaches
Leadership—top management	No awareness of the necessity of change. Solving new problems by means of old methods. Focus on the maintenance of status quo	change in the approach towards …….	Full commitment and support for actions related to Lean and continuous improvement. Lean Leadership
Leadership—immediate superiors	Oriented towards compliance with legal regulations	change in the approach towards …….	Fully supporting actions of employees and teams. Know and apply Lean methods in everyday work. Oriented primarily towards prevention

(continued)

Table 4.7 (continued)

The levels of Lean Culture maturity in higher education	Low maturity Lean Culture (average assessments from 1 to 2.5—low maturity level)	Medium maturity Lean Culture (average assessments from 2.5 to 3.5—medium maturity level)	Mature Lean Culture (average assessments from 3.5 to 5.0—high maturity level)
People	Fear of change. No commitment. Opportunistic attitudes, trained ineptitude	change in the approach towards	Lean methods are method of everyday work. Preventing errors is a priority
Team work and relations	No or sporadic cooperation among departments	change in the approach towards	Team work is the basic form of work. Success is the responsibility of the whole team
Artefacts—language	A language incomprehensible for members of the organisation	change in the approach towards	Comprehensible language. A broad range of understanding and using specialist Lean and continuous improvement terminology

The levels of Lean Culture maturity in higher education	Low maturity Lean Culture (average assessments from 1 to 2.5—low maturity level)	Medium maturity Lean Culture (average assessments from 2.5 to 3.5—medium maturity level)	Mature Lean Culture (average assessments from 3.5 to 5.0—high maturity level)
Tangible artefacts	No or sporadic use of visualisation tools	change in the approach towards	Visual management is a basic work tool
Behavioural artefacts	No meetings, seminars, etc. dedicated to continuous improvement	change in the approach towards	Meetings, events, etc. as a form of sharing knowledge and pursuing improvement. Celebration of small successes
Cooperation with the environment	No manifestations of institutional cooperation. Sporadic cases of individual cooperation. Strong fear of sharing knowledge and experiences	change in the approach towards	Close cooperation with the environment, new inspirations for improving university management processes. Communities of practitioners, international networks, study visits, conferences, informal contacts, etc.

Source The author's own work

- Process driven Lean Culture (Lean Culture based on the organisational-technical dimension—the process approach). Lean Culture is built first of all through the implementation of the process approach and the application of process management systems. Changes are usually imposed on a top-down basis, with strong support of top management; the dominant role is played by specialists and experts, while employees' involvement in the process of changes is rather limited, which carries the risk of their rejection. Changes concern mainly these areas of the university's functioning where information technology tools can be applied. What is expected is measurable results of changes expressed in terms of quantity and value.
- Social-driven Lean Culture (Lean Culture based on the social dimension). Lean Culture is built mainly through social changes introduced on a bottom-up basis and employees' strong involvement in improvement activities. The main carriers of change include training events, meetings, seminars, etc. This approach poses the risk of incomplete support from top management, insufficient resources, or problems with measuring the effects of change. There may also appear a certain barrier to change implementation resulting from the lack of a systemic and holistic approach at the level of the whole university (especially if the university's key and auxiliary processes have not been mapped and the process approach has not been introduced).
- Sustainable Lean Culture. Lean Culture is built through simultaneously implementing the process approach, ensuring a high level of employees' involvement, as well as making use of their initiative and creativity. This approach balances the top-down approach and the bottom-up approach, actions in the organisational-technical system and actions in the social subsystem. Only this approach guarantees the maintenance and permanence of introduced changes.

The research was also aimed at determining the conditions for Lean Culture maturity in the participating institutions. The results of the analysis are presented in the following section.

4.4.2.6 The Determinants of Maturity of Lean Culture— Research Results

Looking for variables determining assessments of Lean Culture maturity in higher education, the author used a multiple regression analysis (Sobczyk 2002; Greń 1984; Luszniewicz 1987; Pluta 1977; Steczkowski and Zeliaś 1997). A multiple regression analysis makes it possible to explain the variability of a selected quantity—a so-called response (dependent Y) variable with respect to other considered features—so-called explanatory (independent X) variables, omitting the problem of spurious correlation among examined variables. In the research, the dependent Y variable was Lean Culture maturity assessment. The independent variables X included variables related to universities and variables related to employees. The independent variables and the results of the multiple regression analysis are presented in Table 4.8.

The multiple regression analysis was conducted by using Statistica and Stata software (Table 4.9).

The author reviewed the results of the multiple regression analysis from two perspectives. She answered the following questions: Which independent factors significantly diversify the assessment of Lean Culture maturity in the universities participating in the research and which factors diversify the assessment of the particular dimensions of Lean Culture?

With respect to the first question, the results of the multiple regression analysis indicate that a general assessment of Lean Culture maturity in higher education depends on the following factors:

- The type of university—in public universities, the average assessment of Lean Culture was 0.548 point lower than in private ones (a 1–5 scale).
- An employee's position in the university—top managers assessed Lean Culture on average 0.509 point higher than the other employees (line managers and subordinates) (a 1–5 scale).
- The university's successful implementation of a quality management system consistent with the requirements of the ISO 9000 standard,

Table 4.8 Independent (explanatory) variables—a description

Name	Description
ucz_kraj	University's home country (1 if Poland)
ucz_plat	Tuition fees (1 if student pays)
ucz_rodz	Type of university (1 if public)
ucz_iso	ISO, EFQM (1 if it is held)
m1_1	Gender (1 if woman)
m2_2	Employment history (1 if 5–10 years)
m2_3	Employment history in university (1 if more than 10 years)
m3_1	Employment history in higher education (1 if up to 5 years)
m3_2	Employment history in higher education (1 if 5–10 years)
m4_1	Position in university (1 if top management)
m4_2	Position in university (1 if line manager…)
m4_3	Position in university (1 if temporary team manager)
m4_4	Position in university (1 if subordinate)
m5_1	Position in university (1 if administration employee)
m5_2	Position in university (1 if academic)
m6_1	Experience in Lean Management (1 if it is held)
_cons	Constant
Additional variables	
m7_1	Place of first contact with Lean Management (1 if higher education institution)
m7_2	Place of first contact with Lean Management (1 if other public organization)
m7_3	Place of first contact with Lean Management (1 if business)
m8_1	Participation in Lean Management training events (1 if regularly)
m8_2	Participation in Lean Management training events (1 if sporadically)
m9_2	Execution of Lean Management projects (1 if sporadically)
m9_3	Execution of Lean Management projects (1 if not applicable)
m10_1	Participation in Lean Management implementation team (1 if participant)
m11_2	Membership in Lean Management implementation support network (1 if not member)

Source The author's own work

the EFQM model, or others—the assessment of Lean Culture in the universities with such systems was on average 0.255 point higher (a 1–5 scale).

- An employee's experience in Lean Management or other process-based concepts—employees holding such experience assessed Lean Culture on average 0.126 point lower than employees without such experience (a 1–5 scale).
- The assessment of Lean Culture maturity was not influenced by whether a respondent was an administration employee or an academic.

Table 4.9 Multiple regression analysis

Independent variable	Dependent variable							
	KL Lean Culture	KL_1 (KL_I) process dimensions	KL_II social dimension	KL_2 top management	KL_3 immediate superiors	KL_4 values and principles	KL_5 employees	KL_6 team work and relations
ucz_kraj	−0.053 (0.30)	**−0.340 (2.22)****	0.085 (0.45)	0.383 (1.63)	0.024 (0.11)	0.162 (0.69)	−0.043 (0.22)	−0.020 (0.10)
ucz_plat	0.133 (0.53)	−0.045 (0.18)	0.219 (0.80)	0.418 (1.28)	0.140 (0.39)	0.050 (0.14)	0.327 (1.18)	0.016 (0.05)
ucz_rodz	**−0.548 (1.87)***	**−0.725 (2.53)****	−0.462 (1.45)	−0.200 (0.54)	−0.626 (1.55)	**−0.771 (1.89)***	−0.279 (0.86)	−0.556 (1.53)
ucz_iso	**0.255 (4.66)*****	**0.246 (4.06)*****	**0.259 (4.51)*****	**0.421 (6.17)*****	**0.159 (1.86)***	**0.348 (5.08)*****	**0.203 (3.60)*****	**0.191 (2.96)*****
m1_1	0.005 (0.10)	0.037 (0.62)	−0.010 (0.18)	−0.001 (0.02)	−0.018 (0.22)	0.022 (0.34)	−0.040 (0.74)	0.031 (0.48)
m2_2	−0.079 (0.57)	0.040 (0.29)	−0.136 (0.91)	**−0.283 (1.66)***	−0.021 (0.10)	−0.175 (0.94)	−0.094 (0.68)	−0.191 (1.22)
m2_3	−0.088 (0.62)	0.089 (0.62)	−0.173 (1.12)	−0.266 (1.54)	−0.084 (0.38)	−0.137 (0.75)	−0.176 (1.22)	−0.269 (1.57)
m3_1	−0.106 (0.73)	−0.011 (0.08)	−0.152 (0.95)	**−0.402 (2.28)****	0.165 (0.72)	−0.247 (1.31)	−0.200 (1.34)	−0.013 (0.08)
m3_2	−0.031 (0.27)	−0.053 (0.44)	−0.021 (0.16)	−0.097 (0.64)	0.114 (0.63)	−0.062 (0.43)	−0.069 (0.57)	0.080 (0.55)
m4_1	**0.509 (1.98)****	0.506 (1.61)	**0.511 (1.80)***	0.486 (1.58)	0.571 (1.57)	0.584 (1.44)	**0.571 (2.41)****	0.050 (0.15)
m4_2	0.042 (0.19)	−0.023 (0.08)	0.074 (0.29)	−0.077 (0.29)	0.276 (0.84)	−0.043 (0.12)	0.157 (0.75)	−0.141 (0.45)
m4_3	−0.194 (0.98)	−0.190 (0.69)	−0.196 (0.86)	−0.326 (1.39)	0.016 (0.05)	−0.261 (0.80)	−0.169 (0.88)	−0.383 (1.25)

(continued)

Table 4.9 (continued)

Independent variable	KL Lean Culture	KL_1 (KL_I) process dimensions	KL_II social dimension	KL_2 top management	KL_3 immediate superiors	KL_4 values and principles	KL_5 employees	KL_6 team work and relations
m4_4	−0.149	−0.140	−0.153	−0.261	0.083	−0.086	−0.162	−0.589
	(0.69)	(0.49)	(0.62)	(1.01)	(0.25)	(0.24)	(0.78)	(1.84)*
m5_1	0.044	0.391	−0.123	−0.238	0.013	−0.622	0.061	0.224
	(0.15)	(1.10)	(0.42)	(0.79)	(0.03)	(1.58)	(0.26)	(0.78)
m5_2	−0.033	0.164	−0.128	−0.392	−0.030	−0.586	0.067	0.432
	(0.11)	(0.46)	(0.44)	(1.30)	(0.06)	(1.48)	(0.29)	(1.49)
m6_1	−0.126	−0.152	−0.113	−0.148	−0.267	−0.135	0.022	−0.150
	(1.78)*	(2.11)**	(1.49)	(1.77)*	(2.47)**	(1.52)	(0.29)	(1.68)*
_cons	3.671	3.551	3.729	3.151	3.816	4.224	3.580	4.027
	(6.74)***	(5.80)***	(6.49)***	(4.88)***	(4.66)***	(5.76)***	(6.54)***	(6.17)***
R^2	0.13	0.14	0.12	0.15	0.05	0.12	0.13	0.10
N	764	764	764	764	764	764	764	764

Source The results of the author's research conducted within the framework of the project: The determinants of the maturity of Lean Management culture in higher education institutions. The project was executed under the research program 'Miniatura 1' financed by the National Science Centre, Poland (the dates of the project: 12 September 2017–12 September 2018) (No. DEC. 2017/01/X/HS/00619)

Legend The parentheses contain the values of Student t statistic for the assessed parameters; statistically significant parameters are marked with asterisks

$*p < 0.1$; $**p < 0.05$; $***p < 0.01$; the standard errors of parameter estimates were calculated using the heteroscedasticity consistent White–Huber method

The obtained research results confirm the hypotheses formulated at the beginning of the chapter. They are also consistent with the results of the author's previous research on Lean Culture in higher education (based on a different research questionnaire) (Maciąg 2016a, 2018). They confirm that the Lean Management concept is more familiar to institutions with typical business operating models. The implementation of quality management solutions causes university organisational culture to become oriented more towards processes, which moves it closer to the Lean Culture model.

In the private universities, Lean Culture maturity was also assessed higher in the dimension "Value". This allows the author to formulate the assumption that private ownership strengthens the values regarded as important from the perspective of Lean Management. This certainly requires further extensive research. The research shows clearly the existence of subculture created by top management of a given university. The assessments of top managers were decidedly higher in the case of Lean Culture maturity, its social dimension, including particularly its element concerning employees. Because of their positions in organisational structures, top managers better understand processes carried out in the university, have more decision making powers, more often participate in training, have better access to information. Hence their higher assessments of this aspect. The research results confirm that top management should enter the work environment of line employees. It is very important for a full understanding of the university's problems (gemba) for the prevention of decision making "from behind a desk". Lean Culture maturity received much higher assessments in the institutions which had implemented quality management models such as ISO 9001, EFQM, and others. The research results show unambiguously that quality management models of this type cause permanent changes in university organisational culture, making it more open to other process-based management concepts, e.g. Lean Management. The research confirms also the hypotheses that employees with experience in Lean Management and other process-based concepts are more critical in their assessments. The conclusions formulated in Chapter 3 were confirmed. Participation in Lean projects irreversibly and permanently changes employees' attitudes and behaviours. The results of the multiple regression analysis negatively verified the hypothesis of the existence of two subcultures in universities—a subculture of administration employees and a subculture of academics. The author is aware that an analysis of representative research results at a level of particular universities could deliver a different result. This issue will definitely become a subject matter of further studies.

In the second part of the review of the multiple regression analysis results, the author answered the following question: Which independent variables differentiate the assessments of Lean Culture maturity with respect to is particular dimensions? The results of the analysis are presented in Fig. 4.5.

It should be noted that the developed model of regression is characterised by the low coefficient of determination R^2 (the maximum value is 1). It shows that the independent variables selected by the author for the purposes of the analysis explain only 13% of the variability of the dependent variable (Lean Culture maturity assessment). The analysis

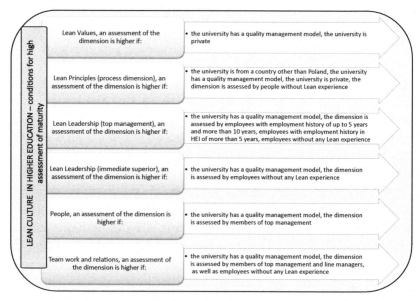

Fig. 4.5 The factors influencing a high assessment of maturity in the Lean Culture dimensions—multiple regression analysis results (*Source* The author's own work)

conducted with respect to the particular institutions which had met the conditions of representativeness (the highest questionnaire return rates were achieved) showed that R^2 equalled respectively: 14, 7, 23, 17, and 29%. What deserves attention is a considerable differentiation in this respect. It should also be noted that in the universities with the implemented process approach based on the ISO 9001 standard or information technology solution, the value of R^2 was higher (29 and 23% respectively). During the course of the analysis the direction of further studies became clearly visible. It is necessary to discover what other external or internal factors may determine the level of Lean Culture maturity assessments. The question arises whether there is a universal set of independent variables appropriate for every higher education institution or whether it is possible that universities are so diversified with respect to organisational culture that such a set cannot be indicated.

Concluding this analysis, the author wants to emphasise that the LCMQ offers considerable diagnostic opportunities in the field of the assessment of Lean Culture maturity in higher education institutions. Nevertheless, there are some limitations in the application of this tool. They are described in the following section.

4.4.2.7 The Conditions for and Limitations of Using the LCMQ for Assessing Maturity of Lean Culture in Higher Education

Developed by the author, the LCMQ allows a multidimensional assessment of Lean Culture maturity in higher education institutions. However, if the proposed research tool is to be used effectively, it is necessary to remember about the limitations in its application. These limitations concern the following issues:

- The selection of research samples.
- The scope of application.
- The subjectivity of employees' assessments.
- The limited scope of comparisons among universities.

A serious challenge in the organisation of research in which the LCMQ is to be used is the identification of appropriate methods of selecting a research sample. It is an important problem connected with the fulfilment of requirements concerning the representativeness and anonymity of research, voluntary participation in research, as well as the costs necessary for the performance of research. Representativeness means that particular qualities of a research sample reflect the qualities of the general population and all members of this population have the same chance to be included in a sample (Babbie 2013b, p. 218). In social research, the following two types of sample selection are used: probabilistic sampling based on probability calculus and non-probabilistic sampling (Babbie 2013b, p. 211; Easterby-Smith et al. 2015, p. 81). In probabilistic sampling, a research sample is selected by means of simple sampling. It provides for sampling from a list containing the names of all persons in a given parent population (a sampling frame is, for example, a list of all employees in a higher education institution, the number of the first person to be selected for research is drawn at random, each subsequent person is drawn according to the adopted sampling interval). The selected persons are asked to fill in the questionnaire. In order to assess the average Lean Culture level in an organisation, with an error of not more than d and with probability α, the minimum sample size can be calculated from the following formula (Sobczyk 2002):

$$n \geq \left(\frac{u_\alpha \cdot s}{d} \right)^2,$$

where u_α is the relevant critical value taken from the tables of the normal cumulative distribution function, and is the standard deviation of the examined variable in the sample.[1] For the most often used probabilities α, the critical values equal ($u_\alpha = 1.64$ for $\alpha = 0.9$; $u_\alpha = 1.96$ for

---

[1]For the most often used probabilities α, the critical values equal ($u_\alpha = 1.64$ for $\alpha = 0.9$; $u_\alpha = 1.96$ for $\alpha = 0.95$; $u_\alpha = 2.58$ for $\alpha = 0.99$). For example, for $d = 0.1$, $\alpha = 0.95$ and $s = 0.6$ (the value close to the mean standard deviation of the Lean Culture level among the institutions participating in the research), the minimum sample size is $n \geq 139$.

$\alpha = 0.95$; $u_\alpha = 2.58$ for $\alpha = 0.99$). For example, for $d = 0.1$, $\alpha = 0.95$ and $s = 0.6$ (the value close to the mean standard deviation of the Lean Culture level among the institutions participating in the research), the minimum sample size is $n \geq 139$.

The method of random sampling ensures the representativeness of research results, but does not ensure the anonymity and voluntary participation in research, does not protect against distortions resulting, for example, from the existence of subcultures in a given institution (e.g. women, men, employment history, superior/subordinate). Anonymity in research based on simple sampling can be ensured by organising it similarly to the process of electing public officials (e.g. by providing ballot boxes, separate rooms, or by sending envelopes with questionnaires to selected employees). Such a solution is, however, labour-intensive, time-consuming, and expensive. If the researcher knows at the stage of sampling that there are subcultures in the examined institution, the population can be divided a priori into relevant groups or layers (e.g. women, men) and the simple sampling procedure can be carried out in such groups. If the researcher has no information on this at the research preparation stage, the research should be conducted as planned and subsequently relevant corrections should be made in the obtained research results. Using regression analysis, it is possible to check which statistically significant factors diversify research results. Next the researcher determines to what extent the studied sample deviates from reality (e.g. 30% of the questionnaire research participants were women, and 70% were men; the regression analysis results show that the respondent's gender is an important factor diversifying the research results; the research results should be corrected by assigning weights to particular factors; such weights are calculated as follows: in the research structure there are 30% of women and 70% of men, there should be 50% of women and 50% of men; the weights are determined as follows: the weight for women's assessments $50/30 = 1.67$, the weight for men's assessments $50/70 = 0.71$; the obtained weights are multiplied by the assessments given in the particular statements).

Taking into consideration the above deliberations, it is possible to conclude that in the adopted research strategy, a research sample based on simple sampling may be difficult to achieve.

Another solution is to use non-probabilistic sampling methods. Such methods include sampling based on participant availability, purposeful or arbitrary sampling, the snowball method, quota sampling (Babbie 2013b, p. 211; Easterby-Smith et al. 2015, p. 81). The analysis conducted by the author indicates two methods which are the most useful from the point of view of research on Lean Culture maturity in higher education.

One of them is research based on participant availability. It consists in surveying the people who are in a given place (physically or virtually) at a given time and are willing to participate in research (Babbie 2013b, p. 211; Easterby-Smith et al. 2015, p. 81). Such research is frequently referred to as incidental or incidental population research. Sampling based on participant availability is relatively simple, inexpensive, anonymous, and voluntary, but it does not ensure sample representativeness and thus does not make it possible to generalise research results. It can be used in pilot research, for example to test the effectiveness of research tools. The author's experience shows that using this sampling method can also result in distortions in research results. Such distortions can result from the fact that a questionnaire is filled in only by university employees representing particular attitudes, e.g. those who are interested in implementing modern process-based concepts, always active and ready to fill in various questionnaires, fierce opponents of those holding top managerial positions, etc. The Internet forum effect can occur.

The other method is quota sampling. In this method, the starting point is information on the qualities of a studied population (e.g. the participation of men and women, superiors and subordinates); the next stage is establishing the percentage structure of a given population with respect to the previously distinguished qualities (Babbie 2013b, p. 211; Easterby-Smith et al. 2015, p. 81). Sampling is conducted in accordance with the percentage structure of the population (e.g. 30% of employees are men and 70% are women, thus in a sample of 100 persons there should be 30 men and 70 women). In higher education institutions, it should not be difficult to determine the percentage structure of a population with respect to such simple qualities as gender, education, etc. On the other hand, in view of the large number and overlapping of various functions fulfilled by subordinates and superiors, especially in the academic sphere, this may constitute a difficulty. In such situations, the author recommends establishing individually a percentage structure for the purpose of particular research, taking into consideration the availability of data concerning employees as well as the sections in which they are collected in a university. Quota sampling ensures anonymity, voluntary participation in research, and relatively low costs; unfortunately, it does not ensure the representativeness of research results.

Summing up, it should be emphasised that the most effective sampling method in social research is random sampling. It allows an optimum increase of probability that a research sample will be representative and makes it possible to analyse research results by means of methods based on probability calculus (Babbie 2013b, p. 218). Furthermore, random sampling allows the avoidance of errors caused by fault of the researcher or resulting from an incorrect assessment of a sample. It should be remembered that the larger a research sample, the greater the representativeness of research results. Consequently, including all university employees in questionnaire research, thus coming close to 100% of the studied population, makes it possible to disregard issues related to sampling. The selection of a sampling method should be a conscious decision of the researcher because, as it has been described above, particular consequences follow a given method.

Another limitation in the application of the LCMQ is the scope of research. The LCMQ does not examine all dimensions of Lean Culture distinguished in the theoretical model. This results first of all from their specific character and problems with assessing maturity using a survey questionnaire as a research tool. This concerns primarily such Lean Culture dimensions as linguistic artefacts, visual artefacts, and relations with the environment. Their maturity can be measured and assessed by means of other research methods and techniques, e.g. descriptive methods, observations, discussions, feedback gathered during the course of conducted research.

The adopted research approach based on employee self-assessment can constitute another limitation. Lean Culture maturity is assessed from the perspective of employees' subjective impressions. This may result in some distortions caused by employees' expectations which increase with time, positions held in the organisation, the current organisational climate, or the time of research. In order to minimise the impact of this factor on the assessment of Lean Culture maturity, research should be conducted on a regular basis, e.g. every other year, so that the researcher is able to notice certain trends and assess the effectiveness of implemented changes. If the researcher suspects that in the studied organisation there are groups (subcultures) or conflict situations which may influence or distort assessment results, then research results should be reviewed, taking into consideration identified divisions (for example, research results could be arranged according to organisational structure units or on the basis of other criteria which should be identified in the survey particulars, e.g. the name of a department, the place in the organisational structure—central administration, departmental administration, superior, subordinate, etc.) The author recommends using the LCMQ at the stage of diagnosing, before starting to implement planned changes, and for a properly long period of time after such implementation in order to achieve maximally objective assessments.

The author does not recommend using Lean Culture maturity assessment results as a basis for direct comparisons among universities or for creating rankings. Every higher education institution functions in particular internal and external contexts, therefore Lean Culture maturity should be assessed in terms of progress in the effectiveness of solutions implemented in a particular university. Research results can be used indirectly in benchmarking groups maintained by communities of practitioners for the purpose of assessing the effectiveness and efficiency of implemented changes, for example information technology support tools, training programmes, changes in the organisation and implementation of a Lean strategy. The organisation of such meetings should follow the Chatham House Rule. When a meeting or a part of a meeting is held under the Chatham House Rule, its participants may freely use received information, but the identities or affiliations of speakers or participants are not disclosed. This allows an open and free discussion and simultaneously the anonymity of people or sources of information to which participants refer during discussions (www7).

Summarising this section, the author would like to emphasise that a diagnosis of Lean Culture maturity in a higher education institution as its process culture is of primary importance in developing a programme for implementing the Lean Management concept.

4.5 The Building of a Mature Lean Culture in a University

4.5.1 A Programme of Change in the Organisational Culture of a Higher Education Institution

Researchers and practitioners implementing the Lean Management concept in higher education institutions pose the following questions: How can organisational culture in higher education institutions be changed? How can Lean Culture be improved? How can a university build organisational culture oriented towards continuous improvement?

The analysis of the literature on the subject shows that there are no unequivocal guidelines in this respect. Nevertheless, there are certain indirect suggestions concerning these issues and included in publications on the shaping of organisational culture and Lean Culture in various organisations, including universities. Problems related to changes in organisational culture were examined in research conducted, among others, by Atkinson (1990), Deal and Kennedy (1982), Schein (2004), Cameron and Quinn (2003), Ott (1989), Sikorski (2006, 2009), Czerska (2003), Sułkowski and Sikorski (2014), and Sułkowski (2012, 2016). Cultural issues related to the implementation of Lean Management were studied, among others, by Czerska (2009), Liker (2005), Womack et al. (1990), Atkinson and Nicholls (2013), Mann (2014), Bhasin (2012), Anvari et al. (2011), Atkinson (2013), Bortolotti et al. (2015), Goodridge et al. (2015), Jaca et al. (2012), Zarbo (2012), Stehn and Höök (2008), Pakdil and Leonard (2015), Clark et al. (2013), and Robinson and Schroeder (2009). In the context of higher education institutions, these problems were investigated by Radnor et al. (2006), Balzer (2010), Emiliani (2015), Waterbury (2011), Murphy (2009), Hines and Lethbridge (2008), and Cano et al. (2016). In the literature on the subject, in order to refer to cultural changes caused by the implementation of Lean Management researchers use such terms as Lean

Culture change (LCC) (Atkinson 2013), Lean transformation (Antony and Kumar 2011), Lean roadmap (Anvari et al. 2011), Lean journey (Zarbo 2012).

The objective of this part of the book is to present a proposal for a programme of change in higher education organisational culture. Proposed by the author, the approach to designing such a programme is conditioned by the functional-systemic research paradigm adopted in this book. In this approach, Lean Culture is treated instrumentally and its change has a purposeful character oriented towards improving the effectiveness and efficiency of the functioning of higher education in a long-term perspective. The author is fully aware of limitations in the shaping of organisational culture and, first of all, the fact that organisational culture cannot be managed in the classical meaning of the word. Czerska formulates a similar recommendation, referring to changes in organisational culture as a "course correction" (Czerska 2003, p. 68). Therefore, the author will use the notion of a change programme. Using the definitions formulated by ISO, a change programme will be understood as follows: *temporary structure of interrelated programme components (project, programme or other related work) managed together that provides advantages, contributes to the achievement of strategic and operational objectives, and realizes benefits* (ISO 21503:2017).

In order to create a theoretical framework describing the implementation of a programme of cultural change in higher education institutions, the author used the Plan-Do-Check-Act (PDCA) cycle (Fig. 4.6). The PDCA cycle was developed by Shewhart and popularised by Deming (2012). Using the PDCA cycle to describe a programme of change in organisational culture emphasises the essence of the Lean Management concept and is perfectly compatible with the paradigmatic premises of this book and the adopted relational definition of organisational culture. The philosophy of PDCA stands in contradiction to the basic premise of Taylorism, according to which the leader should find one optimum way of executing a process and then enforce it on employees (Stoller 2015, p. 63). The PDCA cycle is based on the premise that it is the employee who changes the organisation through their actions, with the assistance and support provided by the leader.

Within the change programme, the existing university organisational culture may be examined in two ways. In the short-term perspective, it

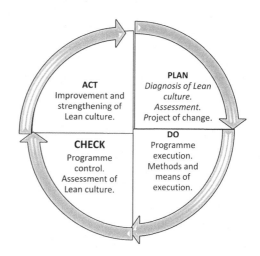

Fig. 4.6 A theoretical framework for the stages of executing a programme of cultural change in a higher education institution (*Source* The author's own work)

is a context for changes to be implemented (it determines their preparation and implementation), while in the long-term perspective, it is the effect of the change process (it has acquired the qualities specified in the change programme) (Czerska 2003, p. 37). The execution of the cultural change programme has both the strategic and operational dimensions (Atkinson and Nicholls 2013). In the author's opinion, in the strategic dimension, change is oriented towards changing employees' attitudes and behaviours in such a way as to ensure that Lean Culture will become everyday work culture. As Zarbo emphasises, it should be based on respect for and development of the people who are responsible for the process of continuous improvement (Zarbo 2012). In the strategic dimension, change depends on the development of Lean leadership. Many authors emphasise the critical importance of this issue (Emiliani 2015; Balzer 2010; Lu et al. 2017; Radnor and Bucci 2011; Atkinson and Nicholls 2013; Mann 2009; Goodridge et al. 2015). It is also important to consolidate such Lean Values as respect for people and continuous improvement as well as the qualities of Lean Culture characterising people's attitudes, for example understanding, questioning, proactivity, and trust. In the operational dimension, change is oriented towards achieving operational excellence on the basis of the Lean Principles. In the author's opinion, the critical factors in this respect include team work, training, and (organisational, technical, social, financial) support. This is also confirmed by other researchers (Cano et al. 2016; Balzer 2010; Radnor and Bucci 2011; Zarbo 2012). The literature presents proposals of various approaches to the improvement of operational activities in higher education institutions on the basis of the Lean Management principles. Waterbury proposes the Educational Lean Improvement Model (ELIM) model based on the PDSA cycle, Sherlock—the Improve Model Sherlock (2009) and Anvari et al. (2011)—the dynamic model for a Lean roadmap.

Summing up this part of the deliberations, the author would like to emphasise that the execution of a cultural change programme is based on the two basic pillars: a long-term perspective and actions within the particular stages of the PDCA cycle. Below, on the basis of her own research, the author discusses the most important activities undertaken by the universities participating in the research within the programme of changing organisational culture towards Lean Culture. Using the results of studies conducted by other researchers, the author assigned such activities to the particular stages of the change programme. The description does not distinguish between the activities in the strategic dimension and those in the operational dimension. During the course of the research the author noticed that these two spheres strongly permeated each other. Describing them separately could distort the idea of the holistic and comprehensive approach to the execution of the organisational culture change programme in higher education institutions. The necessity of a broad institutional approach is also emphasised by other authors (Balzer et al. 2016). In the section below, the author also formulates her own recommendations concerning the execution of the cultural change programme.

The first stage in the PDCA cycle is planning changes in the organisational culture of a higher education institution.

4.5.2 Planning Changes in the Organisational Culture of a Higher Education Institution

The objective of this stage is preparing a plan of changes in the organisational culture of a higher education institution. On the basis of the results of the conducted research, the author proposes that this stage comprises the following actions: becoming aware of and recognising the necessity of changes, conducting a diagnosis of Lean Culture, assessing the level of maturity and the cultural gap, and developing a plan of changes in organisational culture. Planning constitutes a basis for conducting control procedures, and such procedures allow the planning of subsequent actions in the organisational culture change programme which will lead to a decrease in the cultural gap and a higher level of its maturity. Therefore, the diagnostic activities and assessment of Lean Culture using the LCMMHE and LCQM should take place at the planning stage in the first PDCA cycle only. In the subsequent cycles, the diagnosis and assessment of Lean Culture should be carried out at the controlling stage. Many authors emphasise the critical importance of diagnosis in the building of a Lean Culture. Atkinson and Nicholls write that as long as readiness for change is controlled, change is characterised by a low risk.

4.5.2.1 Top University Management's Awareness of the Necessity of Implementing Changes

At the planning stage, it is of key importance that top university managers become aware of the necessity of introducing changes and the possibility of using for this purpose new management methods based on the Lean Management concept and other process-based approaches. Demonstrating the need for change is a critical success factor in the change implementation process. This is emphasised by the researchers specialising in change management (Hayes 2018; Cameron and Green 2015; Jaca et al. 2012). Becoming aware of the need for change concerns both management and regular organisation members. Senior university managers become aware of the need for change and benefits resulting from change implementation. Employees become aware that work becomes less and less comfortable and that this should be changed (then their resistance to change weakens and gradually changes into enthusiasm for change). The author is of the opinion that this critical change implementation dimension is completely neglected in higher education institutions. If a university develops through autopoiesis, it is only a deep awareness of the need for change that can influence its DNA. The university itself undertakes actions as an expression of its autonomous choice. Otherwise, in a situation of pressure on cultural change, it will only pretend to opt for change, maintaining the status quo. The author discussed this topic in Chapter 2 of this book.

The author's research shows that becoming aware of the need for changes is a difficult stage, especially in universities whose models are based on the bureaucratic approach or are characterised by the dominant role of the academic oligarchy in management. In some of the surveyed universities, it was not top management that was the source of impulses for change. Change programmes were also initiated by individuals interested in the concept of Lean Management (they were individual representatives of management, specialists). Such persons are referred to as heroes (Deal and Kennedy 1982) or change agents (Anvari et al. 2011). Many of the surveyed universities had such "heroes" who were responsible for managing the process of change or revealed themselves in this process. They were charismatic people enjoying general respect, experts in the field of Lean Management.

Inspirations for change often had their source in activities undertaken by other universities, public organisations (offices, hospitals) or participation in various networks and professional organisations (e.g. regular meetings of chancellors, presidents, directors). The stage of becoming aware of the necessity of and need for changes was associated in some cases with a long process of persuading top managers. An important factor was to select a proper way of argumentation. At the beginning attention was drawn to benefits resulting from changes illustrated with specific and reliable examples of successfully implemented Lean Management principles. The author observed that at the beginning stage recipients were usually unprepared to understand the culture-creating dimension of Lean Management. Therefore, emphasis was put on issues related to improvements in everyday work and a more methodical approach to problem solving; the results of completed projects were presented (using first of all visual tools and measurable change results such as time, number of actions, etc.). It should be remembered that the higher education sector is characterised by status competition and institutional isomorphism, which the author described in Chapter 2.

Therefore references were made to the universities which are regarded as models worthy of imitation. What also appeared useful was arguments showing the possibility of broadening the university's scope of self-determination with respect to organisational matters.

The author's research shows that the implementation of change is accompanied by numerous fears. Consequently, it was very important to emphasise continually that the objective of the programme was the reduction of waste, and not jobs. The respondents drew attention that a characteristic feature of many schools was their focus on large, groundbreaking changes or strategic projects, while they were not good at smaller projects related to everyday operations. Deal and Kennedy suggest that indicating a real external threat which imposes change could be a useful strategy (Deal and Kennedy 1982). The author noticed the use of this strategy in the institutions participating in her research. The respondents emphasised that there had existed and continued to exist a state of danger caused by such factors as less funds for current activities, competition in rankings, demographic problems, or Brexit.

The management's understanding of the need for change and full support for the selection of Lean Management as a philosophy and method of change implementation were indispensable conditions for eventual success. It is important that all interested parties become convinced of the necessity of change and manifest, as it were, a hunger for change.

4.5.2.2 Diagnosing Lean Culture, Assessing a Level of Maturity, and a Cultural Gap—LCMMHE and LCMQ

In order to diagnose Lean Culture maturity, the author proposes to use the LCMMHE and LCMQ, which were described in Chapter 3. Understanding the context and present organisational culture of a university is a continuous process necessary for determining and improving the key elements of a change programme and the method of its implementation. What is of particular importance is an analysis of risks and opportunities related to the change implementation process.

Each of the surveyed universities had intuitively developed its own model of building a mature Lean Culture. Sometimes activities were undertaken on a trial and error basis, which resulted in false starts caused by the initial resistance on the part of managers and employees. Unlike in manufacturing or business organisations, the universities had to deal with a special challenge because the object of planned transformation was a strong and relatively universal organisational culture. The author's research showed that the majority of the surveyed universities were aware that a model functioning well in a business environment or in another university might prove to be limited in their individual cases.

The occurrence of this attitude is also confirmed by other researchers (Liker and Convis 2012, p. 46; Emiliani 2015). The literature on the subject indicates also that the method of implementing the Lean concept may depend on whether the implementing institution is a so-called old or new university. On the basis of their research, Thirkell and Ashman (2014) showed that old universities implemented Lean mainly in the administrative sphere, avoiding the involvement of academics or human resources departments. In new universities, the Lean concept theoretically comprised a whole institution, human resources departments were active participants of the implementation process, but, in practice, changes were limited to the administrative sphere.

The conducted research and analysis of the literature on the subject allowed the author to pose the following questions which should be answered at the diagnostic stage: At which levels is it possible to carry out a successful transformation of organisational culture? Which levels will not undergo transformation at all? To what extent will this constitute a barrier to the building of a mature Lean Culture? What are the potential places of the occurrence of conflicts causing Lean Culture to be perceived as hostile and repressive? The author recommends preceding a decision concerning the selection of an approach to the building of a mature Lean Culture by a thorough diagnosis of organisational culture and its context and ensuring that the programme itself is continuously modified and improved in accordance with the PDCA cycle. The necessity of a thorough diagnosis of an institution's organisational culture and the factors influencing it is also emphasised by Stehn and Höök (2008) (Pakdil and Leonard 2015).

4.5.2.3 A Project to Change Organisational Culture

Another activity at the planning stage in the PDCA cycle is creating a project of changes in organisational culture. Such a project should comprise activities in the areas of organisational solutions, people management, and managers' work methods (Czerska 2003; Zarbo 2012; Mann 2014; Sherlock 2009). Stoddard and Jarvenpaa (1995) emphasise that in order to carry out a thorough transformation of an organisation, changes have to become visible in all key areas and at all organisational levels: work, skills, structures, values, measuring systems, and information technology (Stoddard and Jarvenpaa 1995). The conducted analysis of the literature on the subject and the results of the author's research show that the building of an organisational framework for the implementation of a change programme (a Lean Management system) and the selection of adequate Lean methods and tools are of particular importance (Balzer et al. 2016; Waterbury 2015).

A Lean Management System

A Lean Management system is an ultimate tool to carry out an organisational culture change programme. The research conducted by the author shows that it usually contains the following elements:

- An organisational structure.
- Procedures (appointing people responsible for concept implementation, selecting appropriate techniques and tools, effectiveness and efficiency indexes, monitoring and improvement methods).
- Resources (human, material, financial, information resources; time).

The research results show that the universities participating in the survey established various organisational structures and solutions of a more or less formal character. On the basis of the collected research material, the author prepared Table 4.10 in which these approaches are systematised and their major strengths and weaknesses are indicated.

The analysis conducted above proves clearly a high level of diversification among the approaches to the implementation of the cultural change programme. The research showed that there had not been one single ideal solution for the implementation of the Lean Management concept in the participating universities. An observation of the evolution of the applied organisational solutions allowed the author to identify certain regularities. After some time the surveyed universities usually replace temporary forms (one-off project, events, etc.) with more permanent organisational forms. The author observed a process of internal institutionalisation in the form of creating specialist teams and departments dealing with the implementation and support for the development of the Lean concept. But it was not a regularity in all institutions. During the research the author drew attention to discussions on whether the establishment of dedicated Lean departments was an effective solution, whether it supported Lean Culture maturity or, just the opposite, restricted the mass character of the concept or reduced personal responsibility of employees and line managers. The respondents indicated the threat of the whole responsibility for the implementation of Lean Management being transferred symbolically to the employees of the deliberately established Lean department. There were also problems with transferring knowledge and competences to organisations. Some interviewees highlighted the problem of the university being dependent on one person, a Lean coach or leader, with respect to Lean affairs. Such a person's resignation could potentially result in the suspension or slowdown of the change programme. Consequently, what contributed more to the effective change of organisational culture was developing information networks of Lean advocates, leaders, facilitators, and specialists. Therefore, the universal character of the change programme and professionalisation with respect to Lean Management through continuous training programmes were very important elements. The respondents emphasised that at its highest maturity level, Lean Culture should become an everyday practice in the university's functioning, and each middle-level manager should become simultaneously a Lean promoter and coach. Lean should be a way of thinking and an integral part of

Table 4.10 Organisational solutions related to the implementation of the Lean Management concept in selected higher education institutions

Organisational solution	Essence and description	Strengths, opportunities	Weaknesses, threats, risks
A dedicated department (continuous improvement, business improvement or others)	In the organisational structure, a dedicated department is created to execute tasks connected with change planning, change management, consultancy, support, training, emergency assistance, monitoring, and control. There may be different scopes of activities	The assignment of tasks, responsibilities, and powers with respect to Lean to a particular unit within the organisational structure. Clarity and accountability of tasks. A high level of professionalisation. Lower costs of external training. Easier planning connected with the university's strategy and cascading of objectives to operating activities. Easier control of resources and funds allocated for improvements. A possibility of merger with other organisational unites, e.g. the teaching quality department	A risk of interruptions in the transfer of knowledge and skills to employees. Responsibility for success of implemented changes lies with department employees; university employees and managers are released from this responsibility. A threat of impermanence of changes in the university's organisational culture; improvement activities are still regarded as episodic events and not as a permanent element of university employees' everyday work
A dedicated employee (a position for Lean affairs) responsible for the implementation of the Lean concept plus a formal team/teams of employees	The university creates a position of a specialist responsible for Lean affairs, i.e. the planning, implementation, monitoring, control, and improvement of all activities related to Lean. The Lean specialist is supported by a formally established team consisting of university employees representing different parts of the institution, who usually combine work in the team with their regular duties	As above A free transfer of knowledge among Lean experts and other employees. Lean experts are perfectly acquainted with the specific character of work in the particular departments of the university. An increased sense of responsibility among university employees	Problems with combining regular duties with activities in the Lean team (lack of time, stress, overwork). Assigning responsibility for Lean implementation to just one person or one team. A threat of impermanent changes in organisational culture

(continued)

Table 4.8 (continued)

Organisational solution	Essence and description	Strengths, opportunities	Weaknesses, threats, risks
A dedicated employee/specialist responsible for the implementation of the Lean concept plus an internal network of Lean specialists and employees interested in continuous improvement	The university creates an internal network which unites employees dealing with Lean and using this concept in their everyday work. The functional objectives of the network are providing support, jointly looking for the best problem solving methods and techniques, sharing experiences. The network should have a leader appointed by top management	Intensive and mass specialist training programme in Lean and other related methodologies. A free transfer of knowledge among Lean experts and other employees. Lean experts are perfectly acquainted with the specific character of work in the particular departments of the university. An increased sense of responsibility among university employees. An extensive knowledge of methodology and ability to use it in everyday work. No barriers with respect to access to Lean experts. A universal character of Lean. A considerable influence on moving organisational culture maturity towards Lean	There may be problems with assessing the implementation of a Lean strategy as it may be watered down during the course of its implementation. Changes can be measured mainly by means of changes in the university's organisational culture, and such changes are difficult to diagnose and measure. Another measure is a level of satisfaction, but it is rather subjective
A dedicated employee (a position for Lean affairs) responsible for the implementation of the Lean concept plus a formal team/teams of employees plus an internal network of Lean specialists and employees interested in continuous improvement	The university creates a position of a specialist responsible for Lean affairs who is supported by the Lean team and the internal network of Lean specialists and employees interested in continuous improvement	As above A universal character and intensity of activities undertaken in connection with the implementation of the Lean strategy	As above

Source The author's own work

organisational culture in higher education institutions. Formal organisational structures could stop existing.

Lean Methods and Tools—The Culture Creative Dimension

The research conducted by the author shows clearly that certain Lean techniques and tools enjoy special popularity in higher education institutions. This may indicate their particular usefulness. Such tools and techniques include Value Stream Mapping (VSM), Suppliers, Inputs, Process, Outputs, Customer (SIPOC), Kanban, Kaizen, 5WHY, Gemba, Andon, Ishikawa Diagram, Pareto Method, Kata, Six Sigma, Hoshin Kanrii. Each of them was used successfully at various stages of executing organisational culture change programmes. In Table 4.11, the author describes these methods and tools, taking into consideration in particular their culture creative dimension.

Implementing Lean methods and tools, the surveyed universities adopted the problem-based approach. The order of their application was determined by the character of problems occurring in a particular organisation. The research conducted by the author shows that universities adapt to their needs more and more Lean Management methods and tool which are traditionally associated with the manufacturing and business sectors. The surveyed universities used various methodologies in the areas of project management (e.g. the PRINCE methodology), Knowledge Management, Change Management, Agile, SCRUM, or Strategic Management. These methodologies were frequently modified and their culture creative potential was strongly utilised. The necessity of adapting Lean Management methods and techniques is also emphasised by such researchers as Emiliani (2005), Radnor et al. (2006), Balzer (2010), and Cano et al. (2016). Bortolotti et al. (2015) emphasise that the use of soft Lean Management methods oriented towards people, relations, problem solving, cooperation, continuous improvement, multitasking, and customers creates better chances of success in the building of a required organisational culture (Bortolotti et al. 2015). Using such methods allows a relatively fast change in the most visible part of university organisational culture. They influence changes in the

Table 4.11 A characterisation and culture creative dimension of selected Lean Management methods and tools

Name	Characterisation	Influence on Lean Culture in higher education
Andon	Andon has its conceptual roots in the Jidoka system created by Sakichi Toyoda. Jidoka refers to an intelligent machine which automatically stops when a problem appears (Liker and Convis 2012, p. 133). It is an integral part of the Toyota production system, an element creating operational excellence (Liker and Convis 2012, p. 133)	The author's own research shows that Andon makes it possible to empower employees who are entitled to interrupt the course of a process if there are too many tasks to perform or too many documents to process
Ishikawa Diagram	Ishikawa Diagram is a very popular tool used in quality management. Its essence is a graphical presentation of an analysis of mutual relations among the reasons for a particular problem. The factors causing problems are usually divided into the following categories: manpower, machines, methods, management, materials, money, environment

Manpower · Materials · Machinery reason cause · A problem (an effect) · reason · cause · Methods · Management · Money · Environment | The author's research shows that the Ishikawa Diagram strengthens team work, stimulates employees' creativity, initiative, and commitment to problem solving. It teaches the user how to identify logical relations between causes and effects. It is used frequently together with the 5Why technique. The use of the Ishikawa Diagram is described, among others, by Sherlock (2009). It is also used in the Six Sigma methodology |
| Gemba | Gemba was created by Taichii Ohno, the father of the Toyota Production System. He believed that people can learn the most from everyday experience gained in work-places (Liker and Convis 2012, p. 98). Gemba is not a method in the exact sense of the word, but an approach to solving problems and undertaking activities in organisations. It is based on the ability to observe and analyse situations without relying on any predetermined judgements. It comprises the following actions on the part of leaders: visiting a workplace, observing a process, talking to people (gemba walk) (Mann 2009, p. 25) | The research conducted by the author shows that the Gemba technique allows university management to understand fully problems occurring in the work environments of particular organisational units. A full understanding takes place through personal experience. This teaches people mutual respect, understanding, and empathy. It motivates observers to look for sources of problems in management systems, and not in people who carry out processes. It encourages people to look for new solutions and teaches experimentation |

Name	Characterisation	Influence on Lean Culture in higher education
Hoshin Kanrii	Hoshin Kanrii is cascading superior strategic objectives down to operational objectives connected with everyday work. Objectives are established by way of intensive data collection and pursuit of consensus among managers at every organisational level; the process of establishing objectives is a dialogue in which all organisational levels (both leaders and employees) participate. Establishing objectives by way of consensus is aimed at ensuring that every employee knows and understands what is to be achieved and how to deal with it (Liker and Convis 2012, p. 195)	Hoshin Kanrii strengthens employees' and leaders' motivation and commitment at every organisational level. Motivation can be built through goal achievement indexes (an individual employee's awareness of how they contribute to the achievement of the whole team's results); emphasis is put first of all on team work; it is teams, not individual employees, that are assessed and rewarded. It also allows employees and leaders to understand better the university's strategic objectives and to focus on their achievement. This topic was researched by Roberts and Tennant (2003). There are close connections between Hoshin Kanrii and Kaizen
Kaizen	In Japanese, Kaizen means good change (kai - good, zen - change). Kaizen assumes that everything can be improved and the pursuit of continuous improvement is the duty of every employee in an organisation (Stoller 2015, p. 65). Kaizen is based on employees' bottom–up initiative and commitment to improving activities and processes by offering proposals for improvement	Kaizen allows a better understanding of processes and activities, a better understanding among team members, a stronger cooperation. It increases employees' initiative and creativity. It was researched, among others, by Emiliani (2005)
Kanban	Kanban is one of the forms of visualising the course of processes and ensuring effective communication during the course of carrying out activities (Hammarberg and Sunden 2015). Kanban is a blend of two Japanese words: kan (to see) and ban (a board) (Stoller 2015, p. 55). Kanban made it possible to convey a pull signal, a signal to start production, or a signal that materials, subassemblies or semi-finished products were needed (Stoller 2015, p. 55)	The visits in the surveyed universities showed that the Kanban board was often used in carrying out administration processes (e.g. public procurement procedures) or improvement processes (the implementation of approved improvement ideas/projects). Kanban allows a full understanding and practical application of the pull principle. It strengthens team work and a sense of responsibility for tasks and processes. It ensures the transparency and clarity of actions and processes in the course of task execution. It facilitates communication

To do	Waiting	Done	Tests	Finished

(continued)

316   J. Maciąg

Table 4.11 (continued)

Name	Characterisation	Influence on Lean Culture in higher education
Value Stream Mapping	Value Stream Mapping (VSM) allows a simultaneous combination of making an organisation lean (for example by eliminating redundant actions or sources of waste) and improving the quality of processes and their output. It consists in analysing all actions within a process, starting from a customer and moving along the value stream towards resources necessary for providing a service. A Value Stream Map is a drawing presenting the flow of information and materials in the process of fulfilling an order for a selected group of products or services (Czerska 2014)	Participation in restructuring projects in which Value Stream Mapping is used gives first of all a sense of value resulting from the possession of specialist and detailed knowledge on analysed processes; employees have a sense of agency and having a real influence on the shape of processes and the methods of their execution. Employees are simultaneously the authors and recipients of changes, which increases the probability of their permanence. Value Stream Mapping stimulates work in interdepartmental teams (Maciąg 2016b, 2019a, b). The benefits of using Value Stream Mapping are also emphasised by Balzer (2010) and Waterbury (2011)

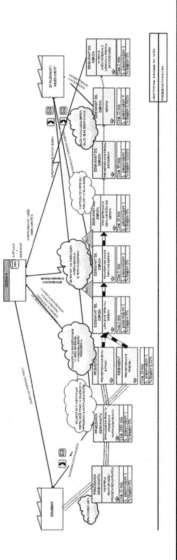

Name	Characterisation	Influence on Lean Culture in higher education
Pareto Method	The Pareto Method and the Pareto-Lorenz Diagram are tools allowing the user to hierarchise factors exerting influence on an examined phenomenon. It is a graphical representation showing both the relative and absolute distribution of the types of errors, problems or their causes. In the practice of management, according to the 80/20 rule, it is necessary to focus on actions correcting the most important 20% of the causes of inconsistencies	The research conducted by the author shows that this method makes it possible to concentrate on the most important causes of problems and facilitates the understanding of such causes. It allows a better allocation of resources in the process of improving the functioning of a university. This is confirmed by various research (Davidoff and Forrest 2007). The Pareto principle is used for example in the Six Sigma methodology

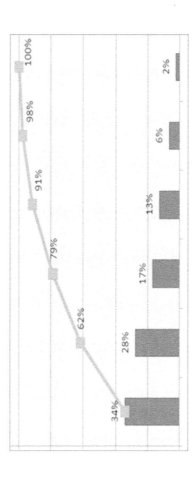

(continued)

Table 4.11 (continued)

Name	Characterisation	Influence on Lean Culture in higher education
SIPOC	Suppliers, Inputs, Process, Outputs, Customer (SIPOC) is based on the assumption that everything that constitutes the content of a process is oriented towards the customer and results from their needs and expectations. Thus processes are developed as links in a chain of creating value for the customer (Grajewski 2007, p. 123)	The author's own research shows that SIPOC is often used to design and organise knowledge of processes taking place in a university. This makes it possible to understand such processes and relations among them, facilitates the work of interdepartmental teams, improves the mutual understanding of the roles and activities of particular departments and employees in the processes. It ensures transparency. SIPOC is used, among others, in the Six Sigma methodology (Murphy 2009)
Six Sigma	The objective of Six Sigma is to improve processes by reducing their changeability by using statistical methods based on measuring standard deviations (the key concept is that of the Six Sigma level). More in this topic in Hamrol (2007, p. 81) and Antony (2014, p. 303)	A cultural change in an organisation (the awareness that everything can be measured; emphasis on the approach in which first we measure, and then we talk and act). LSS has a positive influence on leadership development, continuous improvement, responsibility for resources, processes, transparency, and team work (Antony 2014; Svensson et al. 2015). University employees, leaders, and partners unite around common goals through participation in restructuring projects. LSS strengthens the holistic and comprehensive approach to problem solving by building and strengthening cooperation and communication at the level of processes (Maciąg 2019a, b)

Table within SIPOC cell:

Input		Name of process				Output	
		Process's owner					
Suppliers	Inputs	Process (activities)	Aim of process	Indicators of process	Norms of indicators	Outputs	Customer
S	**I**	**P**				**O**	**C**

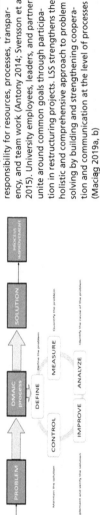

Name	Characterisation	Influence on Lean Culture in higher education
5WHY	The 5WHY technique consists in asking a "why" question five times in the process of looking for the causes of problems occurring in processes in an organisation. It is related to such techniques as the Ishikawa Diagram, Kaizen, Gemba, Six Sigma, Kata, etc.	The research conducted by the author shows that the use of this technique allows the building of a culture of asking questions continually as a basis for improvement. It makes it possible to identify the most deeply hidden phenomena which are not visible in cursory observations. This topic is also examined by Balzer (2010)
5S	This method is used in a multiphase transformation of the way in which an organisation is managed towards improved effectiveness, quality, and work safety. It is applied mostly to organise workstations and offices. It consists of the following 5 phases: "sort", "set in order", "shine", "standardize", and "sustain" (Czerska 2014)	The author's own research shows that the implementation of 5S improves employees' awareness with respect to organising a safe workstation, develops self-discipline and responsibility. Dogan et al. (2014) emphasise that 5S increases employees' satisfaction with work improvements, work safety, and participatory management (Dogan et al. 2014; Balzer 2010)

Source Prepared on the basis of the author's own research and the analysis of the literature on the subject Maciag (2019a, b), Svensson et al. (2015), Stoller (2015), Hammarberg and Sunden (2015), Czerska (2014), Dogan et al. (2014), Antony (2014), Liker and Convis (2012), Waterbury (2011), Balzer (2010), Sherlock (2009), Murphy (2009), Hamrol (2007), Davidoff and Forrest (2007), Grajewski (2007), Antony (2004), Emiliani (2005, and Roberts and Tennant (2003) language or the tangible sphere (visualisation) as well as develop and strengthen particular attitudes and behaviours of leaders and employees through changes in the methods of cooperation (going beyond the previous traditional methods of cooperation).

Summing up this part of the deliberations, the author would like to emphasise the critical importance of the planning stage of a change programme. The research results indicate that errors made at this stage could result in greater fears, resistance, chaos, and risks of sabotaging subsequent attempts to introduce changes. Such errors could also hinder transition to the next stage in the PDCA cycle, i.e. the execution of an organisational culture change programme. As a matter of fact, some of the surveyed universities did not manage to go beyond this stage.

4.5.3 Executing a Programme of Change in Organisational Culture

The execution of a programme of change in organisational culture aims to implement a previously developed plan. It consists of the following three actions (Czerska 2003, p. 74): accepting the plan, preparing the conditions for its implementation, and implementing the plan.

The acceptance of the plan includes its approval by people managing the university as well as its social acceptance. In order to acquire social acceptance, the following three approaches distinguished by Yorkstone can be used (Yorkstone 2016):

- Event-driven Lean in HE—it is based on various events (meetings, workshops, seminars, and conferences) supported by a centrally established team of trained Lean coaches and consultants.
- Advocate-led Lean in HE—it is based on the activities of a team of trained Lean coaches, consultants, and facilitators supporting employees in the execution of improvement projects and the development of a network of Lean advocates.
- Tool-led Lean in HE—it is based on the ad hoc use of Lean tools and techniques to solve problems occurring in the university.

Each of the approaches above is effective provided that it comprises the whole university and has a mass character, i.e. it comprises both academics and administration employees. It is a condition for effecting changes in the organisational—technical, social, and cultural systems of the university.

The results of the research conducted by the author confirm that establishing plans and programmes in cooperation with lower level management leaders and employees is, according to the Hoshin Kanri philosophy, an important factor determining social acceptance for the change programme. As Mann emphasises, it is of critical importance for the shaping of Lean leadership at all organisation management levels (Mann 2009). The author recommends consulting employees dealing with particular issues in their everyday work about the feasibility of change plans. If change plans are ambitious, it is recommended to determine resources necessary for their execution (tangible resources, time, people). The final version of a plan should be based on a consensus to ensure that top-down plans are compatible with bottom-up ones. Typical elements of the organisational culture change programmes in the surveyed universities included training plans, plans concerning the collection and analysis of information on sources of wastage and problems with process execution (problems could be reported by department managers or through the employee suggestion system; complaints filed by employees, students, or other stakeholders were analysed; the places in rankings, the results of audits conducted by external institutions, and the results of benchmark analyses were assessed), process restructuring plans, process improvement plans, etc. In the surveyed universities, Lean became an integral part of operational management. It was a part of problem diagnosing activities, change planning activities, designing, testing, implementing, monitoring, and improving processes (preventive activities), as well as documenting, institutionalising, and training activities.

Creating conditions for change implementation comprised also preparations in the organisational, technical, and financial spheres (the author did not research financial issues within the scope of the project). Examples of organisational solutions in this respect were discussed above in the section dedicated to the Lean Management system. Nevertheless, it should be emphasised that change programmes often comprised only selected processes or departments; there was a visible lack of a comprehensive approach at this stage of change implementation. This is confirmed by other researchers' observations (Balzer et al. 2016).

The respondents often raised the issue of selecting processes to undergo restructuring. It was especially important at the beginning stage of building a Lean Culture. The author also observed that the universities often followed the strategy referred to as the strategy of low-hanging fruit. The restructuring covered first of all processes fulfilling simultaneously a few criteria (this was described in detail in Chapter 2). These criteria included the importance of a process in the university's functioning, a large number of problems related to a process, the mass character of a process, the mass character, repeatability, and susceptibility of a process to standardisation. The identification of the importance of processes was facilitated by the employee suggestion system and the analysis of received complaints and process-related indexes. Efforts were made to ensure the optimally objective character of the selection process from the point of view of the whole university. It was important that possibly the largest group of customers or process users experience positive consequences of introduced changes. The author's research showed that a well promoted individual project and its spectacular success often became a pass to further activities. Resistance among managers and employees decreased, while their motivation, commitment, faith, and trust in implemented changes increased. In the author's opinion, small step changes, which are the essence of Kaizen, foster a climate favourable for deeper changes in organisational culture, alleviate fears of change, and build the awareness of benefits. This topic is also examined by Balzer et al. (2016) and Emiliani (2005).

At the stage of programme execution, the respondents emphasised the significance of communication. The surveyed universities usually published information materials, created dedicated websites, allocated specially equipped and prepared rooms for activities related to Lean Management or Lean simulation games. Offices were equipped with white boards for the purposes of Kanban or team work visualisation.

The research conducted by the author shows that at the stage of change programme execution there appeared problems resulting from a lack of team work culture and skills, incompetent change management, unwillingness to share information, fears of changes in the status quo established by authorities, as well as fears of losing a job. A lack of support from immediate superiors, disregard for the results of teams' work, extending changes in time, a lack of adequate dynamics of change, and process bureaucratisation often constituted serious barriers. Typical for universities, the procedure of providing numerous indispensable opinions on change programmes (by various committees or groups of people unaware of the specificity of programmes undergoing assessment) resulted in series of subsequent amendments taking into consideration various local and group interests, which often diluted the sense of a particular programme and its intended results. This caused problems with the implementation and maintenance of planned changes. Employees did not feel that they were the authors of such changes. The author is of the opinion that the aforementioned risks and limitations need to be taken into consideration at the stage of change programme execution.

The supervision and control of change programme execution constitute another important stage in the PDCA cycle.

4.5.4 Supervising a Programme of Change

Controlling the effectiveness of the execution of an organisational culture change programme concerns the correctness of the implementation process and the depth of implemented changes. The correctness of programme implementation may be measured by means of people's resistance to changes, the effectiveness of communication about the execution of a change process, and the adequacy of available technical and financial resources (Czerska 2003, p. 75). The author proposes measuring the depth of changes in university organisational culture by assessing progress in moving to the higher maturity levels in comparison to other institutions in a benchmarking group or by measuring a cultural gap by means of the LCMQ. The author's research allows her to recommend that such an assessment should be carried out after an adequately long period of time in order to identify permanent changes in individual culture and institutional culture. It should comprise Lean

Culture maturity in all its dimensions specified in the LCMMHE. In the author's opinion, a good moment for examining changes in Lean Culture is the completion of a comprehensive long-term training programme or other long-term projects, for example, those connected with the implementation of the process approach. The selection of such a moment can be facilitated by observations of changes in the university's key performance indicators (KPIs).

KPIs are the derivatives of the university's mission and vision. They usually include indicators concerning the quality of education (e.g. a student satisfaction index, positions in rankings, a number of complaints), recruitment indicators (e.g. a number of enrolled students, a number of students continuing education, a number of started teaching programmes), academic excellence indicators (e.g. positions in international rankings, a number of citations, parametric assessment results, a number of publications per one academic, etc.), operational/administrative excellence indicators (e.g. the average time necessary for dealing with a particular matter), and employee efficiency indicators (e.g. a number of overtime hours, cost indicators). On the basis of the Hoshin Kanrii concept (Liker and Convis 2012, p. 194) or the related technique of the Balanced Score Card (Kaplan and Norton 2001; Tyagi et al. 2013; Rampersad 2004, p. 39), such indicators should be cascaded down to processes and operational plans for particular processes, organisational units, teams, and employees. The necessity of cascading strategic objectives is also emphasised by Antony (2014), Cano et al. (2016), and Mann (2009). The surveyed universities operated reporting systems specifying scopes of responsibility as well as frequencies and formats of reports.

The author indicates that there are a number of methods and approaches to assessing the effectiveness and efficiency of management systems and processes in higher education institutions (Maciąg 2013). Her research shows that more and more universities make use of the Balanced Scored Card to assess progress in the implementation of their strategies. It should be remembered, however, that this tool does not allow an assessment of the direct impact of an organisational culture change programme on strategy implementation indicators with respect to customers, processes, finances, and development (Kaplan and

Norton 2001; Rampersad 2004, p. 39). The influence of an increase in Lean Culture maturity can be measured indirectly only. For example, employees' qualifications (a development perspective) determine the efficiency of processes carried out in an organisation (quality, time, timeliness—a process perspective). A high quality of provided services influences an increase in customer loyalty (a customer perspective), which translates into the university's financial results. The author's research shows that the surveyed universities used simple indicators assessing progress in change processes. Assessments based on quantitative indicators were usually limited to descriptions of reduced actions, documents, and operations, numbers of complaints, amounts of time or costs (but in the case of service provision processes, these indicators are sometimes difficult to measure) (Maciąg 2016b). In their assessments, the universities used the qualitative indicator of satisfaction among employees, students, etc. The conducted research shows deficiencies in measuring instrumentation, which does not allow an assessment of the effectiveness and efficiency of actions undertaken with a view to changes in university organisational culture. This is also confirmed by other researchers (Yorkstone 2016). The used measuring systems make it possible to measure phenomena in the organisational-technical and economic spheres. The assessment of the organisational culture sphere has to be based on different tools, e.g. the LCMQ proposed by the author.

The final stage in the PDCA cycle is improving the maturity of Lean Culture.

4.5.5 Improving the Maturity of Lean Culture

A measure of Lean Culture maturity is a change which occurs in university employees and leaders. Such a change is the effect of continuous improvement. *CI is where all members of the organisation work together on an ongoing basis improving processes and reducing errors to improve overall performance for the customer* (Fryer et al. 2007, p. 498). Atkinson emphasises that LCC is expressed through a sustained commitment to drive continuous and never-ending improvement (Atkinson and Nicholls 2013). Robinson and Schroeder (2009) use the notion of Lean improvement culture to emphasise employees' involvement in everyday improvement activities (Robinson and Schroeder 2009).

The results of the research conducted by the author show that the development of Lean Culture has a long-term, usually linear, evolutionary, and sustainable character. This is confirmed, among others, by Bhasin (2012). The objective is to transform the existing organisational culture towards a culture of continuous improvement. Changes in the organisational-technical (process) dimension are strongly connected with changes in the social dimension (Fig. 4.2). The development of Lean Culture means moving successively to the higher levels of maturity through cyclical activities in the PDCA model. The research conducted by the author allowed her to indicate the conditions for maintaining changes and improving Lean Culture maturity in higher education institutions. Such conditions include the following:

- Consistency in the execution of the organisational culture change programme.
- Emphasis put on permanent changes in the leadership and work style models to be based on cooperation. Development of the Lean leadership model.
- Involvement of all employees through training and various forms of team work in problem identification, which will help them to become aware of the need for change and to stimulate their initiative (the importance of the principle of voluntariness and asking for help).
- Continuous promotion of the change programme and provision of information on changes.
- Motivating and appreciating employees and leaders for their involvement.
- Organisational and technical support for employees, leaders, and facilitators.
- Building internal and external networks in which knowledge is created and shared.
- Visual management (Lean brain).
- Standardisation (giving up management through exceptions).

- The culture of continuous improvement oriented towards problem prevention.

In the interviews, the respondents indicated that ensuring continuous support for university employees was of critical importance for successful change implementation. A frequent error made in Lean implementation was an initial achievement of a high level of commitment and expectations in employees and managers, and a subsequent lack of support for the execution of improvement projects. If employees realised that their ideas remained on paper only, such initial enthusiasm turned into aversion to change in general and to change initiators in particular. Employees felt betrayed. Another important thing was developing a professional system of support for people involved in Lean Culture building programmes. Such support included ensuring access to lean facilitators and/or organisational units and teams, availability of material and technical resources (rooms, office equipment, boards, computer software, etc.), as well as enough time for change preparation and implementation. The respondents indicated that the centralisation of Lean tasks understood as gathering all tasks and relevant knowledge in one organisational unit or by one person constitutes a threat to the change programme. A resignation, dismissal, restructuring, or other changes could potentially threaten the continuity of Lean programme execution. It was important to ensure the support of all university employees for the change programme through their participation in training events and projects.

In the light of the research results, the execution of change programmes caused numerous dilemmas. They are discussed in the following section.

4.5.6 Dilemmas in the Process of Building and Improving Lean Culture

The research conducted by the author allowed her to identify a few dilemmas characteristic of higher education institutions which may reveal themselves in the process of executing a programme aimed at building Lean Culture maturity. Examples of such dilemmas include choosing between the bottom-up approach and the top-down approach, choosing between an external consulting firm and the university's own employees, or the dilemma of time.

The Bottom-Up Approach Versus the Top-Down Approach

The research conducted by the author shows that in the Lean implementation process there appeared a problem consisting in the necessity of ensuring balance between the bottom-up approach and the top-down approach. Threats resulted from the fact that the top-down approach was frequently perceived as an attempt to impose organisational changes on employees. The used language and methods usually met with resistance because employees did not see any additional benefits or value which could be created for them. The implementation of information technology systems in higher education institutions is a typical example of applying the top-down approach. Such systems generated benefits for managers, for example in the form of more effective process metering, faster availability of managerial information, or possibilities of modelling and predicting. But, from the perspective of employees, they were usually a source of additional work as hard copy documentation was not completely eliminated (employees had to perform twice more actions and generate twice more documents). Employees were required to make additional effort to learn how to use the new systems (often on their own, without any formal training, or through e-learning courses). Changes generated fears (e.g. employees felt that they lacked competencies to use the new systems effectively). Hence the author concludes that changes implemented exclusively on a top-down basis, without actively involving employees, may fail to bring about expected results. Employees should feel the need for changes, understand their sense, and be their creators. If changes are forced on employees, they treat them with indifference or hostility.

On the other hand, using the bottom-up approach only may also have a negative impact on an increase in Lean Culture maturity. The author's own research clearly revealed the situation in which a lack of certain central coordination of restructuring activities in a university led to the doubling of restructuring processes and thus the wastage of resources, energy, time, and employees' commitment. Therefore, in the author's opinion, what becomes very important is the coordination and prioritisation of tasks and projects at the level of a whole organisation, in accordance with the adopted mission and strategy. Hoshin kanri, the Balanced Score Card, or process mapping are useful tools for effectively combining the top-down and bottom-up approaches.

Time

The conducted research shows that Lean Management implementation and Lean Culture building are time-consuming. The execution of a small project took 2–3 weeks, a big one—3–4 months. Changing an organisational culture requires a few years of an organisation's effort. During the course of the research the number of 10 years appeared on many occasions as the time necessary for carrying out a cultural organisation change programme. This certainly requires further extensive research.

The problem of time concerns also the previously discussed issue of sharing time between everyday duties and improvement training events or projects.

Universities sometimes try illusorily to shorten the duration of the Lean Culture building process by using external or internal specialist organisational units and experts. They develop and implement ready-made solutions, which allows institutions to save time. However, there is a risk that this is done at the cost of regular employees' and leaders' lost opportunities for learning, personal development, and involvement in interesting projects. And it is through changes in employees' attitudes and behaviours that true and deep changes in organisational culture can take place. Consequently, such changes require long periods of time.

An External Consulting Firm or the University's Employees

The author's research shows that management in the majority of the surveyed universities had to deal with this dilemma. Consulting firms tempted the universities with offers of professional training and assistance, quick and spectacular effects. In the author's opinion, universities should first of all invest in the development of their own employees and leaders with an optional support of external consultants. The conducted research allows the author to recommend that caution should be exercised when considering offers of consulting firms; their services can be bought if the university has no possibilities or resources to develop its own competencies. This recommendation is supported by the following arguments:

1. The majority of consulting firms do not understand the specific character of the functioning of higher education institutions and their organisational culture based on many centuries of academic traditions. If the content of consulting services and training courses is not adjusted to this specificity, the Lean Management may be immediately rejected by both leaders and regular employees.
2. The building of a Lean Culture is a long-term task based on the learning cycle and the PDCA method. Only individual and team commitment may bring about long-lasting effects.
3. Consulting firms focus on data and objectives, and not on people.
4. According to the respondents, the implementation of the Lean concept based on workshops conducted by external consultants using the rapid model of Lean Management (usually quick five days' training events) usually ends in failure. Left alone and without support after such workshops, employees are not able to use effectively knowledge acquired in the course of training. Initial enthusiasm and motivation may soon turn into discouragement.

Summing up the results of the conducted research, the author wants to indicate the major limitations which may occur in higher education institutions in connection with the execution of an organisational culture change programme. They are as follows:

• Strong traditional organisational culture of higher education institutions.

- Time necessary for carrying out effective changes in organisational culture—the research results indicate the time horizon of 10 years.
- No consistency in the implementation of organisational changes (the principle of rotation in office influences the pace of change implementation).
- The first failures usually cause management to give up changes, even those regarded as desirable.
- A limited ability to change university organisational culture holistically (the less visible the organisational culture level, the lower the ability to change it).

Nevertheless, it should be emphasised that Lean Culture and traditional academic culture have many common points. The evolutionary character of change programmes and the use of the PDCA cycle as their basis are compatible with the unique character of the functioning of universities. Furthermore, the results of the research conducted by the author confirm that as a matter of fact, higher education institutions are oriented towards processes and implemented changes, despite the slow pace of the implementation process, will continue to develop. This results from the fact that people are the carriers of change and, because of the character of their work, university employees are aware of changes taking place in their environment, are more mobile and open to how the contemporary world changes. Furthermore, changes are strengthened by the more and more frequent use of information technology systems based on the logic of processes. Thus, it is ultimately university leaders who decide whether changes in organisational culture are to be deliberate and planned, or not.

4.6   Chapter Summary

Lean Culture should eventually become organisational culture in higher education institutions because this will ensure the permanence of the effects of introduced changes. The process of continuous improvement based on the PDCA cycle should become a part of every university's DNA code. The starting point for changes in university organisational culture and the building of its maturity is a comprehensive diagnosis. Performed in this chapter, the analysis of the literature on the subject showed clearly that the organisational culture assessment models and change programmes proposed in the literature were inadequate or insufficient for the purposes of higher education institutions. They concern mainly the visible sphere of Lean Culture (methods, tools, artefacts), but do not measure its manifestations through behaviours and attitudes of people in organisations. Therefore, the author proposed a new approach, method, and tool in this respect. She attempted to answer the following questions: How should Lean Culture maturity be examined and assessed for the purpose of its further improvement? What are the conditions for such assessment? The general objective of this chapter was to present the author's original tool for the assessment of Lean Culture maturity in higher education, to determine the conditions for its application, and to present a concept of a programme for the building of Lean Culture maturity. With a view to achieving the aforementioned objectives, the author first of all outlined a theoretical framework for the intended research. She defined such basic notions as Lean Culture maturity, Lean Culture maturity model, and Lean Culture maturity level and presented the methods of examining maturity of Lean Culture as higher education organisational culture. At the next stage, she developed and tested a tool for assessing Lean Culture maturity in higher education LCMQ. The advantage of this tool over others consists in its function to test Lean Culture as a manifestation of employees' attitudes and behaviours in an organisation. This allowed the examination of Lean Culture at its deeper levels, invisible in the previously used assessment models which focused mainly on the visible sphere. The results of the conducted questionnaire research allowed the author to define approaches to assessment, to describe a Lean Culture typology, and conditions for its assessment and development. Confirmations were also obtained for the formulated hypothesis according to which:

- The LCMQ allows a correct, accurate, and reliable assessment of Lean Culture maturity in higher education.
- Lean Culture maturity assessment is higher in private universities than in public universities and universities implementing quality management models and other process management concepts.
- University managers assess Lean Culture maturity higher than other university employees (they have a separate subculture).
- University employees who have experience in implementing process management concepts are more critical in assessing Lean Culture maturity (an assessment level will be lower).

The conducted research did not confirm the hypothesis that maturity assessment results were significantly statistically diversified with respect to the place of the assessing employee in the university organisational structure (the administrative part, the academic part). In the light of the conducted research, it is not possible to confirm that there are two separate subcultures: that of administration employees and that of academics. The chapter ends with a proposal for a programme of building Lean Culture maturity in higher education institutions, ensuring a comprehensive and holistic approach to changes in higher education organisational culture.

The author is aware of limitations in the examination and shaping of Lean Culture as organisational culture of higher education institutions. Therefore, in this area, she deliberately did not use the notion of strategy because the effects of changes resulting from Lean Management implementation are difficult to measure and dependent on numerous factors located outside management processes. The conducted research allowed the author to indicate the following new areas of research exploration: a more detailed characterisation of the types of Lean Culture, external and internal factors determining a level of Lean Culture maturity, the culture-creating dimension of Lean methods and tools, as well as the effectiveness of the solutions offered by Lean Management systems. They will become the subject matter of the author's further research.

Appendix 1: Lean Culture Maturity Questionnaire—The Final Version of the Research Questionnaire

Dear Madame, Dear Sir

Please review the following statements to help to evaluate the maturity of Lean Culture at the University.

I would like to know how much you agree or disagree with each statement. All responses are confidential. The results of this research I will use to investigate the reliability of the questionnaire as a tool which allows evaluating Lean Culture at a university.

How to complete this questionnaire?

Please formulate an opinion and evaluate the University in which you are working now. In the questionnaire word 'process' means work process, work, work activities. If you act at the University on many positions, please evaluate the statements from the point of view of the position, which is now dominant for you (senior/top manager, middle/operational manager/supervisor, temporarily appointed team manager or subordinate).

I thank you for your feedback.

Dr. Justyna Maciąg

Copyright©Justyna Maciąg

Scale of assessment
5 Strongly agree
4 Agree
3 Neither agree nor disagree
2 Disagree
1 Strongly disagree

THE AREAS OF LEAN CULTURE

Dimension 1—PROCESS APPROACH

1	I understand how the process I execute contributes to the achievement of the objectives of the university	1	2	3	4	5
2	I understand the relationships among the core processes in my university	1	2	3	4	5
3	The efforts which I need to execute the process of my work are sufficient and appropriate (i.e. information, materials, infrastructure, software etc.)	1	2	3	4	5
4	The documents (instructions, procedures and other written rules) which I need and use in my process are useful, easy to understand and appropriate	1	2	3	4	5
5	I can easily find the documents I need for my work	1	2	3	4	5
6	The number of documents in the process is reduced to the necessary minimum	1	2	3	4	5
7	I know the requirements of my customers (internal and external)	1	2	3	4	5
8	My work in the process is sensible and valuable for the final users/customers (staff, students etc.)	1	2	3	4	5
9	I know how to properly act in the process under which I work and I know the stages of its execution	1	2	3	4	5
10	My work is evenly distributed in the process execution (no downtime or excessive workload)	1	2	3	4	5
11	I execute activities in the process when they are needed by my customer/final user	1	2	3	4	5
12	Processes are executed without unnecessary delays (on time)	1	2	3	4	5

13	I don't create data and documents etc. in the process which are useless and unnecessary	1	2	3	4	5
14	Risks in my process are defined	1	2	3	4	5
15	I know how to treat a risk and I know what kind of activities I should take to accept, minimise and/or avoid risks	1	2	3	4	5
16	I have the right to stop my work when I recognise the problems which can cause defects in the process	1	2	3	4	5
17	Communication among the staff members who operate in my unit assures the effective execution of the process	1	2	3	4	5
18	Communication among the departments which operate under the process assures its effective execution	1	2	3	4	5
19	I identify the sources of waste on an ongoing basis	1	2	3	4	5
20	I can take corrective actions to minimise or reduce identified sources of waste	1	2	3	4	5
21	I monitor the level of defects in the process by using different indicators (i.e. time, cost, number of defects etc.) on an ongoing basis	1	2	3	4	5
22	The collected information about defects and problems in the process of work is regularly analysed	1	2	3	4	5
23	The collected information about defects and problems in the process of work constitutes a basis for improvement	1	2	3	4	5
24	Implemented improvements make my work more compliant with my customers' requirements	1	2	3	4	5
25	Implemented improvements make my work better organised and effective	1	2	3	4	5
26	I often use pictures, dashboards, tables and other forms of visualisation in my work	1	2	3	4	5
Dimension 2—LEADERSHIP						
TOP/SENIOR MANAGERS						
27	Via active, open and public support, the senior/top management have created an atmosphere of trust in continuous improvement	1	2	3	4	5
28	The senior/top management are patient and understand that changes in behaviours and attitudes to work and organisational culture take time	1	2	3	4	5
29	The senior/top management actively support and promote the managers and the leaders of change	1	2	3	4	5
30	Changes in the university are complex and complement each other	1	2	3	4	5
31	The improvements of the processes are purposeful and sensible, linked to the vision and mission of the university	1	2	3	4	5
32	Changes in the university are complex and complement each other	1	2	3	4	5
33	The process of communication in the university is simple and does not contain redundant steps/procedures/documents	1	2	3	4	5
34	The process of making decisions about change implementation in the university is simple and does not contain redundant steps	1	2	3	4	5
35	The process of approving change implementation in the university is simple and does not contain redundant steps	1	2	3	4	5

(continued)

(continued)

	LINE MANAGER/ IMMEDIATE SUPERIOR					
36	My superior is my coach/mentor	1	2	3	4	5
37	My superior truly understands the character of the whole process of work that I do	1	2	3	4	5
38	My superior supports me in the improvement of my daily work	1	2	3	4	5
39	Relationships with my superior are open, deformalized, and based on partnership, trust, and authority	1	2	3	4	5
40	The aims of changes are discussed before implementation and are not imposed by the managers	1	2	3	4	5
41	My superior takes my ideas into account and treats them as valuable and important	1	2	3	4	5
42	My superior treats mistakes as an important experience which can be used in the future to prevent other mistakes and to learn	1	2	3	4	5
43	The superior works to sustain the effects of implemented improvements	1	2	3	4	5
44	The superior motivates and engages me in the process of continuous improvement	1	2	3	4	5
45	The superior is personally involved in solving problems at their sources (these are not decisions made "from behind the desk")	1	2	3	4	5
46	The superior plans my work to allow time for developmental activities (i.e. meetings, training, workshops, etc.)	1	2	3	4	5
	Dimension 3—VALUES IN THE UNIVERSITY					
47	An important value in my university is respect for people	1	2	3	4	5
48	An important value in my university is openness to change	1	2	3	4	5
49	The university is proactive, faces changes, and prevents problems and defects	1	2	3	4	5
50	The new methods of solving problems and improvement are continuously checked and tried	1	2	3	4	5
51	A common sense approach is used in management	1	2	3	4	5
52	An evidence-based approach is used in the decision making process in the university	1	2	3	4	5
53	Continuous improvement is an inherent part of all activities and a way of performing everyday work in the university	1	2	3	4	5
54	There is a culture of questioning any ineffective and routine ways and rules of working in the university	1	2	3	4	5
55	There is a culture of trust in the university	1	2	3	4	5
56	Waste identification and reduction is an important value in the university	1	2	3	4	5
57	The main purpose of continuous improvement in the university is changing the behaviours and attitudes of the employees	1	2	3	4	5
	Dimension 4—EMPLOYEES					
58	I can report problems in processes in the University and recommend the prevention and correctness actions (there is a special reports system, a system of work suggestions etc.)	1	2	3	4	5
59	I feel that I am prepared and I have a competency to implement changes which improve the process	1	2	3	4	5

No.	Statement	1	2	3	4	5
60	I understand how my work contributes to the accomplishment, development and the vision for the continuous improvement of the university	1	2	3	4	5
61	I am empowered to show initiative, be involved in projects and implement changes in the processes	1	2	3	4	5
62	All initiatives and changes which I have done, even small ones, are appreciated	1	2	3	4	5
63	All knowledge and abilities acquired in past projects in the university I use in my daily work	1	2	3	4	5
64	The knowledge and abilities acquired from training, workshops and others I use in my daily work	1	2	3	4	5
65	The active participation in improvement of projects have changed my attitude to work and has engaged me more in the process of continuous change	1	2	3	4	5
66	My job is inspirational and interesting. I don't feel bored and stuck in a routine because I can make improvements	1	2	3	4	5
67	I keep the positive effects of changes and don't come back to the old and ineffective ways of working	1	2	3	4	5
68	I deepen my knowledge about continuous improvement of myself	1	2	3	4	5
69	I am not afraid I can lose my job due to process improvements	1	2	3	4	5
70	I am informed on a regular basis about changes in my team/department/organisation	1	2	3	4	5
71	When I have a problem in my work in process improvement, I can expect help from a professional internal specialist, special departments, special teams etc., which are obligated to assistance	1	2	3	4	5
72	I treat every suggestion as an opportunity for change and as a challenge	1	2	3	4	5
73	I feel that we work together for the success of the university	1	2	3	4	5
74	I am evaluated holistically for the results of my actions, also for my engagement in improvement activities (and not for incidents)	1	2	3	4	5
75	I am involved in the evaluation of my work and actions	1	2	3	4	5
Dimension 5—TEAM WORK AND RELATIONSHIPS						
76	The work and achievements of my colleagues are an inspiration for me to make improvements	1	2	3	4	5
77	In my team, I share my knowledge and experience with my colleagues	1	2	3	4	5
78	There are interdepartmental/interdisciplinary teams which help to solve different problems with communication	1	2	3	4	5
79	We celebrate small wins	1	2	3	4	5
80	I can share the results of my own and my colleagues' work improvement initiatives (i.e. at conferences, seminars, meetings, in written and on-line materials, etc.)	1	2	3	4	5

Source The author's own work

References

Al-Najem, M., Dhakal, H., & Bennett, N. (2012). The role of culture and leadership in Lean transformation: A review and assessment model. *International Journal of Lean Thinking, 3*(1), 119–138.

Antony, J. (2014). Readiness factors for the Lean Six Sigma journey in the higher education sector. *International Journal of Productivity and Performance Management, 63*(2), 257–264.

Antony, J., & Kumar, M. (2011). *Lean Six Sigma: Research and practice.* London: Bookboon.

Anthony, S., & Antony, J. (2016). Academic leadership and Lean Six Sigma: A novel approach to systematic literature review using design of experiments. *International Journal of Quality & Reliability Management, 33*(7), 1002–1018.

Anvari, A., Zulkifli, N., Yusuff, R. M., Hojjati, S. M. H., & Ismail, Y. (2011). A proposed dynamic model for a Lean roadmap. *African Journal of Business Management, 5*(16), 6727–6737.

Atkinson, P. E. (1990). *Creating culture change.* Bedford: IFS.

Atkinson, P. E. (2013). Implementation of Lean culture change and continuous improvement. *Operations Management, 39*(3), 16–21.

Atkinson, P., & Nicholls, L. (2013). Demystifying Lean culture change and continuous improvement. *Management Services, 57*(3), 10–15.

Babbie, E. (2013a). Downloaded from: https://www.researchgate.net/post/Should_we_use_a_5_or_7_point_Likert_scale_Whats_better_and_why. Accessed 15 June 2018.

Babbie, E. (2013b). *Podstawy badań społecznych* [The basics of social research]. Warszawa: Wydawnictwo Naukowe PWN.

Balzer, W. K. (2010). *Lean higher education.* New York: CRC Press.

Balzer, W. K., Francis, D. E., Krehbiel, T. C., & Shea, N. (2016). A review and perspective on Lean in higher education. *Quality Assurance in Education, 24*(4), 442–462.

Bessant, J., Caffyn, S., & Gallagher, M. (2001). An evolutionary model of continuous improvement behaviour. *Technovation, 21*(2), 67–77.

Bhasin, S. (2012). An appropriate change strategy for Lean success. *Management Decision, 50*(3), 439–458.

Bitkowska, A., & Weiss, E. (Eds.). (2015). *Zarządzanie procesowe w organizacjach: teoria i praktyka* [Process management in organizations: Theory and practice]. Warszawa: Vizja Press & IT.

Bortolotti, T., Boscari, S., & Danese, P. (2015). Successful lean implementation: Organizational culture and soft lean practices. *International Journal of Production Economics, 160,* 182–201.

Bugdol, M. (2006). *Wartości organizacyjne: szkice z teorii organizacji i zarządzania* [Organizational values. Essays on the theory of organization and management]. Kraków: Wydawnictwo UJ.

Bugdol, M. (2011). *Zarządzanie jakością w urzędach administracji publicznej: teoria i praktyka* [Quality management in public administration offices: Theory and practice]. Warszawa: Difin.

Bugdol, M., & Szczepańska, K. (2016). *Podstawy zarządzania procesami* [Rudiments of process management]. Warszawa: Difin SA.

Caffyn, S. (1999). Development of a continuous improvement self-assessment tool. *International Journal of Operations & Production Management, 19*(11), 1138–1153.

Calvo-Mora, A., Leal, A., & Roldán, J. L. (2005). Relationships between the EFQM model criteria: A study in Spanish universities. *Total Quality Management & Business Excellence, 16*(6), 741–770.

Cameron, K. S., & Quinn, R. E. (2003). *Kultura organizacyjna – diagnoza i zmiana. Model wartości konkurujących* [Diagnosing and changing organizational culture: Based on the competing values framework]. Kraków: Oficyna Wydawnicza Kraków.

Cameron, E., & Green, M. (2015). *Making sense of change management: A complete guide to the models, tools and techniques of organizational change.* London: Kogan Page Publishers.

Cano, M., Moyes, D., & Kobi, A. (2016). A framework for implementing Lean operations management in the higher education sector. In *Toulon-Verona Conference "Excellence in Services".*

Chiarini, A., & Vagnoni, E. (2015). World-class manufacturing by Fiat. Comparison with Toyota production system from a strategic management, management accounting, operations management and performance measurement dimension. *International Journal of Production Research, 53*(2), 590–606.

Clark, D. M., Silvester, K., & Knowles, S. (2013). Lean management systems: Creating a culture of continuous quality improvement. *Journal of Clinical Pathology, 66*(8), 638–643.

Crosby, P. B. (1979). *Quality is free.* New York: McGraw-Hill.

Czerska, M. (2003). *Zmiana kulturowa w organizacji: wyzwanie dla współczesnego menedżera* [Cultural change in the organization. A challenge for the contemporary manager]. Warszawa: Difin.

Czerska, J. (2009). *Doskonalenie strumienia wartości* [The improvement of value streams]. Warszawa: Difin.

Czerska, J. (2014). *Podstawowe narzędzia lean manufacturing* [The basic tools of Lean manufacturing]. Gdańsk: LeanQ Team.

Davidoff, D. J., & Forrest, L. A. (2007). Library web site assessment: From focus groups to pareto charts. *Indiana Libraries, 26*(4), 26–28.

Deal, T. E., & Kennedy, A. A. (1982). *Corporate cultures: The rites and rituals of organizational life* (Vol. 2, pp. 98–103). Reading, MA: Addison-Wesley.

Deming, W. E. (2012). *Wyjście z kryzysu: Out of the crisis.* OpExBooks.pl.

Dogan, Y., Ozkutuk, A., & Dogan, O. (2014). Implementation of "5S" methodology in laboratory safety and its effect on employee satisfaction. *Mikrobiyoloji Bulteni, 48*(2), 300–310.

Doolen, T. L., & Hacker, M. E. (2005). A review of Lean assessment in organizations: An exploratory study of Lean practices by electronics manufacturers. *Journal of Manufacturing Systems, 24*(1), 55–67.

Dos Santos Bento, G., & Tontini, G. (2018). Developing an instrument to measure Lean manufacturing maturity and its relationship with operational performance. *Total Quality Management & Business Excellence, 29*(9–10), 977–995.

Easterby-Smith, M., Thorpe, R., & Jackson, P. R. (2015). *Management and business research.* London: Sage.

Emiliani, M. L. (2005). Using kaizen to improve graduate business school degree programs. *Quality Assurance in Education, 13*(1), 37–52.

Emiliani, B. (2015). *Lean university: A guide to renewal and prosperity.* Wethersfield: CLBM, LLC.

Fryer, K. J., Antony, J., & Douglas, A. (2007). Critical success factors of continuous improvement in the public sector: A literature review and some key findings. *The TQM Magazine, 19*(5), 497–517.

Garceau, L. R., Pointer, M., & Tarnoff, K. (2015). A proposed model of assessment maturity: A paradigm shift. *Journal of Business and Behavioral Sciences, 27*(1), 134.

Goodridge, D., Westhorp, G., Rotter, T., Dobson, R., & Bath, B. (2015). Lean and leadership practices: Development of an initial realist program theory. *BMC Health Services Research, 15*(1), 362.

Grajewski, P. (2007). *Organizacja procesowa. Projektowanie i konfiguracja* [A process organization. Designing and configuration]. Warszawa: PWE.

Grajewski, P. (2012). *Procesowe zarządzanie organizacją* [Process management in organizations]. Warszawa: PWE.

Greń, J. (1984). *Statystyka matematyczna* [Mathematical statistics]. Warszawa: PWN.

Hammarberg, M., & Sunden, J. (2015). *Kanban. Zobacz jak skutecznie zarządzać pracą* [Kanban. See how work can be managed effectively]. Warszawa: Helion.

Hamrol, A. (2007). *Zarządzanie jakością z przykładami* [Quality Management on Examples]. Warszawa: WN PWN.

Harmon, P. (2010). *Business process change: A guide for business managers and BPM and Six Sigma professionals.* Amsterdam: Elsevier.

Hayes, J. (2018). *The theory and practice of change management.* London, UK: Macmillan.

Hines, P., & Lethbridge, S. (2008). New development: Creating a Lean University. *Public Money and Management, 28*(1), 53–56.

ISO 10014:2006. (En)Quality management—Guidelines for realizing financial and economic benefits.

ISO/TR 13054:2012. (En)Knowledge management of health information standards.

ISO/TR 14639-2:2014. (En)Health informatics—Capacity-based eHealth architecture roadmap—Part 2: Architectural components and maturity model.

ISO 9001:2015. Quality management systems—Requirements.

ISO/IEC 33001:2015. (En)Information technology—Process assessment—Concepts and terminology.

ISO 21503:2017. (En)Project, programme and portfolio management—Guidance on programme management.

Jaca, C., Santos, J., Errasti, A., & Viles, E. (2012). Lean thinking with improvement teams in retail distribution: A case study. *Total Quality Management & Business Excellence, 23*(3–4), 449–465.

Jedynak, P. (2007). *Ocena normalizowanych systemów zarządzania jakością. Instrumenty i uwarunkowania wartości* [Assessment of standardized quality management systems. Instruments and conditions of value]. Kraków: Wyd. Uniwersytetu Jagiellońskiego.

Jeston, J., & Nelis, J. (2008). *Business process management: Practical guidelines to successful implementations.* Las Vegas, NV: Elsevier.

Jørgensen, F., Matthiesen, R., Nielsen, J., & Johansen, J. (2007). Lean maturity, Lean sustainability. In J. Olhager & F. Persson (Eds.), *Advances in production management systems* (pp. 371–378). Boston: Springer.

Kaltenbrunner, M., Bengtsson, L., Mathiassen, S. E., & Engström, M. (2017). A questionnaire measuring staff perceptions of Lean adoption in healthcare: Development and psychometric testing. *BMC Health Services Research, 17*(1), 235.

Kaplan, R. S., & Norton, D. P. (2001). *Strategiczna Karta Wyników* [The strategic scorecard]. Warszawa: Wyd. Naukowe PWN.

Kostera, M. (2003). *Antropologia organizacji. Metodologia badań terenowych* [Anthropology of organizations. Field research methodology]. Warszawa: WN PWN.

Lameijer, B. A., De Mast, J., & Does, R. J. (2017). Lean Six Sigma deployment and maturity models: A critical review. *Quality Management Journal, 24*(4), 6–20.

Liker, J. K. (2005). *The Toyota Way.* Warsaw: MT Biznes.

Liker, J. K., & Convis, G. L. (2012). *Droga Toyoty do lean leadership* [The Toyota way to Lean leadership]. Warszawa: MT Biznes.

Lisiecka, K. (2009). *Systemy zarządzania jakością produktów. Metody analizy i oceny* [Product quality management systems. Analysis and assessment methods]. Katowice: Wyd. Akademii Ekonomicznej w Katowicach.

Lu, J., Laux, C., & Antony, J. (2017). Lean Six Sigma leadership in higher education institutions. *International Journal of Productivity and Performance Management, 66*(5), 638–650.

Luszniewicz, A. (1987). *Statystyka ogólna* [General statistics]. Warszawa: PWN.

Maciąg, J. (2013, June 24–25). Methods of quality management system efficiency measurement in HEIs, FICL6σ. In *First International Conference on Lean Six Sigma for Higher Education.* Glasgow, Scotland, UK. Theme: Enhancing Process Efficiency and Effectiveness in Higher Education Using Lean Six Sigma.

Maciąg, J. (2016a). The determining role of organizational culture in the implementation of the Lean management concept as exemplified by Polish universities. In *Lean Conference 2016 "People, Culture and Lean in Higher Education".* University of Stirling, Scotland, 1–3 November 2016. Downloaded from: http://www.leanhehub.ac.uk/conference/former-hosts.

Maciąg, J. (2016b). Mapowanie strumienia wartości w procesie kształcenia w szkole wyższej: wyzwania teorii i praktyki [Value Stream Mapping in the higher education teaching process: Challenges to theory and practice]. In T. Wawak (Ed.), *Zarządzanie w szkołach wyższych i innowacje w gospodarce.* Kraków: Wydawnictwo Uniwersytetu Jagiellońskiego.

Maciąg, J. (2018). Kultura Lean Management w polskich szkołach wyższych (wyniki badań pilotażowych) [Lean management culture in Polish higher education institutions (pilot research results)]. *Nauka i Szkolnictwo Wyższe, 1*(51), 69–95.

Maciąg, J. (2019a). Six Sigma as a tool of improving processes in the university for example of academic assessment process (case study). In S. Yorkstone

(Ed.), *Global Lean for higher education: A themed anthology of case studies, approaches, and tools.* Taylor & Francis and a Productivity Press book (accepted for publication).

Maciąg, J. (2019b). *Value stream mapping (VSM) as a tool for creating a Lean culture in a university.* Global Lean for Higher Education, Taylor & Francis and a Productivity Press book (accepted for publication).

Mann, D. (2009). The missing link: Lean leadership. *Frontiers of Health Services Management, 26*(1), 15–26.

Mann, D. (2014). *Creating a Lean culture: Tools to sustain lean conversions.* New York: Productivity Press.

Mashhadi, M. M., Mohajeri, K., & Nayeri, M. D. (2008). A quality-oriented approach toward strategic positioning in higher education institutions. *World Academy of Science, Engineering and Technology, 37*(1), 338–342.

Meybodi, M. Z. (2010). On the links between Lean manufacturing practices and consistency of organizational benchmarking performance measures. *B > Quest.*

Murphy, S. A. (2009). Leveraging Lean Six Sigma to culture, nurture, and sustain assessment and change in the academic library environment. *College & Research Libraries, 70*(3), 215–226.

Nawanir, G., Lim, K. T., Othman, S. N., & Adeleke, A. Q. (2018). Developing and validating Lean manufacturing constructs: An SEM approach. *Benchmarking: An International Journal, 25*(5), 1382–1405.

Ott, J. S. (1989). *The organizational culture perspective.* Chicago, IL: The Dorsey Press.

Pakdil, F., & Leonard, K. M. (2015). The effect of organizational culture on implementing and sustaining Lean processes. *Journal of Manufacturing Technology Management, 26*(5), 725–743.

Perera, P. S. T., & Perera, H. S. C. (2013). Developing a performance measurement system for apparel sector Lean manufacturing organizations in Sri Lanka. *Vision, 17*(4), 293–301.

Perkins, L. N., Abdimomunova, L., Valerdi, R., Shields, T., & Nightingale, D. (2010). Insights from enterprise assessment: How to analyze LESAT results for enterprise transformation. *Information Knowledge Systems Management, 9*(3–4), 153–174.

Pluta, W. (1977). *Wielowymiarowa analiza porównawcza w badaniach ekonomicznych* [Multidimensional comparative analysis in economic research]. Warszawa: PWE.

Radnor, Z., & Bucci, G. (2011). *Analysis of Lean implementation in UK business schools and universities*. London: Association of Business Schools.

Radnor, Z., Walley, P., Stephens, A., & Bucci, G. (2006). Evaluation of the Lean approach to business management and its use in the public sector. *Scottish Executive Social Research, 20*.

Rampersad, H. K. (2004). *Kompleksowa karta wyników* [Total performance scorecard]. Warszawa: Placet.

Roberts, P., & Tennant, C. (2003). Application of the Hoshin Kanri methodology at a higher education establishment in the UK. *The TQM Magazine, 15*(2), 82–87.

Robinson, A. G., & Schroeder, D. M. (2009). The role of front-line ideas in Lean performance improvement. *Quality Management Journal, 16*(4), 27–40.

Rosemann, M., & De Bruin, T. (2005). *Application of a Holistic model for determining BPM maturity*. Downloaded from: http://citeseerx.ist.psu.edu/viewdoc/download?doi=10.1.1.225.9386&rep=rep1&type=pdf.

Rummler, G. A., & Brache, A. P. (2000). *Podnoszenie efektywności organizacji* [Improving performance]. Warszawa: PWE.

Schein, E. H. (2004). *Organizational culture and leadership (Jossey-Bass business & management series)*. San Francisco: Jossey-Bass.

Shah, R., & Ward, P. T. (2007). Defining and developing measures of Lean production. *Journal of Operations Management, 25*(4), 785–805.

Sherlock, B. J. (2009). *Integrating planning, assessment, and improvement in higher education*. Washington, DC: National Association of College and University Business Officers.

Sikorski, C. (2006). *Kultura organizacyjna. Efektywnie wykorzystaj możliwości swoich pracowników* [Organizational culture. Use your employees' skills efficiently]. Warszawa: C.H. Beck.

Sikorski, C. (2009). *Kształtowanie kultury organizacyjnej: filozofia, strategie, metody* [The shaping of organizational culture: Philosophy, strategies, methods]. Łódź: Wydawnictwo Uniwersytetu Łódzkiego.

Sobczyk, M. (2002). *Statystyka. (wyd. IV)* [Statistics (Edition IV)]. Warszawa: PWN.

Spencer, N. H. (2013). *Essentials of multivariate data analysis*. Boca Raton: Chapman & Hall and CRC Press.

Steczkowski, J., & Zeliaś, A. (1997). *Metody statystyczne w badaniu zjawisk jakościowych* [Statistical methods in research on qualitative phenomena]. Kraków: Wyd. Akademii Ekonomicznej w Krakowie.

Stehn, L., & Höök, M. (2008). Lean principles in industrialized housing production: The need for a cultural change. *Lean Construction Journal, 2*, 20–33. https://www.leanconstruction.org/learning/publications/lean-construction-journal/lcj-back-issues/2008-issue/.

Stoddard, D. B., & Jarvenpaa, S. L. (1995). Business process redesign: Tactics for managing radical change. *Journal of Management Information Systems, 12*(1), 81–107.

Stoller, J. (2015). *Lean Ceo: w drodze do doskonałości* [The Lean CEO: Leading the way to world-class excellence]. Warszawa: MT Biznes.

Sułkowski, Ł. (2012). *Kulturowe procesy zarządzania* [Cultural management processes]. Warszawa: Difin.

Sułkowski, Ł. (2016). *Kultura akademicka: koniec utopii?* [The academic culture. The end of a utopia?] Warszawa: Wydawnictwo Naukowe PWN.

Sułkowski, Ł., & Sikorski, C. (2014). *Metody zarządzania kulturą organizacyjną* [Organizational culture management methods]. Warszawa: Difin.

Svensson, C., Antony, J., Ba-Essa, M., Bakhsh, M., & Albliwi, S. (2015). A Lean Six Sigma program in higher education. *International Journal of Quality & Reliability Management, 32*(9), 951–969.

Tabachnick, B. G., & Fidel, L. S. (2014). *Using multivariate statistics* (6th ed.). Harlow: Pearson.

Thirkell, E., & Ashman, I. (2014). Lean towards learning: Connecting Lean thinking and human resource management in UK higher education. *The International Journal of Human Resource Management, 25*(21), 2957–2977.

Tyagi, R. K., Gupta, P., & Jaworska, A. (2013). *Strategiczna karta wyników firm usługowych* [The strategic scorecard in service enterprises]. Warszawa: Wydawnictwo Naukowe PWN.

Urban, W. (2015). The Lean management maturity self-assessment tool based on organizational culture diagnosis. *Procedia-Social and Behavioral Sciences, 213*, 728–733.

Van Looy, A., De Backer, M., & Poels, G. (2011). Defining business process maturity. A journey towards excellence. *Total Quality Management & Business Excellence, 22*(11), 1119–1137.

Vimal, K. E. K., & Vinodh, S. (2012). Leanness evaluation using IF–THEN rules. *The International Journal of Advanced Manufacturing Technology, 63*(1–4), 407–413.

Vinodh, S., & Chintha, S. K. (2011). Leanness assessment using multi-grade fuzzy approach. *International Journal of Production Research, 49*(2), 431–445.

Waterbury, T. (2011). *Educational Lean for higher education: Theory and practice*. Lulu.com.

Waterbury, T. (2015). Learning from the pioneers: A multiple-case analysis of implementing Lean in higher education. *International Journal of Quality & Reliability Management, 32*(9), 934–950.

Womack, J. P., Jones, D. T., & Roos, D. (1990). *Machine that changed the world*. New York: Simon & Schuster.

Wu, C. W., & Chen, C. L. (2006). An integrated structural model toward successful continuous improvement activity. *Technovation, 26*(5–6), 697–707.

Yorkstone, S. (2016). Lean universities. In T. Netland & D. J. Powell (Eds.), *The Routledge companion to Lean management*. New York: Taylor & Francis and Routledge.

Zarbo, R. J. (2012). Creating and sustaining a Lean culture of continuous process improvement. *American Journal of Clinical Pathology, 138*(3), 321–326.

(www1) https://dictionary.cambridge.org/dictionary/english/maturity. Accessed 5 October 2018.

(www2) https://www.merriam-webster.com/dictionary/maturity. Accessed 10 November 2018.

(www3) https://www.iso.org/obp/ui/#search. Accessed 30 November 2018.

(www4) https://www.investorsinpeople.com/. Accessed 30 November 2018.

(www5) https://www.iso.org/news/Ref2187.htm. Accessed 5 October 2018.

(www6) Business Process Maturity Model (BPMM) https://pdti.pbh.gov.br/sites/pdti.pbh.gov.br/files/Business%20Process%20Maturity%20Model%20(BPMM)_v1.0.pdf.

(www7) https://www.chathamhouse.org/chatham-house-rule.

5

Summary, Conclusions, and Directions of Further Research on Lean Culture in Higher Education

5.1 Research Summary and Conclusions

A growing number of research reports as well as observations of experiences of universities experimenting with Lean Management show an increasing interest in the implementation of this concept. This results from changes in the context in which universities function and the fact that other approaches such as Total Quality Management or Business Process Reengineering are perceived as production and business concepts which constitute a threat to academic principles and traditions. Because of their top-down method of implementation, they cause changes mainly in the technical and organisational sphere without simultaneously making them permanent by building a culture of continuous improvement. Therefore, universities make use of the Lean Management concept, believing in its culture creative character, because in its implementation, considerable emphasis is put on the bottom-up approach in which employees' natural initiative, creativity, and natural commitment is applied. Employees become both the authors and recipients of changes. The research conducted by the author in higher

© The Author(s) 2019
J. Maciąg, *Lean Culture in Higher Education,*
https://doi.org/10.1007/978-3-030-05686-5_5

education institutions which have implemented or are implementing this concept confirms that a level of Lean Culture maturity is of critical importance for successful implementation of changes based on the process approach. Therefore, there is a need to diagnose Lean Culture maturity and to measure progress in the process of its change. The research proved that the continuity and permanence of the effects of restructuring activities can be ensured only if organisational and technical changes are strongly connected with social changes. The implementation of the Lean Management concept requires undertaking actions associated with particular expenditures (funds, assets, employees' working time, etc.). University management and stakeholders expect such actions to be effective and efficient. However, there are problems with measuring the effects of such actions. In the organisational-technical sphere, various ratios related to time, costs, quantity of actions or documents are used. But so far there has been a lack of models, methods, and tools used to measure changes in the social sphere with respect to organisational culture maturity. This book fills the gap.

The author showed how the Lean Management concept changed academic organisational culture, how such changes could be diagnosed and managed, and also how the meaning and understanding of the Lean Management concept changed in the process of its implementation in higher education institutions.

The main objective of the book was to define the notion of Lean Culture maturity in higher education institutions as well as to determine its key dimensions and descriptors in the light of the adopted ontological and epistemological premises. In the book, the author adopted a new approach to research on Lean Culture, broadening the previously dominant functionalist paradigm with a humanistic perspective based on the interpretative-symbolic paradigm. In this approach, the researcher focused her attention on an individual human being—a university employee, assuming that organisational culture was created in the networks of mutual relations, meanings, and interpretations. The adopted ontological premises allowed the author to use the approach based on epistemological pluralism. Such a research attitude made it possible to achieve all established cognitive and methodological objectives.

The achievements resulting from the conducted research are presented in the subsequent sections.

5.1.1 A Theoretical Contribution to Management Sciences

The main cognitive objective of the book was to define the notion of Lean Culture, as well as the dimensions and descriptors of its maturity. This objective was fulfilled by creating a theoretical framework for the testing of Lean Culture maturity in higher education institutions. Filling the identified research gap, the author defined new notions, systematised the already existing approaches, and proposed new model approaches and concepts. The achievements in the theoretical-cognitive sphere are the following:

- Characterising processes conducted in higher education institutions, indicating their specific nature, and proposing new criteria for their classification.
- Showing differences between business organisations and higher education institutions which determine the implementation of process management concepts in universities.
- Defining the notion of a Lean University and proposing a model concept of a Lean University, as well as determining the scope and directions of necessary changes in the university management model.
- Defining the notion of Lean Culture as well as the dimensions and descriptors of Lean Culture maturity in the form of the Lean Culture Maturity Model in Higher Education (LCMMHE).
- Establishing which factors of the external and internal contexts in which higher education institutions function determine Lean Culture maturity, as well as establishing mutual relations, interdependences, and gaps in higher education organisational culture and Lean Culture.
- Defining the notions of Lean Culture maturity, Lean Culture maturity model, and Lean Culture maturity assessment level.

- Proposing new approaches to Lean Culture typology, taking into consideration Lean Culture maturity and change implementation methods.

The author also reflected on not only how higher education organisational culture changes in the process of implementing the Lean concept but also the degree to which the Lean Management concept changes in the process of its implementation in higher education. The proposals in the theoretical-cognitive sphere were accompanied by methodological recommendations.

5.1.2 A Methodological Contribution

The main methodological objective of the book was to develop and test the author's original model of assessing the maturity of Lean Culture in higher education (LCMMHE), as well as to develop and test a tool for examining the maturity of Lean Culture (Lean Culture Maturity Questionnaire [LCMQ]), and to determine conditions for their implementation. A novelty in the methodological dimension is the author's adopted research perspective which so far has not been applied in research on Lean Culture and Lean Culture in higher education. Keeping in mind restrictions resulting from basing her research on Lean Culture on the functionalist paradigm only, the author supplemented it with the relational approach to defining Lean Culture, which is close to the interpretative-symbolic approach. Adopting this ontological attitude allowed the author to broaden the research perspective with the humanistic approach and to assume the position of epistemological pluralism. In the research, the author used the whole spectrum of social research methods used in management, going beyond the standard methods of researching organisational culture as well as using the elements of the grounded theory methodology and the open coding method. This allowed the examination of Lean Culture at its deeper levels, invisible in the previously used assessment models which focused mainly on the visible and tangible sphere. Filling the identified gap concerning research on and assessment of Lean Culture, the author systematised the existing research methods and tools, and proposed new ones. The achievements in the methodological sphere are the following:

- Making use of the elements of the methodology of the grounded theory and the open coding method in the research on Lean Culture.
- Creating a tool for assessing Lean Culture maturity in higher education (LCMQ) on the basis of the author's original LCMMHE. The advantage of this tool over others consists in its function to test Lean Culture maturity as a reflection of employees' attitudes and behaviours in an organisation.
- Formulating a methodology of using the LCQM to establish a Lean Culture maturity level in higher education institutions.
- Identifying the conditions for Lean Culture maturity.
- Defining and preliminarily characterising the levels of Lean Culture maturity in higher education institutions.
- Establishing a typology of approaches to assessment of Lean Culture in higher education.
- Establishing a typology of Lean Culture in higher education.
- Creating a project of changes in higher education organisational culture towards building a Lean Culture and its continuous improvement and determining the conditions for its execution.

In the conducted analyses, the author took into consideration the perspective of American experiences and the Anglo-Saxon student-centred model, as well as the European tradition of the continental university based on faculty-centred Humboldt's model oriented towards combining teaching and research and fulfilling the needs of the faculty. This allowed the author to develop the LCQM as a solid and reliable research tool and to propose programmes of changes in organisational culture which can be carried out in any higher education institution irrespective of its location, management model, organisational and legal form, or the state of advancement in implementing the Lean Management concept. This indicates the applicative dimension of the book.

The conducted studies of the literature on the subject and the results of the research allowed the author to indicate the directions of further research on Lean Management, higher education organisational culture, change management, and Lean Culture development.

5.2   The Directions of Further Research

The research conducted by the author showed that resistance appeared in universities against changes connected with Lean Management, but it was still not clear what caused such resistance. Is it a lack of understanding of the essence of process management and Lean Management, or an inappropriate selection of change implementation methods, or a lack of understanding of the essence of higher education processes, or an insufficient modification of process management methods in higher education institutions? Are people the carriers of resistance or does it result more from the nature of the university determined by the autotelic character of knowledge and the combination of teaching and research? In-depth research of the organisational culture of particular universities using the LCMMHE and LCMQ provides opportunities for obtaining answers to the above questions.

Another area is research on a more detailed characterisation of the types of Lean Culture, external and internal factors determining a level of Lean Culture maturity, the culture-creating dimension of Lean methods and tools, as well as the effectiveness of the solutions offered by Lean Management systems.

The very concept of Lean Management constitutes another important direction in research. In its primary essence, it is based on foundations other than those of higher education organisational culture. It is based on the viewpoint of business and manufacturing. Hence the recurring question about the usefulness and justifiability of applying this concept in higher education in the light of its specific qualities resulting from tradition and the nature of the knowledge creation process. The conducted research shows that certain solutions which constitute the foundation of Lean Culture, e.g. those related to leadership or the Lean Principles, may appear to be very difficult or impossible to implement in their original versions in higher education institutions or may require a wide range of changes or adjustments. There is a serious risk that the concept will become very much distorted and its original sense will be lost. This definitely requires further research.

The author is of the opinion that in the light of its interdisciplinary character, Lean Culture should become a subject of in-depth research combining the disciplines of management, psychology, sociology, linguistics, and others.

Eventually, summing up the results of the deliberations presented in this book and rejecting the position of the opponents of applying Lean Management in higher education, the author is of the opinion that this concept allows universities to return to their true identity as well as the essence and core of the processes on which they are founded and defined in terms of the master–disciple and new–known (ignorance–knowledge) relations. Lean makes it possible to eliminate bureaucratic, corporate or NPM-related degeneration and to fight against the two curses of contemporary higher education, i.e. bureaucratisation and economisation. In the author's opinion, it is a considerable challenge because it requires an unconditional undertaking to create value and assume responsibility for this process. In the light of the conducted research, the Lean concept appears to be compatible with the specific character of higher education. On the one hand, it is well received by employees as a common sense idea consistent with human nature. On the other hand, it is based on some kind of consensus built on a bottom-up basis by participants of processes. Thus Lean Culture becomes their own individual culture of work. Lean Culture is created simultaneously in the individual and organisational dimensions, and associated changes have a rolling character typical of continuous improvement processes.

Index